*Revolutionary Change and
Democratic Religion*

Revolutionary Change and Democratic Religion

CHRISTIANITY, VODOU, AND SECULARISM

Celucien L. Joseph

☙PICKWICK *Publications* • Eugene, Oregon

REVOLUTIONARY CHANGE AND DEMOCRATIC RELIGION
Christianity, Vodou, and Secularism

Copyright © 2020 Celucien L. Joseph. All rights reserved. Except for brief quotations in critical publications or reviews, no part of this book may be reproduced in any manner without prior written permission from the publisher. Write: Permissions, Wipf and Stock Publishers, 199 W. 8th Ave., Suite 3, Eugene, OR 97401.

Pickwick Publications
An Imprint of Wipf and Stock Publishers
199 W. 8th Ave., Suite 3
Eugene, OR 97401

www.wipfandstock.com

PAPERBACK ISBN: 978-1-4982-2470-3
HARDCOVER ISBN: 978-1-4982-2472-7
EBOOK ISBN: 978-1-4982-2471-0

Cataloguing-in-Publication data:

Names: Joseph, Celucien L., author.

Title: Revolutionary change and democratic religion : Christianity, vodou, and secularism / Celucien L. Joseph.

Description: Eugene, OR : Pickwick Publications, 2020 | Includes bibliographical references and index.

Identifiers: ISBN 978-1-4982-2470-3 (paperback) | ISBN 978-1-4982-2472-7 (hardcover) | ISBN 978-1-4982-2471-0 (ebook)

Subjects: LCSH: Religion and politics—Haiti. | Social conflict—Religious aspects—Haiti. | Social conflict—Haiti. | Haiti—Religion. | Haiti—Politics and government. | Christianity—Haiti. | Vodou—Haiti.

Classification: BL2350 .C44 2020 (print) | BL2350 .C44 (ebook)

Manufactured in the U.S.A.   APRIL 10, 2020

To my children: Terrence, Josh, Abby, and Emily
You have graced my life with love and happiness

Contents

List of Tables | ix
Acknowledgments | xi
Introduction | 1

PART I: Radical Change in the Time of Slavery and Freedom

1. Changing Slavery and Defending Human Rights: Toussaint Louverture and the Challenge of Freedom | 13

2. To Write for Change, Freedom, and Human Dignity: The Historic Letter of July 1792 | 46

3. Changing Western Historiography and Epistemology: Anténor Firmin, the Egyptian Question, and Afrocentric Imagination | 57

PART II: Faith, Secularism, and the Problem of Change

4. Revolution of the Mind: Religion, Marxist Humanism, and Development; An Analysis of Roumain's Religious Feeling and Marxist Rhetoric | 105

5. Democratic Faith as Religious Freedom: The Possibility of Christian-Vodouist Dialogue in Hurbon and Fils-Aime | 146

6. Holistic Transformation: Justice as Solidarity and the Poor in Aristide's Theological Tradition | 172

Bibliography | 213
Index | 227

Tables

TABLE 1. Parallel reading of Louverture's declaration and Isaiah 1:1 | 30

TABLE 2. Rhetorical categories group #1. Toussaint Louverture and fragments of revolutionary rhetoric of freedom. Textual articulation and visual representation | 42

TABLE 3. Rhetorical classification group #2. Toussaint Louverture and fragments of revolutionary rhetoric of freedom. Textual articulation and visual representation | 43

Acknowledgments

Revolutionary Change and Democratic Religion: Christianity, Vodou, and Secularism engages Haiti's intellectual history by focusing on the ideas and writings of six brilliant thinkers: Toussaint Louverture (abolitionist), Joseph Antenor Firmin (anthropologist), Jacques Roumain (Marxist and Communist thinker), Jean-Fils Aime (Protestant theologian), Laënnec Hurbon (Catholic theologian), and Jean-Bertrand Aristide (former president of Haiti and liberation theologian). This present text articulates the idea that postcolonial Haiti has produced a robust intellectual tradition—from the colonial period to the postcolonial present—and that Haitian thought is/has not been homogeneous or fixed. As a result, *Revolutionary Change and Democratic Religion* is an investigation of the rich diversity in Haitian intellectual history with special attention to its cross-disciplinary, liberative intent, and global perspective. The underlying idea of this book is arguably the advocacy of drastic social and political change, the transformation of the mind and the human condition in both colonial Saint-Domingue and postcolonial Haiti, and an alternative epistemology rooted in precolonial African history and achievement, as well as the black experience in modernity. The instrumentalization of religion and secular ideas are deployed in achieving these objectives.

I wish to express my gratitude to friends and colleagues who have commented on the early drafts of this book. My thanks and appreciation go to many individuals whose scholarship on the role of religion in society and Haitian studies have shaped my own scholarship; second, I am appreciative to all the anonymous reviewers of previously published articles represented in this book. They have offered constructive feedback to make this book more understandable and scholarly astute. I would like to express my appreciation for the permission granted to reprint the previously published article "The Religious Philosophy of Jean Price-Mars," *Journal of Black Studies* 43.6 (2012) 620–45.

Finally, I would like to offer my profound appreciation to my loving and patient wife, Katia Joseph, my love and companion in life, whose kindness, understanding, and support make life an exciting journey with her and our wonderful children: Terrence, Josh, Abby, and Emily. Without you, this life would not be worth living.

Introduction

REVOLUTIONARY CHANGE AND DEMOCRATIC *Religion: Christianity, Vodou, and Secularism* is a critical assessment on the triumph of human reason and secularism in the Haitian life, with an emphasis on the performative role of religion and the place of intellectual activism to foster social change and the revolution of the mind—within the historical trajectories of slavery and post-slavery, colonial Saint-Domingue and postcolonial Haiti, religion and no-religion. On one hand, this book makes an urgent call for greater democratic freedom of religion in the Haitian society; on the other hand, it makes a clarion call to the use of religion and emancipative humanist ideas to mobilize individuals toward social mobility, the common good, and holistic radical transformation.

Revolutionary Change and Democratic Religion also reevaluates the history of ideas in Modern European (Western) intellectual history by challenging some of the premises and antecedents that have shaped Western intellectual narratives, discourses, and ideologies. By confronting the rhetorical discourses that exclude the history and achievements of other peoples and nations in modernity, such as those of precolonial Africa and the African people, and people of African descent in the Black Diaspora, this book seeks to reframe the intellectual trajectories of Western thought and reconstitute its intellectual antecedents. It is in this respect, we can speak brazenly of the revolution of the mind and the reshifting of the Western conscience and epistemology, as will be observed in the case of Joseph Anténor Firmin who called for a proper contextual decolonization of knowledge, Western history, and global history.

The dominant idea of this book, which it also advocates, is arguably holistic "change." The idea of revolutionary change in the title is associated with the watershed events leading to the Haitian Revolution (1791 to 1804) and the founding of the postcolonial state and Republic of Haiti.

The accent is on the utilization of rhetorical language as a performative device to activate drastic transformation in the colonial milieu, and the public and political spheres of Saint-Domingue and France, the mother land—as will be observed in the close reading of Toussaint Louverture's political speeches and political actions. We can also speak of rhetorical activism as a strategic means deployed by abolitionists (i.e., Toussaint) to destroy the institution of slavery and to conscientize French legislators and slave masters on the imperative need for policy change. The second level of the practice of rhetorical activism aims at conscientizing the African slaves to question the ethics of slavery and to reject it simultaneously, as well as to throw away the values of the colonial life. Toussaint Louverture, Jean-Francois Boissou, and Belair champion this rhetorical approach. Consequently, we use the concept of conscientization as "a process of becoming aware of one's place in the world and its forms of oppression and then of committing to act as a historical agent of social liberation. Reaching beyond 'awareness,' conscientization is only achieved when it acts with imagination and commitment to change oppressive social structures."[1]

A complementary usage of the notion of change in this book pertains to the symbolic and functionalist practice of religion in effecting and sustaining democracy, civility, and solidarity in the Haitian society. We advocate the concept of "democratic religion" as a reasonable practice in society; we affirm that various religious traditions, when used and practiced selfishly and generously, could enhance both civil and political societies, and enrich social interactions between people of faith and no-faith. We recognize that both religion and secularism could be deployed strategically and meaningfully for the welfare of community and the common good. This approach does not, by any means, indicate that we are undermining the obvious tension between radical religion and radical secularism. Religion and secularism can also be used to oppress and exploit people. For example, in the context of the Haitian experience, it is possible for the two dominant religions, Vodou and Christianity, to coexist and be used responsibly and effectively for the welfare of the Haitian people and the progress of human condition in the Haitian society. The critical reader should also know that we recognize there are sharp differences between Vodou and Christianity, and between Vodou theology and Christian theology, Vodou ethical worldview and Christian ethical

---

1. Groome, "Take and Read."

worldview. For example, many Christians believe firmly in the deity and humanity of Jesus Christ, and his exclusive functional role as the only Savior and Lord. The exclusive claim of Christianity is that Jesus Christ is the only way to God, and because he provides sacrificial and substitutionary atonement to every individual through his blood, without him, it is impossible for any one or religion to have direct access to God.

By contrast, both Vodouists and secular humanists reject this audacious Christian confession and the noted exclusive and absolute claims of Christianity; rather, they have embraced a more liberal definition of religion and a more inclusive path to God. Without undermining doctrinal or theological distinctions, our objective here is to encourage interreligious and interfaith dialogue between Vodou and Christianity, as represented in the work of Jean Fils-Aimé and Laennec Hurbon. We are also convinced that there is room for those who profess no dogma or no faith at all, in the case of Jacques Roumain. Finally, we concur that religion can be used instrumentally for community outreach and to foster social development; this is the case of Jean-Bertrand Aristide who deliberately employs both the promises of Christian tradition of liberation theology and secular liberalism and democratic ideals to mobilize individuals from different sectors and social stratum in the Haitian society to serve, love, and walk in solidarity with the poor and the oppressed. The call to purposefully love people, bear one another burden, affirm the humanity and dignity of the outcast, and be in solidarity with those who are weak and the least among us knows no religion; rather, it is a duty of all individuals because we are all—with no exception—our brother's/sister's keepers.

As noted above, *Revolutionary Change and Democratic Religion* is presented as a work of intellectual history of Haiti, that is a critical reflection on the history of ideas and an attempt to grasp the intersections of rhetoric, religious ideas, the race question, and secular humanism in Haiti's intellectual history, as well as the various ways they crisscross each other. As a scholar and interpreter of the human experience, I seek to analyze the thought of Haitian writers and intellectuals in their regional, international, and cosmopolitan context, and with all their complexity and paradoxes.

Revolutionary Change and Democratic Religion is equally a discourse on the convergences and confluences of ideas, and the appeal of human reason, democratic ideals, and communitarian ethics to rethink about the values of modernity and reconsider the complexity of European intellectual history and human history. Toward this goal, we suggest that the general interweaving themes of rhetoric, the race concept, race vindication, universal emancipation, religious unorthodoxy, secular humanism, the particular and the universal, and cosmopolitanism are representative of Haiti's intellectual tradition.

Recently, the argument for a rich intellectual tradition in Haiti has been well taken by non-Haitian writers such as Gordon K. Lewis, *Main Currents in Caribbean Thought: The Historical Evolution of Caribbean Society in Its Ideological Aspects, 1492–1900* (1983, 2004); Joan Dayan, *Haiti, History and the Gods* (1995); Silvio Torres-Saillant, *Caribbean Poetics: Toward an Aesthetic of West Indian Literature* (1997), and *An Intellectual History of the Caribbean* (2004); Nick Nesbitt, *Universal Emancipation: The Haitian Revolution and the Radical Enlightenment* (2008), and *Caribbean Critique: Antillean Critical Theory from Toussaint to Glissant* (2013), Valerie Kaussen, *Migrant Revolutions: Haitian Literature, Globalization, and U.S. Imperialism* (2008), Kiama L. Glover, *Haiti Unbound: A Spiralist Challenge to the Postcolonial Canon* (2010), Deborah Jenson, *Beyond the Slave Narrative: Politics, Sex, and Manuscripts in the Haitian Revolution* (2011).

In our intellectual history, Toussaint is not only a man of deep commitment to his people but also the great Haitian anti-racist and public intellectual, radical social activist and anticolonial prophet of Black Freedom and Human rights in the eighteenth century. Haiti has given the world a man of great mind, Joseph Anténor Firmin. He is the most rigorous Haitian intellectual, anti-racist writer, and the first black anthropologist who countered with force, clarity, and intellectual breadth Western racism and epistemic apartheid in the nineteenth century. In the footsteps of Toussaint and Firmin, Jacques Roumain and Jean Price-Mars continued the intellectual legacy in the twentieth century. If Roumain is the most important Marxist writer and novelist the country has produced in the twentieth century, Price-Mars and Firmin are intellectuals par excellence who had interrogated the supremacy of Western cultural hegemony and values in the world. Both Firmin and Price-Mars in *Ainsi parla l'Oncle*, published in 1928, had sought to create an alternative modernity in Black Atlantic thought and culture, based on the achievements of the African people and their ancestry in the African Diaspora in the modern world.

In *The Equality of the Human Races: Positivist Anthropology*, a foundational text in the discipline of anthropology which was published in 1885, Joseph Anténor Firmin, the first black anthropologist in the Western world, had shaken the intellectual foundations of Western intellectual history when he puts for the scientific evidence for the triumph of precolonial African civilizations and the indebtedness ancient Greece and Roman owed to Africa. If Toussaint had defended human rights and championed universal emancipation and equality for all, Firmin, Roumain, and Price-Mars had influenced several generations of black intellectuals and writers across the Black Atlantic, as well as freedom and cultural movements in the Black Diaspora. Correspondingly, in the sphere of religion, Laennec Hurbon, Jean Fils-Aimé, and Jean-Bertrand Aristide have shed new light on the performative function of religion in society and the imperative of interreligious dialogue and interfaith friendship in the context of the two dominant religions in Haiti: Vodou and Christianity. They have called for greater religious tolerance and religious inclusivism. While Hurbon and Fils-Aimé emphasize the prior usage of the Vodouist tradition in the time of slavery to change the course of black destiny from slavery to freedom, Aristide appeals to the Christian tradition and secular humanism to alleviate human suffering and poverty and walk in solidarity with the poor and the oppressed. These Haitian thinkers and theologians champion democratic religion and the freedom of faith to cultivate relational friendship and love, as well as to foster cultural and political change.

Revolutionary Change and Democratic Religion is divided into three parts and six interdisciplinary chapters. While Haiti's intellectual tradition is interdisciplinary, global, and transnational. Arguably, with the rise of Haitian indigenism, and the *noirisme* as a cultural nationalism movement in the twentieth century, Haitian writers began to accentuate Marxism, socialist communism, and peasantry as complementary literary themes in their tradition. We should remember that Haitian writers and intellectuals have appealed to these theoretical notions and critical theory as tools of analysis to address the fragility of human existence, to make sense of the human experience in Haiti, and to struggle against Western imperialism, racism, and systemic oppression of all kinds that continue to oppress individuals and those living in the margins of modernity in this postcolonial era.

Subsequently, part 1 of the book is an analysis of the theme of black freedom, race vindication, and collective agency leading to revolutionary change in the political writings of Toussaint Louverture and other revolutionary writers during the era of the Haitian Revolution. Part 2 and part 3 focus predominantly on the history of ideas in postcolonial Haiti. While part 2 continues with the notion of race vindication and historiographic shift in the thought of Firmin, with special attention to his Afrocentric imagination and his argument for the African origin of the ancient Egyptian civilization, part 3 considers the significance of secular and religious ideas in the writings of Jacques Roumain, Laenner Hurbon, Jean Fils-Aimé, and Jean-Bertrand Aristide. In other words, the last three chapters of the book seek to establish the rich diversity of religious ideas, religious pluralism, and religious perspectives in Haiti's intellectual history. Hence, there is no sense of intellectual uniformity in Haiti's religious discourse or intellectual history. For example, Haitian writers (i.e., Dorsainvil, Price-Mars, Roumain, Jacques Stephen Alexis, etc.) in the twentieth century were divided over the precise nature and religiosity of Haiti's popular religion. Certainly, they expressed competing ideas and contradictory opinions in regard to the Vodou faith and Christianity.

Chapter 1 examines three important roles that underscore Toussaint Louverture's entire career and public function as public intellectual, social activist, and anticolonial prophet of black freedom and human rights in Saint-Domingue's public sphere. Toward this goal, I also explore how Toussaint's strategic use of language as a generative force and creative-performative act to foster revolutionary ideas—what we might call "the revolutionary rhetoric of freedom"—and to articulate his idea of freedom and understanding of being a public servant to the people, the enslaved African population in the French colony of Saint-Domingue-Haiti. We shall therefore study critically and carefully Louverture's rhetorical and theoretical genius as a chief propagator of human liberty and equality for all men and women, and, in particular, for the unreserved general emancipation of his people from the domination of slavery and the colonial system. In this inquiry, the focus is on my critical reading and interpretation of his political writings including selected public speeches and letters. In my reading of these documents, I pay close attention to their content and the various ways they might assist us to understand and reveal Toussaint's ambition to build the postcolonial nation of Haiti as well as his articulation of an ethics of human liberation and cosmopolitanism based on human dignity, self-determination, and social justice. What remains historically true about Toussaint is his zeal for radical change and efforts to alter the inhumane situation of his African brothers and sisters in colonial Saint-Domingue. Toussaint Louverture is the symbol of holistic transformation in Saint-Dominguan politics and public sphere.

Chapter 2 looks closely to the complementary themes explored in the previous chapter. It studies an important letter that was penned by a committee of three insurgent leaders: Jean-Francois Papillon, Georges Biassou, and Charles Belair (Toussaint Louverture), leading successors of Dutty Boukman, the eminent resurrectionist-instigator of the general revolt of 1791. In my exegetical analysis of the July 1792 letter, which was sent to the French General Assembly, I argue that this eloquent document represents the most exhaustive statement of the specific demands of the slave population at Saint-Domingue. It symbolizes the organized will of the people. These slave or former slaves asserted their natural right for general liberty and independence from slavery and the colonial system.

Furthermore, the letter attacks the entire racial system of slavery and is predicated upon the theoretical ideas of fundamental human right to freedom and liberty, and principles of justice and human equality, which revolutionary France symbolizes. Its authors demonstrate their incredible knowledge of the dominant political theories of the period and substantially their familiarity with the French Government policies. They do that in the most sophisticated manner. What is notable about this letter is its authors' undivided commitment to *la libération des Nègres*, black freedom. Arguably, in the most blatant way, it articulates the voice and desire of the people and embodies the spirit of the general will. The insistence of the letter is on the primacy of popular self-determination, and the collective action to creatively will their destiny. Arguably, the goal of this letter is to stimulate political change in public policy both in colonial Saint-Domingue and France.

Chapter 3 is an exploration of the intellectual reasoning and contours of Joseph Anténor Firmin with special attention given to conceptual decolonization of Western historiography and epistemology. Firmin calls for a radical transformation of the mind and the conscience in modernity by his active engagement with the achievements of precolonial African civilizations, and the racial situation of the ancient Egypt. Consequently, the chapter underscore Firmin's major claims for the Black African origin of the ancient Egyptian civilization—a paradigm shift in global history. This chapter also presents Firmin as a man of science, and accentuates his intellectual breath of and familiarity with Western intellectual traditions (both ancient and modern) in the emerging disciplines of humanities, especially anthropology. My analysis also considers Firmin's thought along the line of Afrocentric scholars and their argument for the substantial contributions of the Kemetic culture to classical Greece and world civilizations. From this vantage point, I bring forth Firmin's plea for the "formal recognition" of the achievement of the "Black race" in the cultural and intellectual developments of the modern world. My reading is based on Firmin's major work, *Equality of the Human Races: Positivist Anthropology*. Firmin inaugurates a radical shift in Western historiography and argues for an intellectual reconceptualization of colonial epistemology toward decoloniality and postcoloniality.

Chapter 4 is a critical inquiry of the intersections of religion, social transformation, and Marxist social theory in the thought of Jacques Roumain. It argues that Roumain's radical perspective on religion, development, and his critiques of institutionalized Christianity were substantially influenced by a Marxist conception of historical materialism and secular humanist approach to faith and human progress. Roumain rejects Christianity for its ineffective role in society in fostering social change. This chapter also contends that Roumain's rejection of religious supernaturalism and divine intervention in human affairs and history was shaped by his non-theistic humanism and secular worldview on faith. Ultimately, the chapter demonstrates that Roumain believes that only through effective human solidarity and collaboration can serious social transformation and real human freedom take place. He downplays the potential role of religion to deal adequately with the ambiguities of life in this world. Roumain holds that man was the measure of all things and his own agent of liberation. Consequently, individuals themselves must cooperate and unite in order to alter the social order toward a fruitful life of peace, harmony, and freedom.

As observed, religious orthodoxy is a problem in Roumain's writings. Haitian scholars in the twentieth century have inherited the tension or conflict between Vodou and Christianity in the Haitian experience. It is in this perspective that the subsequent chapter seeks to explore the possibility of a Vodouist-Christian dialogue in the Haitian society.

Chapter 5 is a critical examination of the writings of two prominent progressive Haitian theologians: Laënnec Hurbon, a Catholic theologian and former priest, and Jean Fils-Aimé, a Protestant theologian and former pastor, and their interaction with the Vodou religion. These Haitian thinkers have written prolifically about the three major religious expressions in Haiti and the enduring religious conflict between Protestantism, Catholicism, and Vodou in the Caribbean nation. The history of relations between Christianity—both Protestant and Catholic—and Vodou in Haiti is marked by a high degree of combativeness, hostility, and discomfort.

As a result, this current chapter suggests that Hurbon has inaugurated what we might phrase the Christian-Vodouist compromissory tradition. Following the footsteps of Hurbon, Fils-Aimé has done for Haitian Protestantism what Hurbon has achieved for Haitian Catholicism—pushing forward the idea of the inculturation of Vodou culture and practices in Protestant Christianity in Haiti—within the framework of a Protestant-Vodouist compromissory tradition. In this respect, these Haitian theologians have called for an alternative thinking and radical reorientation of the Haitian mind.

Chapter 6 creatively interprets Aristide's theological ethics as a theology of radical relationality and generous inclusion because it is grounded exclusively in the God of Life and God the Liberator who does not reject anyone, but invites all to himself. Aristide maintains that liberation theology as a discourse about God and his relationship with the outcast and disheartened in our communities is a liberative discourse. This chapter then considers how a politico-theology of relationality will serve and benefit the poor, the oppressed, and the underrepresented individuals and families. It compels the reader to embrace an ethics of justice and solidarity in order to relate to and empower those living in dire poverty and in the margins of society. As previously seen in the writings of Toussaint and others, slavery, globalization, imperialism, and other forms of human oppressions have created enormous suffering and existential poverty in the world, Aristide offers the ethical principles of human connectedness, interdependence, and relationality as various possibilities that could potentially lead to radical and holistic transformation, as well as human strategies and resources to cope with the problem of pain and suffering in this life, and to participate in the plight of the Haitian people, and the global poor and oppressed.

PART I

*Radical Change
in the Time of Slavery and Freedom*

CHAPTER ONE

Changing Slavery and Defending Human Rights

Toussaint Louverture and the Challenge of Freedom

THE FIRST CHAPTER OF the book examines three important roles that underscore Toussaint Louverture's entire career and public function as public intellectual, social activist, and anticolonial prophet of black freedom and human rights in Saint-Domingue's public sphere. Toward this goal, we will also explore how Louverture's strategic use of language as a generative force and creative-performative[1] act to foster revolutionary ideas—what we might call "the revolutionary rhetoric of freedom"—and to articulate his idea of freedom and understanding of being a public servant to the people, the enslaved Africans in the French colony of Saint-Domingue-Haiti. We shall therefore study critically and carefully Louverture's rhetorical and theoretical genius as a chief propagator of human liberty and equality for all men and women, and, in particular, for the unreserved general emancipation of his people from the domination of slavery and the colonial system. In this inquiry, the focus is on my critical reading and interpretation of his political writings including selected public speeches and letters toward the importance and possibilities of creating a postcolonial people and identity, and the project of fostering an ethics of human liberation and cosmopolitanism based on human dignity, self-determination, and social justice.

---

1. British philosopher J. L. Austin was probably the first to introduce and to popularize the idea of performative utterances to suggest that language is generative or creates things; for further comments on this theory, see his little book, *How to Do Things with Words*.

The Making of a Public Intellectual and Social Activist

Nick Nesbitt states that "Toussaint would dictate as many as 300 letters in a single day."[2] One contemporary account reveals how Toussaint has reinvented himself into a prominent figure and public intellectual of the Haitian and French Revolutions:[3]

> I saw him in few words verbally lay out the summary of his addresses [to his secretaries]; rework the poorly conceived, poorly executed sentences; confront several secretaries presenting their work by turns; redo the ineffective sections; transpose parts to place them to better effect; making himself worthy, all in all, of the natural foretold by Raynal.[4]

Toussaint was born in the Age of Revolution in which Saint-Domingue was the most prosperous colony of the French empire. Historian David Geggus informs us that the Caribbean island substantially boosted up the economy of the Americas and Europe:

> In the period between the American and French revolutions, Saint Domingue produced close to one-half of all the sugar and coffee consumed in Europe and the Americas, as well as substantial amounts of cotton, indigo, and ground provisions. Through scarcely larger than Maryland, and the little more than twice the size of Jamaica, it had long been the wealthiest colony

---

2. Nesbitt, *Toussaint L'Ouverture*, xxliv. Nesbitt has translated into English several letters by Toussaint from the French as well his political writings and speeches. I shall heavily rely on Nesbitt's text for my engagement with and analysis of Toussaint's political ideas and writings. In the opening page of his "Note on the Texts," Nesbitt writes, "The correspondence of Toussaint L'Ouverture is vast, and remains to a great degree unpublished, dispersed across the globe in various archives and private collections, awaiting a critical edition." David Patrick Geggus voices similar concerns about Toussaint's correspondence, *Haitian Revolutionary Studies*.

I am also relying on the French original letters, speeches, and political writings, as edited by Gerard Mentor Laurent, *Toussaint Louverture à travers sa correspondence, 1794-1798*. C. L. R. James in his classic work, *The Black Jacobins*, on the Haitian Revolution, had translated into English two important letters by Toussaint: the October 28, 1797, and November 5, 1797, letters. These same correspondences in English translation can be found in George F. Tyson, *Toussaint L'Ouverture*. There is also another significant letter dated July 1792 by Toussaint which biographer Madison Smartt Bell had translated and incorporated in his new biography on the Haitian revolutionary leader, *Toussaint Louverture: A Biography*. Throughout this chapter, I shall be referring to and quoting these texts or authors.

3. Nesbitt, *Toussaint L'Ouverture*, xxliv.

4. Quoted in Nesbitt, *Toussaint L'Ouverture*, xxliv.

in the Caribbean and was hailed by publicists as the "Pearl of the Antilles'" or the "Eden of the Western World." ... By 1789 Saint Domingue had about 8,000 plantations producing crops for export. They generated some two-fifths of France's foreign trade, a proportion rarely equaled in any colonial empire. Saint Domingue's importance to France was not just economic, but fiscal (in customs revenue) and strategic, too, since the colonial trade provided naval stores from northern Europe (hemp, mast trees, saltpeter). In the Mole Saint Nicolas, the colony also contained the most secure naval base in the West Indies.[5]

Arguably, slavery as a system that exploited black labor was the foundation of the colonial economy and the problem of slavery was the crisis of modernity. Colonizers and pro-slavery proponents would fight fiercely to sustain the institution and to maintain the unpaid work of enslaved African men, women, and children, and to keep them from freedom.

Born in slavery on the plantation of Bréda in the northern plain, Toussaint was born François Dominique Toussaint Bréda of African parents. He later assumes the surname Louverture meaning "The Opener of the way," a floating signifier that would give grand imports to the Haitian epic.[6] To emphasize the textual symbolism and significance of his name, I will use "Louverture" throughout the remaining part of the chapter, instead of "Toussaint" as it is traditionally done. As a brilliant political and military leader, Louverture was truly the "Master of the Crossroads" as novelist Madison Smartt Bell recounts in his imaginative and brilliant novel.[7] The "Black Spartacus" was a multilinguist. He spoke the colonizer's language French, the slaves' tongue Haitian Creole, and his father's (unknown) African dialect. He served as a coachman, an esteemed position for a slave, which allowed him to establish inter-plantation contacts and carry important messages across plantations for his master, Baron de Libertat, who granted him freedom at thirty-three, sometime in the 1770s. Louverture was fifty years old when he taught himself to read. In a short autobiographical statement date 1801, he affirmed, "I felt that I was destined for great things. When I received this divine portent, I was fifty-four years old; I did not how to read or write . . . in a few moths I knew how to sign my name and read correctly."[8] He was a man of faith,

5. Geggus, *Haitian Revolutionary Studies*, 5.
6. Clavin, *Toussaint Louverture*, 6.
7. See Bell, *Master of the Crossroads*.
8. Nesbitt, "Self-Portrait, 1801," in *Toussaint Louverture*, 40.

a devout Catholic. Louverture was himself a slave owner, as in 1777 he emancipated the African-born slave named Jean-Baptiste.[9]

Louverture's former status as a slave owner and former slave, however, provided him with a deep understanding of slave life and the meaning of liberty/freedom. A contemporary American consul, Tobias Lear, describes his admiration, "By all the inhabitants of all colours; whether this proceeds from fear or love I cannot yet tell; but all speak of him as a just man."[10] Louverture "believed that to rule men they must be lashed and caressed in turns."[11] Quoting a contemporary source, historian Laurent Dubois comments he "greatly impressed most who met him."[12] In the 1796 letter to Etienne Laveaux—which we will return later—Louverture acknowledged the positive public perception of him as a committed social activist and the champion of black self-determination and human rights: "I asked them if they knew me and whether they were glad to see me. They answered yes, that they knew that I was the father of all the blacks, and that they also knew that I had never ceased to work for their happiness and for their liberty."[13] He continued by informing us about a public meeting he had with the people in which "one of them spoke and said to me: 'General, all of us look upon you as our father, it is you after God who are dearest to us and in whom we have the most confidence.'"[14]

As the conscience and represented voice of the slave population's will and desire for freedom, Louverture took the causes and suffering of the people seriously: "But they begged me to listen to them and that perhaps I would see that they perhaps were not so in the wrong as I believed. I was quiet and listened to them.[15]

Being an eloquent orator, Louverture had substantial influence upon the slave community and the military forces he led. It is believed that he was an avid reader, especially the abolitionist writings of Abbé Raynal.[16] Louverture deliberately acted upon Raynal's words and let the language of this apocalyptic prophecy guide his destiny,

9. Dubois, *Avengers of the New World*, 171.
10. Ott, *Haitian Revolution*, 128.
11. Ott, *Haitian Revolution*, 128.
12. Dubois, *Avengers of the New World*, 172.
13. L'Ouverture, "Letter to Laveaux, 20 February 1796," 22.
14. L'Ouverture, "Letter to Laveaux, 20 February 1796," 22.
15. L'Ouverture, "Letter to Laveaux, 20 February 1796," 22.
16. Guillaume-Thomas-Francois Raynal first published his ten-volume work, *L'Histoire philosophique et politique des établissements et du commerce des Européens dans les deux Indes*, in 1770.

> All that the negroes lack is a leader courageous enough to carry them to vengeance and carnage.... Where is he, this great man that nature owes to its vexed, oppressed, tormented children? Where is he? He will appear, do not doubt it. He will show himself and will raise the sacred banner of liberty. This venerable leader will gather around him his comrades in misfortune. More impetuous than torrents, they will leave everywhere ineffaceable traces of their just anger.[17]

In his 1801 "Self-Portrait" which he probably wrote in his prison cell at Fort de Joux, France, Louverture penned the following words, confirmed Raynal's prediction, and presented himself as the self-emancipatory and self-righteous hero whom Raynal predicted above:

> I felt that I was destined for great things. When I received this divine portent.... The revolution of St-Domingue was going its way; I saw that the writes could not hold out, because they were divided among themselves and crushed by superior members; I congratulated myself on being black.... A secret voice said to me: "Since the blacks are free, they need a chief," and it is I who must be the chief predicted by Abbé Raynal. I returned, transported by this sentiment.[18]

French dramatist and writer Louis-Sébastien Mercier also dreamed in 1771—the dignified "negro" who would "deliver the world from the most atrocious, longest, and most insulting tyranny of all"—he (Louverture) was also the one who had "broken the chains of his compatriots and transformed the oppressed by the most odious slavery into heroes."[19] Based on this brief evaluation of the person and incredible accomplishments of Toussaint Louverture, in the interim I want to articulate this singular proposition: The entrance of Louverture into the Haitian drama might be interpreted as a pivotal era in Black Atlantic political thought and freedom movements. In his intervention in the 1790s, Louverture radically reorients the Haitian experience.[20] As a towering figure in the unfolding events leading to the Haitian Revolution, Louverture was

---

17. Quoted in Dubois, *Avengers of the New World*, 57–58; Raynal, *L'Histoire philosophique et politique*, 3:204–5.

18. Nesbitt, "Self-Portrait, 1801," 40–41.

19. Dubois, *Avengers of the New World*, 57.

20. Yet, we must stress that the revolutionary effort of Louverture and his counterparts (i.e., Makandal, Boukman, Jean-François, Biassou, Belair, etc.) and the courageous maroons must be studied jointly.

committed fearlessly to black freedom and made "the black problem" at Saint-Domingue his own political interest and ambition. Consider, for example, the following excerpt from the letter of November 1797. Louverture pledges:

> I shall never hesitate between the safety of San Domingo and my personal happiness; but I have nothing to fear. It is to the solicitude of the French Government that I have confided my children.... I would tremble with horror if it was into the hands of the colonists that I had sent them as hostages; but even if it were so, let them know that in punishing them for the fidelity of their father, they would only add one degree more to their barbarism, without any hope of ever making me fail in my duty.[21]

Fragments of Rhetoric of Freedom in Louverture's Thought

Louverture conceptualized freedom and its meaning through the art of persuasion and through the rhetoric of resistance. As Kenneth Burke articulates, "The basic function of rhetoric, the use of words, by human agents to form attitudes or to induce actions in other human agents, is certainly not magical."[22] The revolutionary rhetoric of freedom is the mere idea of imagining the meaning of freedom from the perspective of the slave masses. The expression accentuates the indigenous influences on the Haitian Revolution; that does not mean we undermine external influences upon the slaves in the event of the Haitian Revolution. As we shall see, Louverture in particular directly and indirectly was impacted by the libertarian ideology and radical rhetoric of the French Revolution, and the language of the Enlightenment. But Louverture and the slave community at Saint-Domingue were the agents of their own freedom.

Louverture used various rhetorical strategies to stress autonomous slave agency, collective self-determination, and collective self-expression. For Louverture, the act of speaking and writing was inexorably an act of individual and communal liberation, as this was the case particularly for many literate ex-slaves and slaves such as the abolitionist and race leader Frederic Douglas.[23]

21. James, *Black Jacobins*, 196.
22. Burke, *Rhetoric of Motives*, 41.
23. For further research on Douglass, see his *Narrative of the Life of Frederick Douglass* and *My Bondage and My Freedom*.

Freedom from the perspective of Louverture and former slaves and ex-slaves at Saint-Domingue was both an imagining process and a reality. The kind of freedom Louverture envisioned which led successfully to general emancipation out of slavery was ideologically constructed and culturally nurtured. As we will observe in his political letters, this way of thinking of human moral capability and autonomy exercised through collective self-expression was first imagined through language or performative utterances which I already identified as the *revolutionary rhetoric of freedom* (RRF). My basic argument is twofold. First, I advance the idea that revolutionary rhetoric of freedom produced by Louverture had considerable cognitive effects on his audience: the French colonial authorities and the entire slave population. By this position, I suggest that Louverture acted upon words or language with an emancipative intent. Second, I propose through the practice of various rhetorical techniques, Louverture was able to orchestrate new ways for social organization, racial alliance and unity, and political solidarity.

Revolutionary rhetoric of freedom is chiefly concerned with "building community, reaffirming human dignity, enhancing the life of the people" of the enslaved Africans at Saint-Domingue, and equally promoting the interest of all people.[24] Public discourse, as Maulana Karenga suggests, is part of the ancient African rhetorical heritage, in which rhetoric is employed "as a practice to reaffirm not only the creative power of the word but also rootedness in a world historical community and culture, which provides the foundation and framework for self-understanding and self-assertion in the world."[25] This *rhetoric of community*, as Karenga and Molefi Asante call it, is "a rhetoric of communal deliberation, discourse, and action, directed toward bringing good into the community and the world."[26] In this framework, the revolutionary rhetoric of freedom also seeks to assert, create, persuade, but also "to search for and explore possibilities in the social and human condition . . . and expand maximum human freedom and human flourishing, and constantly bring good into the world."[27]

---

24. Karenga, "Nommo, Kawaida, and Communicative Practice," 5.

25. Karenga, "Nommo, Kawaida, and Communicative Practice," 5.

26. Karenga, "Nommo, Kawaida, and Communicative Practice," 6; Asante, *Afrocentric Idea*.

27. Karenga, "Nommo, Kawaida, and Communicative Practice," 6.

Yet with Toussaint Louverture's turning point in the epic of Haitian history, the revolution moves steadily with liberative discourses.[28] (The Haitian Revolution was one of the few successful achievements in the human struggle toward freedom—the right to life and to live—which in its own unique way contributed potentially to the forward flow of human emancipation and a better world, especially the affirmation of the basic rights of dignity, respect, and equality for all men and women and its substantial impact in eradicating slavery both in North America and Latin America. For the impact and after effects of the Haitian Revolution in the Americas and the Atlantic World.) From this vantage point, I contend that to write about the politics of revolutionary rhetoric of freedom at Saint-Domingue is in effect and necessarily to engage particularly the activistic thought of Toussaint Louverture. Louverture's political vision and his self-conscious vocation as the apostle of Haitian liberty were thoroughly grounded in the grammar of revolutionary rhetoric; his military genius was ancillary.

In summary, his political writings as we will observe below are statements or declarations that wage war against any form of human injustice and human oppression. The vigor of the language employed therein constitutes perhaps the most succinct and compelling testimony of Louverture's unflinching devotion to practical freedom, the theoretical aspects of participatory democracy and universal emancipation. Nick Nesbitt declares that

> like his French counterparts, Sieyes, Mirabeau, Danton and above all Robespierre, Toussaint's correspondence shows the development of a tactical mastery of the art of communication. He developed this mastery in the context of a transformation in the nature of political power in 1790s France, when mastery over symbolic political capital—the rhetoric of Liberty, Equality, and Fraternity—itself became a means of winning political power.[29]

The meaning of freedom and its vision contested here is not presented merely as a function of space or people, be it France or French citizens; but how we concomitantly and deliberately pursue justice on behalf of all men and women. In other words, Toussaint's correspondence bears significance for contemporary times. In addition, the aspiration for liberty expressed in the pages of these documents is the paramount

---

28. See the various texts cited above as well these influential two studies: Hunt, *Haiti's Influence on Antebellum America*; Geggus, *Impact of the Haitian Revolution*.

29. Nesbitt, "Notes on the Texts," in *Toussaint Louverture*, xlv.

determination to get rid of slavery itself. As David Scott observes, "The problem of emancipation entailed. . . . The project of imagining and constructing a sustainable freedom with new forms of life" for the Saint-Dominguan slaves.[30]

Furthermore, we must situate Louverture's first "real" attempt toward radical freedom and the postcolonial push in the year of 1793. The transformative moments of this epoch have placed him on both the national and international level as a social activist for human rights, and an anti-racist and anticolonial fighter. The events of 1793 were a defining moment in transatlantic history and in the story of human strivings toward a democratic order, world peace, and subsequently the creation of a future world without slavery. The ideal of human collaboration and transnational affiliation, networking, and political activism have succeeded in various cultural circles and sociopolitical movements both in the Americas and in Western Europe. The international and transnational dimensions of racial difference and cultural racism (both as social categories), anti-oppressive government, and issues pertaining to national identity and citizenship were critical concerns facing the majority peoples in the world. These national and global phenomena reveal in the clearest sense the paradoxical character of modernity and human nature, and the fragility of human existence.

In this epoch-making period, human demands for peace and the cost for freedom and human rights intensified. The United States Congress passed the Fugitive Slave Act of 1793 that forced escaped slaves to return to their slave owners; this law also allowed the pursuit of runaways in another state or territory. The invention of Whitney's cotton grin in 1793 "revived the institution of slavery." It not only radically increased slave labor in the South, but also required more demands for African slaves and augmented transatlantic slave trade transactions.[31] In this same time frame, the peasants in France revolted against the French revolutionary government, pressing their cause for economic equality and representation in the new political order. On June 24, the first Republican Constitution (known as the Constitution of 1793) was adopted in the "New France," which would bear significant repercussions for the political rights of the French overseas colonies, especially in Saint-Domingue.[32] In

30. Scott, *Conscripts of Modernity*, 133.

31. Rodriguez, *Slavery in the United States*, 516; On the relationship between slavery and Atlantic economy, see Ratner et al., *Evolution of the American Economy*.

32. For further studies, see Aldrich, *Greater France*.

this same year, the Jacobins initiated what is traditionally called the "The Reign of Terror" in the history of the French Revolution. In February 1793, France and Spain warred over the sovereignty of the island of Saint-Domingue, which included both geographical locations: Haiti and the Dominican Republic. On June 20, the city of Cap François was destroyed through a series of wars between European powers, and African forces.[33] Seeking political hegemony in the island, on September 20, 1793, British troops under the direction of Major-General Williamson invaded and occupied Saint-Domingue for the next five years.[34]

In August 29, 1793, French civil commissioner Léger-Félicité Sonthonax proclaimed the abolition of slavery in the Northern Province of the colony, which would assure the equality of all men, white or any other color in the colony, a project that was not fulfilled.[35] It was in the same year, and exactly on the same day, that Louverture's inaugural moment is marked by this illustrious speech: "Brothers and Friends. I am Toussaint Louverture. My Name is perhaps known to you. I have undertaken vengeance. I want liberty and Equality to reign in Saint Domingue. I work to bring them into existence. Unite yourselves to us, brothers, and fight with us for the same cause."[36] I interpret this public appearance as Louverture's significant critique of colonial modernity and the embedded structures sustaining it. Louverture ventures to engage the whole edifice of the colonial order by setting things right, and hence to (re-)create an alternative modernity in black.[37] The idea of a black intellectual in modernity describes the public vocation of Louverture both as social critic of the colonial regime in Saint-Domingue's public sphere and the Haitian intellectual par excellence who leads his people to the way of freedom. Edward Said in *Representation of the Intellectual articulates the role of* the intellectual which echoes in clear terms the totality of Louverture's life and his moral values:

> An individual endowed with a faculty for representing, embodying, articulating a message, a view, an attitude, philosophy

---

33. The most comprehensive and detailed study on this watershed moment in 1793 is treated in Popkin's brilliant book, *You Are All Free*.

34. David Geggus wrote the best work on the British occupation of the French island of Saint-Domingue, *Slavery, War and Revolution*.

35. Nesbitt, *Universal Emancipation*, 202–3.

36. Nesbitt, "Proclamation," 1.

37. I borrow the expression "modernity in black" from Kirkland, "Modernity and Intellectual Life in Black," 136–66.

> or opinion to, as well as for, a public. And this role has an edge to it, and cannot be played without a sense of being someone whose place it is publicly to raise embarrassing questions, to confront orthodoxy and dogma (rather than to produce them), to be someone who cannot easily be co-opted by governments or corporations, and whose *raison d'etre* is to represent those people and issues that are routinely forgotten or swept under the rug. The intellectual does so on the basis of universal principles: that all human beings are entitled to expect decent standards of behavior concerning freedom and justice from worldly powers or nations, and that deliberate or inadvertent violations of these standards need to be testified and fought against courageously.[38]

Toussaint Louverture championed the human cause in the land of his birth as a critic, observer and participant in the Haitian drama. He persuasively defended the cause of human freedom, human rights, justice, dignity, and ultimately contributed to the reconstruction of black life at Saint-Domingue. What is significant about this historic day is the enduring psychological impression of the speech on its hearers, and the process of actualizing this prophetic hope into a reality. First, the declaration reveals Louverture's undivided commitment to general emancipation, a consensus that is agreed upon by most Haitianist historians. Second, Louverture sees himself as an anticolonial leader in the process of recreating African history in the Saint-Dominguan landscape, and reconstructing a coherent human community. Finally, Louverture's call for robust solidarity, greater unity and communal loyalty are intrinsically linked to a shared vision and purpose, among the members of the slave community.

Louverture's momentous summons is rooted in the common experiences of colonial racial injustice and deliberate social exclusion and the marginalization of African blacks. His political solidarity is also predicated on the historical oppression of slavery, black labor exploitation, and colonial imperialism. In *Shadow and Act*, Ralph Ellison reminds us that

> it is not culture which binds the peoples who are of partially African origin now scattered throughout the world, but an identity of passions. We share a hatred for the alienation forced upon us by Europeans during the process of colonization and empire and we are bound by our common suffering more than by our pigmentation. But even this identification is shared by

---

38. Said, *Representations of the Intellectual*, 11–12.

most non-white peoples, and while it has political value of great potency, its cultural value is almost nil.[39]

Therefore, it will be hermeneutically plausible to construe the saliency of this act of summoning as one of the decisive moments in black political unity in the New World. Louverture's general emancipation decree is in essence predicated on the idea that to become free is equally to become human, a necessary predisposition to "enter into and transform a preexisting social order."[40] What Haitianist historians have often overlooked in Louverture's political writings and his speeches and letters is the "invisible will of the people" he frames. The foremost general of the Haitian Revolution embodies symbolically the voice of the people through his own inflection, and concretely articulates their fears, joys, triumphs, and ultimately their desire for general emancipation.

In a letter dated August 25, 1794, Louverture's self-conscious messianism is revealed when he pronounces to a group of *gens de couleurs* ("free people of color") that he had been "the first to stand up for" general emancipation, a cause he had begun, supported, and "will finish."[41] I suggest that the language of this text can be deduced in two different ways. First, it reportedly discloses the details about Louverture's personal arrogance and his historical amnesia of the resilience of those who preceded him. If this is so, then, this interpretation would confirm Pierre Pluchon's direct denial of the universal dimension of Louverture's liberative political vision. In his groundbreaking biography on Toussaint, Pluchon argues that Toussaint was *un profiteur du régime colonial* ("an opportunist of the colonial regime") who unremittingly fought for *le droit de l'homme* ("human right"), *la justice* ("principles of justice") and not for *la liberté générale* ("general emancipation").[42] Based on the Pluchonian logic, Louverture was simultaneously a "power-seeker" and a "sincere-abolitionist."[43] Both positions attempt to demonstrate the complex personality of Haiti's leading revolutionary hero, but both authors have failed to look beyond what they affirmed. A second convenient interpretation suggests that Louverture's pronouncement counters the unconventional

39. Ellison, *Shadow and Act*, 255.
40. Nesbitt, "Troping Toussaint, Reading Revolution," 22.
41. Geggus, *Haitian Revolutionary Studies*, 127.
42. Pluchon, *Toussaint Louverture, de l'esclavage au pouvoir*, 21; Piquionne, "Lettre de Jean-François."
43. Ott, *Haitian Revolution*, 83.

idea that Sonthonax the abolitionist was "The Author of Haitian freedom." Whether Louverture was fairly concerned about black liberation (Beaubrun Ardouin) or always strove to achieve an emancipatory agenda (H. Pauleus Sannon, Aimé Césaire, C. L. R. James, and Stephen Alexis) says very little about the politics of Louverture's rhetorics.[44]

Toussaint Louveture strategically employed various language techniques that are egocentric such as rhetoric of intimidation to provoke revolutionary fear and concurrently advance the revolution to its culmination. Rhetorical persuasions are specifically goal oriented. Such way of speaking was not unknown in the world of Louverture and the world before. Orators with a political goal make use of persuasive discourse to inform, describe, and convince. The ancient sophists for example who functioned as philosophers, professional public speakers, and political scientists championed the political use of language toward participatory democracy and the nurturing of civic virtue in the *polis*. Protagoras, for example, took a similar path when he declared:

> By art which they possessed, men soon discovered articulate speech and names, and invented houses and clothes and shoes and bedding and got food from the earth. Thus provided for, they lived at first in scattered groups; these were no cities. Consequently they were devoured by wild beasts, since they were in every respect the weaker, and their technical skill, though a sufficient aid to their nurture, did not extend to making war on the beasts, for they had not the art of politics, of which the art of war is a part. They sought therefore to save themselves by coming together and founding fortified cities, but when they gathered in communities they injured one another for want of political skill, and so scattered again and continued to be devoured. Zeus therefore, fearing the total destruction of our race, sent Hermes to impart to men the qualities of respect for others [aidos] and a sense of justice [dike], so as to bring order into our cities and create a bond of friendship and union.[45]

Though rhetoric is not directly mentioned in the statement, it is implied. Carolyn Miller states that "participation here can only be rhetorical; it takes place through debate and deliberation. Through speech the virtues of justice and respect are tested, enacted, and developed, and

---

44. Geggus provides the most succinct summary of the various theories on this issue in *Haitian Revolutionary Studies*, 119–36.

45. Hamilton and Cairns, *Collected Dialogues of Plato*, 319.

through speech the community itself is created and recreated."[46] In other words, for Protagoras, rhetoric is indispensable for operating the democratic polis, and the realization of an effective civil society. A thorough analysis of Louverture's political writings, speeches and letters reveal that the latter employs constructive rhetorical discourses to accomplish two basic goals: the triumph of human freedom through the Haitian Revolution, and the process of constructing a new Black citizenry in the new republic. He seeks to eradicate the colonial evils, as he makes known in a public speech to the black community at Saint-Domingue: "The moment has arrived when the veil obscuring the light must fall."[47] Although, the evil of slavery, the veil of darkness and colonialism had caused many pains and sufferings to African slaves in the colony, the courageous and determined Louverture, as he declared, was "animated by feelings of humanity and fraternity" and believed that "there can exist no possibility of the destruction of this sacred edifice ... [the] love for freedom."[48] This particular conviction illuminates further his declaration that "I am utterly unlike many others who witness scenes of horror in cold blood. I have always held humanity in common to all, and I suffer whenever I cannot prevent evil."[49]

As the public intellectual of the Haitian Revolution, Louverture conceptualizes and defines the new Haitian identity through the articulation and nurturing of political speeches, which disclose his democratic vision and ideals as both revolutionary leader and Governor-in-chief of the island. Article 1 in Louverture's 1801 constitution affirms the new republic's commitment to universal freedom for all. The article envisions a new and postcolonial nation without slavery—a surprising new identity for former slaves—by declaring its end in the colony: "There cannot exist slaves on this territory, servitude is therein forever abolished. All men are born, live and die free and French." This particular text bears a performative functionality, fulfilling the new republic's decisive goal and national loyalty toward universal emancipation in an era where racial slavery was intrinsic to New World societies and their cultural identity.

As he boards *L'Héros* for France, the imperial ship that would turn him into a transnational maroon in the Atlantic seas and ultimately a

---

46. Miller, "Polis as Rhetorical Community," 222.
47. L'Ouverture, "Toussaint L'Ouverture to His Brothers and Sisters," 13.
48. L'Ouverture, "Toussaint L'Ouverture to His Brothers and Sisters," 13.
49. L'Ouverture, "Letter to General Laveaux, 18 May 1794," 10.

forced expatriate in the *Metropole*, Louverture pronounces to his captors these memorable words: "In overthrowing me, you have cut down in Saint-Domingue only the trunk of the tree of the liberty of the blacks; it will spring back from the roots, for they are numerous and deep."[50] One can only imagine these thirty-four words would push forward the spirit of "the tree of the liberty of the blacks" to the final phase of the revolution. At this juncture, Louverture tries to accomplish two things, symbolically. The first move he undertakes is the yielding of the revolutionary spirit of freedom of the enslaved and the voice he incarnates. This is expressed in the first part of the dictum: "In overthrowing me, you have cut down in Saint-Domingue only the trunk of the tree of the liberty of the blacks." His forced exile would mean that Louverture must also surrender his conscience to his people.

The second move, much anticipated by the one who is going away, foretells the triumph of the spirit of the revolution. Yet "you have cut down," Louverture tells his kidnappers, "only the trunk of the tree of the liberty of the blacks." Louverture is undergoing an oceanic voyage, signaling the Middle Passage and the aquatic route their ancestors experienced a while ago. He is going away involuntarily, in the same manner that some slaves sold themselves into the peculiar institution to Western merchants and others were giving into slavery. In a surprising way, Louverture presents his life as a sacrifice for the liberty of his people. For example, in his long poet, *Cahier d'un retour au pays natal*, the anticolonial poet Aimé Césaire honors Louverture with a moving eulogy. In fact, he interprets the life of Toussaint Louverture as a life of service and of sacrifice for the black race, and elsewhere Louverture, "The Opener of the way," is depicted as "*Le Sacrifice du peuple*" ("The Sacrifice of the people").[51] Césaire continues to inform us that Louverture the martyr disappeared in order to unite and reunite the people. Moreover, he reports that Louverture died ("*Mourir comme Brissot. Comme Robespiere*") like Jacques-Pierre Brissot, a seminal figure of the Girondist movement during the French Revolution and one of the founding members of the abolitionist movement known as *La Société des Amis des Noirs*, and like Maximilien Robespierre, a member of the Jacobin Club and one of the most influential leaders of the French Revolution. Césaire interprets the

---

50. Bell, *Toussaint Louverture*, 265; Clavin, *Toussaint Louverture*, 2.
51. Césaire, *Toussaint Louverture*, 309–14.

surrender of Toussaint Louverture to France "as the sacrifice of a life, his own, that of a leader, is an act of faith, for the salvation of his people."[52]

The suffering and death of Toussaint Louverture is the ground for creating bonds of solidarity and racial consciousness as well as the catalyst for black unity in the island, forecasting Louverture's "New branches will spring forth and bear fruit from the old root." To the moment of death, Louverture remained loyal to his people. "Forever faithful to the masses of slaves, and committed to building alliances to reach his goal, he abandoned whoever that he, Toussaint, could be used against his people."[53] As a social activist, he must foster unity among the people and lead them toward the same objective. Louverture believed that the unification of the slave community could reduce social tensions among them and was important in their struggle for liberty and equality, which he stressed, would not actualize unless the people are united for a common cause:

> I have worked since the beginning [of the revolt] to make that happen, and to bring happiness to all. Unite yourselves to us, brothers, and fight with us for the same cause. [. . .] You say that you are fighting for liberty and equality? Is it possible that we could destroy ourselves, one against the other, and all fighting for the same cause? It is I who have undertaken [this struggle] and I wish to fight until it [liberty] exists [. . .] among us. Equality cannot exist without liberty. And for liberty to exist, we must have unity.[54]

While Louverture is stressing the importance for the slaves to unite in order to escape the evils and labyrinth of slavery and hegemonic Western colonialism, Louverture believed strongly that equality and liberty are inseparable human rights and "essential to any conceivable progress towards emancipation."[55] In his letter to Govenor General Laveaux of Saint-Domingue—an issues which would take up in subsequent paragraphs—Louverture speaks fearlessly on behalf of his people to the General; he laments over social injustice against blacks in the colony and particularly on the problem of equality and liberty that has been denied to his people. Notice his playful rhetoric in the first few lines, as he makes this forceful declaration:

52. Davis, *Aimé Césaire*, 140.
53. Jean Bertrand-Aristide, introduction to Nesbitt, *Toussaint L'Ouverture*, xiv.
54. L'Ouverture, "Proclamation, 29 August 1793," 1–2.
55. Nesbitt, "Note on the Texts," in Nesbitt, *Toussaint L'Ouverture*, xlv.

CHANGING SLAVERY AND DEFENDING HUMAN RIGHTS 29

> Alas, general, they wish as well to make us slaves; there is not equality here, as it seems there is with you. Look how the whites and coloured men who are with you are good and are united with the blacks. One would think they were brothers from the same mother. That, general, is what we call equality. Here it is not the same. We are looked down upon, they vex us at every turn. They don't pay us what we are owed for the food we grow. They force us to give away our chicken and pigs for nothing when go to sell them in the city, and if we complain, they have us arrested by the police, and they throw us in prison without giving us anything to eat, and then make us pay to get out. You see, general, that one is not free if he is treated like this.[56]

Louverture's role as public intellectual here echoes to Michel Foucault's general definition of the public intellectual:

> The role of the intellectual is not to tell others what they have to do. [It is] a question over and over again what is postulated as self-evident, to disturb people's mental habits, the way they do and think certain things, to dissipate what is familiar and accepted, to reexamine rules and institutions.[57]

Nonetheless, Louverture as the voice and reflecting conscience of the will of the people often guided and told them exactly what they must to do in their fight toward liberation. Louverture acted as a moral force and catalyst in Saint-Domingue's public sphere, challenged the slave system, the colonial order and colonial laws and authorities to take responsibility for social justice, black freedom and equality. He had depicted himself as a seeker of "truth about humanity and social justice, and for the betterment of blacks and all humanity.[58]

Briefly, I want to take us back to the 1801 statement already mentioned above. Remarkably, in my perspective, it is the elevation of Louverture's speech tone that deserves our most attention: "I am only a branch" out of many. New branches will spring forth and bear fruit from the old root.[59] The meaning of the first metaphor is not clear. I would like to propose that Louverture construes his activist work in the anti-slavery tradition of his predecessors and contemporaries (i.e., Makandal,

---

56. L'Ouverture, "Letter to Laveaux, 20 February 1796," 23.
57. Quoted in Banner-Haley, *From Du Bois to Obama*, 2.
58. Banner-Haley, *From Du Bois to Obama*, 3.
59. Isa 11:1: "A shoot will come up from the stump of Jesse; from his roots a Branch will bear fruit" (NIV).

Boukman, Biasou, Jean-Francois, etc). The second imagery is a biblical illusion found in the prophetic book of Isaiah 11:1. Observe below the textual parallel between Isaiah's prophecy and Louverture's proclamation:

TABLE 1. PARALLEL READING OF LOUVERTURE'S
DECLARATION AND ISAIAH 11:1

"A shoot will come up from the stump of Jesse"	"I am only a branch out of many"
"From his roots a Branch will bear fruit"	"New branches will spring forth and bear fruit from the old root"

The Isaianic prophecy foresees the coming of the expected Jewish Messiah proceeded directly from the Davidic dynasty. Walter Brueggemann advises that this particular promise along others in the Hebrew Bible anticipates the eschatological new king, a practitioner of justice, who will assure the rehabilitation of the nation of Israel and restore the cosmic order.[60] Furthermore, Brueggemann posits that "from a theological perspective, what is important about these prophetic promises, whatever the specific content and whenever they may be dated, is that they are situated in the presence of prophetic judgment and threats."[61] It is quite possible that Louverture knew about this prophetic passage in Isaiah, as a result he saw himself fulfilling a messianic mission in the context of the Haitian Revolution as the triumph of human freedom. At this point of his life, Louverture practices contextual biblical. He alludes to this particular prophetic text and interprets the history of the Haitian Revolution as the execution of this biblical promise. Louverture biographers inform us that "the Catholic religion became his own . . . and Louverture was outwardly an extremely devout Catholic."[62] Substantially, Louverture probably invoked the Isaiah's passage to foretell the forthcoming divine judgment upon the French empire and correspondingly to forecast the ending of slavery in the colony. At any rate, Louverture and his radical religious predecessors such as Francois Makandal and Dutty Boukman practiced the politics of God and used religion for their own gain.

In addition, this Louverturian forceful declaration in its anticolonial bent provokes horrors in the psychology of the French troops who heard

60. Brueggemann, *Theology of the Old Testament*, 171.
61. Brueggemann, *Theology of the Old Testament*, 171.
62. Bell, *Toussaint Louverture*, 21, 59; Dubois, *Avengers of the New World*, 173.

CHANGING SLAVERY AND DEFENDING HUMAN RIGHTS   31

him. The Black liberator insists that freedom is not a function of geography. Elsewhere in an address to soldiers for the universal destruction of slavery, Louverture employs the metaphor of "the tree of liberty" to declare his unqualified commitment to universal emancipation and his idea of freedom:

> Let the sacred flame of liberty that we have won lead all our acts. [. . .] Let us go forth to plan the tree of liberty, breaking the chains of those of our brothers still held captive under the shameful yoke of slavery. Let us bring them under the compass of our rights, the imprescriptible and inalienable rights of free men. [Let us overcome] the barriers that separate nations, and unite human species into a single brotherhood. We seek only to bring to men the liberty that [God] has given them, and that other men have taken from them only by transgressing His immutable will.[63]

The contour of (black) liberty is beyond the Saint-Dominguan landscape, his words imply. If these words are self-revealing truths, then the border of the tree of (black) liberty would have transnational effects: "it will spring back from the roots, for they are numerous and deep" and "Let us bring them under the compass of our rights, the imprescriptible and inalienable rights of free men." These two phrases are inseparable; they establish Louverture's theoretical and central conception of freedom. Freedom, for the latter, is geographically unrestricted and globally stretched, which points to the repercussions of freedom story as the Haitian Revolution or other world revolutions (i.e., the American and French Revolutions). For Louverture, practical freedom must entail bringing the gift of freedom to other enslaved peoples and nations beyond Haitian boundaries. He emphasized that God as Creator has given liberty as a natural right to men and nations. As we have observed, these declarations signify Louverture's philosophy of democracy and his strong belief in the doctrine of universal emancipation.

Yet Louverture's other meaning of freedom might be understood the same way a text's meaning works. Sybille Fischer, in her excellent study on the Haitian revolution observes the conflicts between "text and reality" in revolutionary accounts.[64] I suggest that texts only have "meaning potential" as the theorization of freedom might be metaphorized as a

---

63. L'Ouverture, "Address to Soldiers," 28.
64. Fischer, *Modernity Disavowed*, 228.

multi-series episode, engaging a multiple of actors playing different roles. In this way, we can further think through freedom's meaning as being multivalent and equally as being contextual. Meaning is always contextual, as freedom is best thought of in its *Sitz im Leben*. Freedom and meaning must always be a *discovery* and *self-creation*. Both are evolutionary events, in process of being. In this way, Louverture can justify his cause that the social location of freedom of enslaved Africans is colonial Saint-Domingue; its context is racial slavery and colonialism, and its border is international. Even as he leaves Saint-Domingue in chains to be confined in the dungeon of Fort de Joux in "high in the Jura mountains,"[65] Louverture believes his oppressed compatriots will actualize the freedom event. His last words were not his last breaths! Louverture's revolutionary spirit will live in the people, as theirs will indwell him to the end.

I want to point out Louverture's continual use of the rhetoric of intimidation to strike further fear upon his opponents so he could win the war. In this last occasion, he is more determined to finish the course: "you have cut down . . . only the trunk of the tree of the liberty of the blacks." When the French troops heard the news from the eyewitness, they were conscious that they would face radical deaths by Dessalines's powerful indigenous army, as the Africans themselves suffered a double death: slavery and revolutionary war killing. "It will spring back from the roots, for they are numerous and deep" articulates the rising of new revolutionaries and a new ideal of human cooperation. The ideological texture embodied in most of Louverture's extant letters demonstrates the multiple uses of various rhetorical tropes. Louverture's three most important letters in his entire political career as leader and military chief have been examined inadequately by researchers. Those who have shown interest have given scant attention to the militant rhetoric of revolution the black general frequently deploys. Louverture constructs a conglomeration of rhetorical strategies that could be characterized as rhetoric of desire, rhetoric of conspiracy, and rhetoric of intimidation and terror.[66] A possible way to organize all these linguistic strategies is to suggest their contributive chief purpose: the revolutionary rhetoric of freedom.

Subsequent to his installation as commander-in-chief, in Saint-Domingue on May 2, 1797, Louverture wrote two apologetic letters to the French Directory, which date from October 28, 1797, and November 5, 1797, for two basic reasons. Both letters were written to defend

---

65. Bell, *Toussaint Louverture*, 267.

66. Individual definition for each particular phrase is followed in the last chart below.

the intents of the revolutionary slaves, and to rebuke erroneous charges made against Louverture and the enslaved community. These accusations were advanced both by the plantation owner Viennot Vaublanc, and the French general Donatien Rochambeau. It is good to point out here that the last phase of the revolution ended in 1804. It was because of Napoleon Bonaparte's ultimate goal to reinstitute slavery in Saint-Domingue, which he did successfully in French colonies of Martinique and Guadeloupe. With Louverture's deportation to France in 1802, Napoleon invaded Saint-Domingue with his powerful army. In short, the indigenous army won the last war of independence and Jean-Jacques Dessalines declared the independence of Haiti on January 1, 1804. The second letter (November 5, 1797) is well documented in by James and Tyson.[67] The first letter is also found in Tyson; yet, both authors have insufficiently dealt with the rhetoric of these extraordinary letters. Nonetheless, what I hope to do in closing is to briefly illustrate Louverture's skillful use of the rhetorical modalities in the interest of his people and in their struggle for social justice, human rights, and equality. The second letter is the most radical and is often viewed by historians as a symbolic representation of Louverture's total commitment to general liberty and his absolute devotion to black freedom and human rights.

Several points need to be made. First of all, these letters were motivated by the collective interest and libertarian ideology of the enslaved community. The voice of the people through Louverture is made absolutely clear. The documents epitomize the slaves' natural desire for freedom, a phenomenon that has been with them from the beginning. The intellectual preoccupation of the first letter is race vindication, whereas, the overarching theme of the second one is general emancipation. Observe below this provocative statement by Louverture, from the November 1792 letter:

> We know that they seek to impose some of them on you by illusory and specious promises in order to see renewed in this colony its former scenes of terror.... But they will not succeed. I swear it by all that liberty holds most sacred.... My knowledge of the blacks, make it my duty not to leave you ignorant either the crimes which they mediate or the oath that we renew, to bury ourselves under the ruins of a country revived by liberty rather than suffer the return of slavery.[68]

67. James, *Black Jacobins*, 195–97; Tyson, *Toussaint Louverture*, 43–45.
68. James, *Black Jacobins*, 195.

It is plain in the text that Louverture and the black masses under his leadership had decided to experience death at any cost; they feared the intention of some former French planters, slave owners, and landholders to restore slavery in the island. General liberty is the consequence of the affirmation and the justification of black humanity and dignity, and "the possibility of becoming subjects to a universal right to freedom"[69] The struggle for black sovereignty and collective subjectivity was the product of historical consciousness, group imagination, and ideological revelations. The militant black resistance expressed in Louverture's brilliant rhetoric also frustrated the French hegemony in the island. Louverture's intellectual integrity and moral courage lead him to oppose any future attempt of violence and/or the restoration of slavery in the colony. To refute various accusations and racist attacks made by Vienot Vaublanc, a member of the new elected right-ring French assembly of 1797, Louverture determines to defend republican ideals, the right of blacks to resist oppression, and ultimately the freedom of his people and the revolution. Vaublanc and several members of the Assembly questioned the capacity of black Africans for liberty and self-determination. Consequently, in the October 28 letter, Louverture "exposes the double standards by which colonial nations have always condemned the colonized people while justifying their own crimes and hypocrisy."[70] Below is one of his most provocative texts:

> Far be it from me to want to excuse the crimes of the revolution in St. Domingue by comparing them to even greater crimes, but citizen Vaublanc, while threatening us . . . didn't bother to justify the crimes that have afflicted us and which could only be attributed to a small number. . . . However, this former proprietor of slaves couldn't ignore what slavery was like; perhaps he had witnessed the cruelties exercised upon the miserable blacks, victims of their capricious masters, some of whom were kind but the greatest number of whom were true tyrants. And what would Vaublanc say . . . if, having only the same natural rights as us, he was in his turn reduced to slavery? Would he endure without complaint the insults, the miseries, the tortures, the whippings? And if he had the good fortune to recover his liberty, would he listen without shuddering to the howls of those who wished to tear if from him?[71]

69. Nesbitt, *Universal Emancipation*, 139.
70. Tyson, *Toussaint L'Ouverture*, 35.
71. Tyson, *Toussaint L'Ouverture*, 43.

Louverture continues his argument by insisting on human ontological sameness and the right of every individual or people to be evaluated not on the basis of social categories of color and/or race but on the content of their character and on their action:

> Certainly not; in the same way he so indecently accuses the black people of the excesses of a few of their members, we would unjustly accuse the entirety of France of the excesses of a small number of partisans of the old system. Less enlightened than citizen Vaublanc, we know, nevertheless, that whatever their color, only one distinction must exist between men, that of good and evil. When blacks, men of color, and whites are under the same laws, they must be equally protected and they must be equally repressed when they deviate from them. Such is my opinion; such are my desires.[72]

The letters of October 28 and November 5 forcefully attacked institutional slavery in Saint-Domingue. Louverture made it obvious to the French Directory that the forces of slavery came to an end in the colony. He remarks, "But to-day when they have left it [slavery], if they had a thousand lives they would sacrifice them all rather be forced into slavery again.... But no, the same hand which has broken our chains will not enslave us anew."[73] In the same line of thought, these two documents along with other important letters written by slaves are the political Manifestoes of the general will of the enslaved community at Saint-Domingue. Together these critical texts, directly addressed the representative body of the French government, interrogate the promise of the 1789 Constitution and the Declaration of the Rights of man and its application in the colonial territory. To reiterate the cause of black freedom, Louverture appealed to the "French Freedom Principle" as well as the conscience of the Nation's authorities:

> France will not revoke her principles, she will not withdraw from us the greatest of her benefits.... She will not permit her sublime morality to be perverted, those principles which do her most honour to be destroyed, her most beautiful achievement to be degraded, and her Decree of 16 Pluviose which so honours humanity to be revoked.[74]

---

72. Tyson, *Toussaint L'Ouverture*, 43.
73. James, *Black Jacobins*, 196.
74. James, *Black Jacobins*, 197.

At this point, Louverturian rhetorical tone and seemingly, his undivided faith in France, and the unprecedented conviction that the Empire will not deny these rights and freedoms to blacks are puzzling. On the other hand, for Toussaint the rhetoric of *liberté, égalité, fraternité* would become for the slaves a means for political empowerment, political action, revolutionary freedom, and their deliberate pursuit of self-governance. If France would not respond appropriately, then the enslaved people would be forced to "make the way by walking it."[75]

In the November 1797 letter, Toussaint Louverture took a daring stand on republican values and this was the key turning point for him as general leader in bolstering Saint-Domingue's liberty.[76] Toussaint overtly challenged the ontological foundations of colonial imperialism, racial slavery, and white supremacy altogether. When the threat was made to reimpose racial slavery at Saint-Domingue, Louverture deliberately manipulated language and used it as a deadly weapon to make known the community's decisive commitment to liberty and common loyalty: "The oath that we renew, [is] to bury ourselves under the ruins of a country revived by liberty rather than suffer the return of slavery."[77] It is evident that the Commander-in-chief had compromised his unconditional dedication to universal justice and the aspiration for freedom on behalf of his race in the colony. For the latter, freedom means the pure categorical imperative of human emancipation, that is, general liberty and the physical transition from slavery to liberty.

The famous letter dated July 1792 under the title *Lettre de Jean-François, Biassou et Belair* was written by Toussaint and two radical leaders and generals of the Haitian Revolution—Jean-François Papillon and Georges Biassou who had served as mentors to Louverture. Louverture signed in the name of, the third signature on the letter, his fourteen-year-old nephew Charles Belair.[78] The letter was written a little over a year succeeding the August 1791 insurrection, and thirty-five years after the Makandal conspiracy in 1757. It indicates these engaged freedom fighters were striving for the same cause and have shared visions of emancipation

---

75. Hallward, "Will of the People," 1.

76. Fick, "Saint-Domingue Slave Revolution and the Unfolding Independence, 1791–1804," in Geggus and Fiering, *World of the Haitian Revolution*, 178–81.

77. James, *Black Jacobins*, 195.

78. For more on its historical context, see Piquionne, "Lettre de Jean-François"; Piquionne reproduced the unedited original French version of the letter in her article. Here, I will be following the English translation in Bell, *Toussaint Louverture*, 39–41.

and human rights for the people. For these race leaders, the collective sense of responsibility (or duty) and the preoccupation to secure the unconditional freedom and the recognition of people of African origin at Saint-Domingue can be interpreted as an effort rooted in common experience and common consciousness and sprung from common pain, and the hardship of slave life. This powerful document was addressed to the representatives of the French government: the French Assembly General, the national commissioner, and the citizens of the colony.

This well-written document contains the most exhaustive statement of the specific demands by Louverture, the radical leaders, and the slave community at large. It represents the collective will of the enslaved population by giving prominence to the necessity of general liberty, *un idéal très précis* that the Assembly would have to confront. The following statement is worth observing. It exhibits the moral outrage of the slave population:

> For too long we have borne your chains without thinking of shaking them off, but any authority which is not founded on virtue and humanity, and which only tends to subject one's fellowman to slavery, must come to an end, and that end is yours.[79]

Further, the letter attacks the entire racial system of slavery and is predicated upon the theoretical ideas of fundamental human right to freedom and liberty, and principles of justice and human equality. The legal motif, juridical language, and forensic metaphors are important features of the text. The entire Western civilization is put on trial. In the letter, Louverture calls into question the universal justice and emancipation of all Africans enslaved by American and European forces.

> For a very long time, we have been victims of your greed and your avarice. Under the blows of your barbarous whip we have accumulated for you the treasures you enjoy in this colony; the human race has suffered to see what barbarity you have treated men like yourself—yes, men—over whom you have no right except that you are stronger and more barbaric than we are; you've engaged in [slave] traffic, you have sold men for horses, and even that is the least of your shortcomings in the eyes of humanity; our lives depend on your caprice, and when it's a question of amusing yourselves, it falls on a man like us [sic] who most often guilty of no other crime than to be under your orders.[80]

79. Piquionne, "Lettre de Jean-François," 133; Bell, *Toussaint Louverture*, 40.
80. Bell, *Toussaint Louverture*, 39.

Louverture and the authors of the document demonstrate their deep knowledge of the dominant political theories of the period; their familiarity with the French Government policies is outstanding. They do that in the most sophisticated manner. What is notable about this letter is its authors' undivided commitment to *la libération des Nègres*. Arguably, in the most blatant way, it symbolizes the voice of the people and embodies the spirit of the general will. The writers insist on the primacy of popular self-determination and collective action to creatively will the destiny of the slave community: "Here, Sirs, is the request of men who are your equals, and here their last resolution: they are resolved to live free or die."[81] Maulana Karenga states that a rhetoric of communal deliberation is a discourse for the good of the community and for the human race.[82]

In short, the letter underscores the psychological state (and condition or transition) of the slave community, their fears, boldness and desires, and equally the relentless motivation to revolutionary self-expression. As a rhetorical piece that questions, informs, and persuades, its authors employ Aristotelian persuasive rhetoric as the appeal to reason, the appeal to the emotions, and the appeal to character to drive the addressee to desired conclusions.

> Firstly: General liberty for all men held in slavery.
> Secondly: General amnesty for the past.
> Thirdly: The guarantee of these articles by the Spanish Government.
> Fourthly: The three articles above are the basis and the only means to be able to have a peace which would be respected by the two parties . . .[83]

The act of naming is of paramount significance in the process of revolutionary rhetoric of freedom, and performative speech acts. Dexter B. Gordon defines "naming" as "the first step in the rhetorical process of controlling and constraining the rhetorical."[84] The demands of the letter can be classified as a rhetoric of desire which underlines the community's vision to build communal balance and reconstruct themselves as free men and women. These political freedoms and rights were not new ideas to enlightened Europe or civilized France; the only exception was that these benefits, though natural as they are or seem, were only inclusive

---

81. Piquionne, "Lettre de Jean-François," 135.
82. Maulana Karenga, "Nommo, Kawaida," 3.
83. Piquionne, "Lettre de Jean-François," 134.
84. Gordon, *Black Identity*, 109.

to the citizens of the Motherland and European white men elsewhere. As Cornell West observes the "notion that black people are human beings is a relatively new discovery in the modern West. The idea of black equality in beauty, culture, and intellectual capacity remains problematic and controversial within prestigious halls of learning and sophisticated intellectual circles."[85] I propose that the dilemma is not the notion of a modern breakthrough concerning black humanity; rather it is the politics of equal recognition and the acknowledgement of human equality and ontological sameness.

As this piece of writing seeks to effectively confront France and its responsibility, the July 1792 document is perhaps the first comprehensive written statement of black consciousness and black resistance in the New World. Further, Louverture attacks the entire racial system of slavery and is predicated upon the theoretical ideas of fundamental human right to freedom and liberty, and principles of justice and human equality. However, the thrust of the document is the radical demands of general liberty for all black slaves in the colony and correspondingly the uncompromising affirmation of their humanity and equality with the civilized French. As a rhetoric of resistance, the letter responds militantly to oppression of racial slavery and the prevalent injustices of the colonial regime. But the language of the letter is crafted to reflect conclusively the experiences of the enslaved—i.e., "the property of the white man," and "men whom you have sold for horses")—and embodies the spirit of Enlightenment principles of political freedoms and rights; among which are natural rights, justice, truth, and the basic commitment to human equality.

The lawsuit imagery, "men whom you have sold for horses," denoting the crime of slave traders is simultaneously a clarion call to judgment and vindication. While it addresses openly the injustice of slavery and interrogates the transatlantic slave commerce, this lawsuit motif suggests the participatory experience of these writers as eyewitnesses and as those who testify. The phrase exposes both the degraded nature of the system and the character of those involved in the exchange. The forensic tone of the text is constructed as to draw attention to the pressing charges against France, and to narrate the slave-master relationship, the sociopsychological scenery and the condition of slavery as a functional system of production, exchange and trade controls, and ultimately the horrendous substitution of animals for persons. As Frank M. Kirkland reasons, "Slavery is morally minimized. . . . The question of injustice as

85. West, *Prophesy Deliverance!*, 48.

a functional rule pertinent to the machinery of slavery is never tendered because such a question raises matters dysfunctional to slavery."[86] Yet the most revealing human sentiment about this accusation is undoubtedly the moral outrage toward slave masters and the governing political body that supports the institution. African people in the New World were violently forced into modernity "with a serviceable connection to a historical past," chiefly the peculiar institution of slavery.[87] The evil and terror of African slavery was a precondition for progressive breakthroughs in the modern world; global capitalism, Euro-American expansion, the blossoming of Euro-American democracy, civilizations, and cultures remain the great paradox and legacy of Western modernity today.[88] From this framework, Louverture and the chief insurgents highlight the "Freedom Principle" which France symbolizes and employ almost the same rhetorical strategies of the French *Déclaration des droits de l'Homme et du Citoyen* of 1789: "Have you forgotten that you have formally vowed the declaration of the rights of man which says that men are born free, equal in their rights; that the natural rights include liberty, property, security and resistance to oppression?"

This protest document reveals in striking ways the slaves' frustrations and passionate discontent with the colonial order, the system of racial slavery, and the physical and psychological terrors and horrors defining and distinguishing slave life in the New World. Finally, Five bold strokes/questions form a dialectical progression have been observed: First, "What is the law that says that the black man must belong to and be the property of the white man?" This forceful statement calls for a public debate and simultaneously anticipates the qualified answer: Yes, our skin color is black but we are your equals and are (or should be) free like you. Second, "You Gentlemen who pretend to subject us to slavery—have you not sworn to uphold the French Constitution of which you are members?" The third question is in a form of a rhetoric of intimation, which interrogates the human failure to administer justice in the social sphere, as John Rawls defines "justice as fairness."[89] It follows a logical sequence: "What does it say, this respectable Constitution?" The second and third interrogations are the heart of the Memo. They are the essence of the

---

86. Kirkland, "Modernity and Intellectual Life in Black," 146–47.
87. Kirkland, "Modernity and Intellectual Life in Black," 148.
88. West, *Cornel West Reader*, 51–54.
89. For an intelligent study on this topic, see Rawls, *Theory of Justice*.

conversation, the real deal! After they have read this line, it must have been clear to the members of the French Assembly that Louverture and these radical leaders have studied the laws of the Metropole scrupulously. They quote them effortlessly even memorize the greatest maxim of the Declaration: "Men are born free, equal in their rights."

Some Concluding Thoughts

The excerpts and the chart below are written reports or discursive representations of the various linguistic techniques used in Louverture's political writings and letters. I suggest that we read them in light of t Louverture's single principle: the universal abolition of slavery in the island and the destruction of the plantation system that sustained it, and his role as public intellectual, social activist and anticolonial prophet of black freedom and human rights.[90] Nick Nesbitt, in his evaluation of Louverturian rhetoric and its effects, observes that "rhetorical intervention here became constitutive investment, founding at once a political subjectivity, both singular and collective, and a singular universal."[91] Notably, these rhetorical statements complement the proposed theory of "revolutionary rhetoric of freedom." Hence, I identify below in Appendix I the rhetorics in twelve classifications or categories. I divide them into two equal groups (Rhetorical Categories Group 1 and Rhetorical Categories Group 2) based on their characteristic and close association. While "Rhetorical Categories Group 1" puts forth moral arguments or ethical judgment, "Rhetorical Categories Group 2" appeals to the psychological, the realm of human emotion. In due course in the essay, I shall provide other instances of the use of these rhetorical strategies. The documentations below from fragments of letters and selected speeches and writings by Toussaint Louverture arguably depict his public roles as black intellectual, social activist, and anticolonial prophet of black freedom. They also tell us about this idea of freedom, liberty, and equality, key theoretical concepts which we shall return later.

90. Nesbitt, *Universal Emancipation*, 78–80.
91. Nesbitt, *Universal Emancipation*, 79.

TABLE 2.

Rhetorical categories group # 1. Toussaint Louverture and fragments of revolutionary rhetoric of freedom. Textual articulation and visual representation.

Rhetorical Categories Group 1	Meaning	Example
Rhetoric of self-assertion/ re-affirmation	The rhetoric of self-assertion underlines the human agency to self-action and self-determination.	"The oath that we renew, to bury ourselves under the ruins of a country revived by liberty rather than suffer the return of slavery" (James, 195).
Rhetoric of freedom	It could be perceived as a psychological state or a condition.	"We are within our rights . . . by your decrees you recognize that all men are free." (*Lettre de Jean-François, Biassou, Toussaint*)
Rhetoric of possibility	It assumes human incompleteness and explores the various possible ways to bringing wholeness, and fostering human growth.	"This is reassuring news for friends of humanity, and I hope that in the future all will feel more at ease and that, if we are able to enjoy peace and tranquility, the colony will flourish to an unparalleled degree." (Nesbitt, 12)
Rhetoric of desire/ intent	In these various instances, language is used to inform and clarity the revolutionaries' plan, desire, and determination.	"They are resolved to live free or die" (*Lettre de Jean-François, Biassou, Toussaint*) "It is for you, Citizens Directors, to run from over our heads the storm which the eternal enemies of our liberty are preparing in the shades of silence. . . . Do not allow our brothers, our friends, to be sacrificed to men who wish to reign over the ruins of the human species" (James, 195)
Rhetoric of warning	This rhetorical strategy communicates crucial information and projects the speaker's objective.	"You will see a resolution, unequivocal and carefully constructed, for the restoration of slavery" (James, 196). "They will be forced to defend their liberty that the Constitution guarantees" (Tyson, 39).
Rhetoric of conspiracy	This concept pertains to the actions of plots including fatal words and secrecy. It is very deliberate when demands are not met.	"The oath that we renew, to bury ourselves under the ruins of a country revived by liberty rather than suffer the return of slavery" (James, 195).

TABLE 3.

Rhetorical classification group # 2. Toussaint Louverture and fragments of revolutionary rhetoric of freedom. Textual articulation and visual representation.

Rhetorical Categories Group 2	Meaning	Example
Rhetoric of reversal	This rhetorical technique expresses profound discontent with the social order; it aims not at reforming but demolishing the complete system.	"Having perceived their treachery, I saw clearly that they intended for us to set upon each other to diminish our number and to enchain those who remained to return them to their former slavery. No, never would they achieve their infamous goal! And we will have revenge on these contemptible beings in our turn in every way" (Nesbitt, 10).
Rhetoric of terror/fear/intimidation	In these various instances, language functions as a weapon to incite obsessive fear, extreme terror, and provoke the opponent.	"Do they think that men who have been able to enjoy the blessing of liberty will calmly see it snatched away?" (James, 196).
Rhetoric of violence	Language at these various moments functions revolutionarily or radically. It is quite provocative and simultaneously challenging. The ultimate goal is to totally destroy.	"Let us unite forever, therefore, and, forgetting the past, let us seek henceforth only to crush our enemies and to avenge ourselves against our treacherous neighbours" (Nesbitt, 10).
Rhetoric of resistance	This particular rhetoric mechanism dominates the whole of the Haitian Revolutionary narrative to its culmination. It is both self-conscious and intentional.	"But if, to re-establish slavery in San Domingo, this was done, then I declare to you it would be to attempt the impossible: we have known how to face dangers to obtain our liberty, we shall know how to brave death to maintain it" (Tyson, 45).
Rhetoric of warning	This rhetorical strategy communicates crucial information and projects the speaker's objective.	"You will see a resolution, unequivocal and carefully constructed, for the restoration of slavery" (James, 196). "They will be forced to defend their liberty that the Constitution guarantees" (Tyson, 39).
Rhetoric of indignation	This rhetorical strategy discloses the revolutionaries' psychological state and points to passionate anger, terror, and the readiness to vindicate.	"You will see there that their determination to succeed has led them to envelop themselves in the mantle of liberty in order to strike it more deadly blows" (James, 196).

Throughout this chapter, we have argued to understand Louverture's role as public intellectual, social activist, and anticolonial prophet of black freedom and human rights. Through our close reading of his political writings, we were able to see how his ideas contributed to the theoretical concept of the revolutionary rhetoric of freedom. We have been able to trace some key words and phrases in the radical language of Louverture as the revolutionary leader of the Haitian Revolution par excellence. We have also observed a pattern of ideological links and thought that reflect Louverture's grand commitment to the principles of justice and natural rights. We have contended that Louverture had ambitious drive toward freedom and a desire for the slave community to live in a free society without slavery. Ideological sentiments in the collective sense against the institution of slavery and toward freedom are dominant features of this discourse. We have also pointed out various textual connections (i.e., textuality, echoes, allusions, textual parallels) and the ideological connections particularly in all three letters by Toussaint—July 1792, August 1797, and November 1797—and his other political ideas.

Freedom for Louverture meant the articulated vision of general emancipation as the general will of the slave community. As he stressed elsewhere his political ideology and philosophy of freedom: "We are free by natural right . . . who could dare claim the right to reduce into servitude men made like them and whom nature has made free."[92] However, freedom as general liberty meant different things in application to various segments of the slave population. The letter dated July 1792 represents the organized will of the slave community through the forceful ideas of Louverture. It indicates in clear terms the collective renunciation of slavery by the masses and their aspiration for collective emancipation. Louverture's first public announcement, "I want liberty and equality to reign in Saint-Domingue" is perhaps the most comprehensive statement of general emancipation in the epic of the Haitian Revolution, comparable to the letter dated July 1792. Louverture's many statements bore a pragmatic force, characterizing the revolution's rhetoric. In a sense, his rhetoric contributed to the birth of the new republic—the postcolonial Haiti—that was to be.

The ideological motives and rhetorical motifs associated with Louverture's writings and the literature of Haitian Revolution represent a rich vocabulary including but not limited to the following concepts:

92. Nesbitt, "Letter to Jean Francois, 13 June 1795," 16.

liberty, emancipation, independence, free, people, death, slave, human rights, hearts, master, slavery, black, white, live, free, die, etc. Toussaint Louverture exploited these rhetorical declaratives to call to arms, to incite fear to motivate, but also to encourage, desire, and resolve. The Revolutionary rhetoric of freedom embodied in creative speech acts, had performed its intended objective, the will of the slaved community. Finally, the Haitian Revolution—through the voice and rhetorical precision of Louverture—and its success was a particular vision of the good life and a particular conception of the good, in the interest of humanity—which were both defined by the revolution's historical trajectories and social location. In seeking total emancipation, Toussaint through his political writings and public functions had sacrificed his individual interests in order to actualize the general welfare of the slave community. These symbolic gestures are consistent with the principles that guided and sustained his commitment: collective self-determination, shared purpose, and self-expression. Toussaint Louverture's various roles as the public intellectual par excellence of the Haitian Revolution, social activist, and anticolonial prophet of black freedom and human rights are rooted in a robust form of human solidarity of shared values of communal determination and mutual commitment, and in his immediate and unflagging commitment to human liberty and decolonization.

The following chapter provides an exegetical reading of the letter mentioned in our previous analysis with an emphasis on the concept of collective freedom, emancipation, self-determination, and independence.

CHAPTER TWO

To Write for Change, Freedom, and Human Dignity

The Historic Letter of July 1792

IN THE FIELD OF Haitian revolutionary studies, the idea of general liberty and universal emancipation has been contested by a minority but powerful voices. Particularly, some Haitian historians have argued that the enslaved Africans in colonial Saint-Domingue had not been preoccupied with an early notion of general emancipation and neither had the natural drive to rupture the shackles of slavery and put an end to the French colonial regime. Many have unconvincingly relentlessly contented that *Liberté générale* was a latter manifestation and progressive thought, as the slaves themselves moved swiftly toward freedom, independence, and decolonization. In this chapter, I argue that the resolution to general liberty and independence were one singular commitment for the enslaved Africans. These twin and inseparable ideas did not develop in the later phase of the revolution. My contention is that general emancipation as total independence was already an early goal that came to fruition in the unfolding events leading to the Haitian Revolution.[1] However, it was

---

1. This position was recently argued by French historian Yves Benot, "Insurgents of 1791." I found Benot's conclusion in the article quite reasonable. He writes, "As long as universal liberty had not yet been won, first by defeating the French and then the Spanish and the English—that is, until 1794—differences of opinion and values had to take second phase to the necessity of unity in the struggle. Yes, such differences were already present in embryo. My intention here has not been to speculate what black independence in 1791 or 1792 might have led to or to judge in any way what the leaders conceived to be good government. My intention is simply to make clear that the aspiration toward independence was present from the beginning, although the leaders

conditioned by a range of contingent circumstances and events in which Saint-Dominguan slaves were obliged to fight for freedom, which translated into a matter of practical reality.

As we have observed in the previous chapter, the concept of independence is manifest more clearly in the rhetorical language and rhetorical force of the July 1792 letter. In this chapter, we shall continue our analysis of this letter, hoping to strengthen our argument. Haitianist historian David Geggus has proven that that the concept of general emancipation as it relates to black freedom in colonial Saint-Domingue began with Toussaint Louverture;[2] prominence is given particularly to Toussaint's military intervention in the spring 1794, which he insists like other historians in the field was a vital moment toward the Haitian freedom.[3] Nonetheless, many historians have overlooked the significance of the historic letter of July 1792. Below, I explore the meaning of freedom by examining this piece of document. Toward this objective, I analyze the rhetoric of freedom and race and underscore the various rhetorical devices embedded in the letter. A second objective here is to think through the idea of freedom, as the writers of this famous piece do so through the act of writing.

The July 1792 letter was first discovered by the French scholar Nathalie Piquionne ("Lettre de Jean-François, Biassou et Belair") in 1998. The illustrious document, according to Piquionne, was first published in February 9, 1793, in a Parisian journal, *Le Créole Patriote*, by the journalist and colonist writer Michel-Claude Louis Milscent de Mussé, who himself was born in Saint-Domingue in 1740. It is observed that Milscent was an active participant in various insurrectionist movements associated with the island's maroons, even before the French Revolution of 1789.[4] Consequently, we can also state that he also witnessed the early unfolding events of pre-revolutionary Haiti. Since he left Saint-Domingue for Angers, France in July 28, 1791, it is uncertain how Milscent received the letter which he shortly made known in less than a year to a European audience, when revolutionary France was still in the nascent process of national recovery from her tragic revolution. Nonetheless, undoubtedly, the journalist knew about the famous letter, also knew those who

---

would take that step until Bonaparte's attempted restoration left them no other choice" (Geggus and Fiering, *World of the Haitian Revolution*, 108).

2. See Geggus, "'Volte-Face' of Toussaint Louverture."
3. See Girard, *Slaves Who Defeated Napoleon*.
4. Piquionne, "Lettre de Jean-François," 132.

have penned it and demonstrably were in solidarity and alliance with the general masses, fighting for the same cause of black freedom. The truth remains that Milscent owned a personal copy of the letter, while freedom talks occupied the intellectual process of revolutionary slaves in the island of Saint-Domingue.

The significance of the letter is paramount, since it has completely reconfigured "the ideological chronology of the Haitian Revolution" as Nick Nesbitt correctly observes.[5] Piquionne comments that the letter absolutely contradicts the famous French biographer Pierre Pluchon's categorical denial of the prevalence of general liberty among the slaves at Saint-Domingue.[6] Another important note is that the letter might help us to look at the narratives of the revolution from different centers and from different perspectives of the individuals who made it a successful world event. Notably, it might also assist us to decentralize the heroic focus on the person and activities of Toussaint Louverture whom C. L. R. James, Aimé Césaire, and others have effectively and triumphalistically produced in their oeuvre. In short, the document reveals equally that the Saint-Dominguan general masses and the insurgent leaders were obsessively preoccupied with the concept we call general emancipation—the inner desire of the enslaved to escape the bondage of slavery and thereby to obtain their own freedom—and that freedom is itself intrinsically unquantifiable.[7]

As already pointed above, some historians in the field of Haitian studies have argued against the idea of general liberty. For example, David Geggus articulates that slaves' notions about freedom were all ambiguous, and "conditioned by their perception of what was possible or probable."[8] Yves Debbasch, Gabriel Debien, and Francois Girod, in varying degrees, implausibly contend that the urge for freedom was not strong among Saint-Dominguan slaves or counted very little to the Haitian independence.[9] Even radical political theorist Jean-Jacques Rousseau who championed human liberty and once declared that "man is born

---

5. Nesbitt, *Universal Emancipation*, 14; Nesbitt, *Caribbean Critique*.
6. Pluchon, *Toussaint Louverture*, 137.
7. Fick, *Making of Saint Domingue*, 6.
8. Geggus, *Slavery, War, and Revolution*, 32.
9. Quoted in Fick, *Making of Haïti*, 6; Geggus, *Slavery, War, and Revolution*, 29; for further studies, consider Debbasch, *Le marronage*; Debien, *Les esclaves aux Antilles françaises*; Girod, *La vie quotidienne de la société créole*.

free, and everywhere he is in chains"[10] suggested that slavery destroyed in the enslaved the natural drive for freedom. A careful reading of the text will help us answer precisely the daunting question: whether slaves at Saint-Domingue had a natural drive for liberty? Or was the desire for independence was there from the beginning? Evidently, the African slaves in Saint-Domingue from Makandal to Dessalines had a natural drive for freedom and decolonization. They established the first postcolonial order and government in the Americas.

As mentioned in the previous chapter, the letter was written in July 1792. The Memo was directed to three key entities: the French Assembly General, the National Commissioner, and the Citizens of the colony. The original reads: *Lettre originale des chefs des Nègres révoltés, à l'assemblée générale, aux commissaires nationaux et aux citoyens de la partie française de Saint-Domingue du mois de juillet 1792.*

This well-eloquent document represents the most exhaustive statement of the specific demands of the slave population at Saint-Domingue. As an organized will, they make the bold assertion of their natural right for general liberty, *un idéal très précis*, the Assembly would have to confront. Further, the letter attacks the entire racial system of slavery and is predicated upon the theoretical ideas of fundamental human right to freedom and liberty, and principles of justice and human equality. Its authors demonstrate their incredible knowledge of the dominant political theories of the period and substantially their familiarity with the French Government policies. They do that in the most sophisticated manner. What is notable about this letter is its authors' undivided commitment to *la libération des Nègres*, black freedom. Arguably, in the most blatant way, it symbolizes the voice of the people and embodies the spirit of the general will. The insistence of the letter is on the primacy of popular self-determination, and the collective action to creatively will their own destiny.[11] In short, the letter privileges the slave masses, their fears, boldness and desires, and equally the relentless motivation to revolutionary self-expression. The July 1792 document is indisputably the first manifesto of a comprehensive written statement of black consciousness and black resistance in the New World. After all, it was an epoch-making document.

The letter was penned by a committee of three insurgent leaders: Jean-Francois Papillon, Georges Biassou, and Charles Belair who were

---

10. Rousseau, *Social Contract*, 41.
11. Hallward, "Will of the People," 17–19.

leading successors of Dutty Boukman, the eminent resurrectionist-instigator of the general revolt of 1791. Favorably honored by the masses, the three were the most influential leaders in the northern plain. They were also present at the August 1791 meeting. Traditions tell us that Jean-Francois was an intelligent slave and became a runaway before the revolution.[12] Biassou was known to be an ambitious man, loved women and vindictive at times. Being the general leader of the rebel army, it was Biassou who launched Louverture's military career when the latter served under his order. James states that Jean-Francois and Biassou "were men who were born to command."[13] As a native from the North, Belair was an intelligent young man and Louverture's nephew by blood or adoption.[14] He was probably nineteen years old in 1792 when his signature appears on the famous letter;[15] which means he would have been twenty-three years old in 1801;[16] shortly a year before Napoleon Bonaparte ordered his uncle to be deported to France and be left in solitude in the depths of Fort-de Joux prison. In what follows, I will demonstrate by a careful reading of the letter that the African slaves in colonial Saint-Domingue exhibited both intellectually and practically an early conviction for their freedom because of the fundamental belief that they were human beings equal in essence and value and that no man should be enslaved by another, and that the commitment for independence was with them from the beginning. The English translation is followed below with further exegetical commentary.

> Gentlemen,
>
> Those who have the honor to present you with these Memoirs are a class of men whom up to the present you have failed to recognize as like unto you, and whom you have covered in opprobrium by heaping upon them the ignominy attached to their unfortunate

---

12. James, *Black Jacobins*, 93.
13. James, *Black Jacobins*, 94.
14. Bell, *Toussaint Louverture*, 43.
15. Bell believes that the name Belair, the third signature on the letter, was used "as a screen." Toussaint was the actual third author of the document (43). If this was the case, then Bell's assumption that Toussaint was a figure "capable of absolute treachery, absolute ruthlessness, and absolute hypocrisy" (106), coupled with rhetorical brilliance, logical clarity, and military genius (Nick 145) is plausible. I contend that there's neither legitimate nor historical reason to assume the third signatory was neither Toussaint's nor any adequate evidence to doubt Belair as its original author.
16. Heinl and Heinl, *Written in Blood*, 94.

lot. These are the men who don't know how to choose big words, but who are going to show you and all the world the justice of their cause; finally, they are those whom you call your slaves and who claim the rights to which all men may aspire.

For too long, Gentlemen, by way of abuses which one can never too strongly accuse to have taken place because our lack of understanding and our ignorance—for a very long time, I say, we have been victims of your greed and your avarice.

Under the blows of your barbarous whip we have accumulated for you the treasures you enjoy in this colony; the human race has suffered to see with what barbarity you have treated men like yourself—yes, men—over whom you have no other right except that you are stronger and more barbaric that we; you've engaged in [slave] traffic, you have sold men for horses, and even that is the least on your shortcomings in the eyes of humanity; our lives depend on your caprice, and it's a question of amusing yourselves it falls on a man like us [sic] who most often is guilty of no other crime than to be under your orders.

We are black, it is true, but tell us, Gentlemen, you who are so judicious, what is the law that says that the black man must belong to and be the property of the white man? Certainly you will not be able to make us see where that exists, if it is not in your imagination—always ready to form new [phantasms] so long as they are to your advantage. Yes, Gentlemen, we are free like you, and it is only by your avarice and our ignorance that anyone is still held in slavery up to this day, and we can neither see nor find the right which you pretend to have over us, nor anything that could prove it to us, set down on the earth like you, all being children of the same father created in the same image. We are your equals then, by natural right, and if nature pleases itself to diversity colors within the human race, it is not a crime to be born black nor an advantage to be white. If the abuses in the Colony have gone on for several years, that was before the fortunate revolution which has taken place in the Motherland, which has opened for us the road which our courage and labor will enable us to ascend, to arrive at the temple of Liberty, like those brave Frenchmen who are our models and whom all the universe is contemplating.

For too long we have borne your chains without thinking of shaking them off, but any authority which is not founded on virtue and humanity and which only tends to subject one's fellowman to slavery, must come to an end, and that end is yours. You Gentlemen who pretend to subject us to slavery—have you not sworn to uphold the French Constitution of which you are members? What does it say, this respectable Constitution?—what is the fundamental law?; have you forgotten that you have formally vowed the declaration of the rights of man which says that men are born free, equal in their rights; that the natural rights include liberty, property, security and resistance to oppression? So then, you cannot deny what you have sworn, we are within our rights, and you ought to recognize yourselves as perjurers; by your decrees you recognize that all men are free, but you want to maintain servitude for four hundred and eighty thousand individuals who allow you to enjoy all that you possess; by your creatures you offer us only to give liberty to our chiefs; but it still one of your maxims of politics that is to say that those who have been the half of our work would be delivered by us to be your victims. No, we prefer a thousand deaths to acting that way toward our own kind. And you want to accord us the benefits which are due to us, they must also shower onto all of our brothers. . . .

Gentlemen, in very few words you have seen our way of thinking—it is unanimous and it is after consulting everyone to whom are connected in the same cause that we present to you our demands, as follows.

First: General Liberty for all men detained in slavery.

Second: General amnesty for the past.

Third: The guarantee of these articles by the Spanish Government.

Fourth: the three articles above are the basis and the sole means to be able to have a peach which would be respected by the two parties, and only after the approbation that would be made in the name of the Colony and approved by M. the Lieutenant General and the National Civil Commissioners to present it to the King, and to the National Assembly. If like us, you desire that the articles above be accepted, we will commit ourselves to the following: first, to lay down our arms; second that each of us will return to the plantation to which he belongs and resume his work on condition of a wage which will be set by the year for each Cultivator who will begin to work for a fixed term.

Here, Gentlemen, is the request of men who are like you, and here is their final resolution: they are resolved to live free or die.

We have the honor to be, Gentlemen, you very humble and obedient servants.

(Signed)
Biassou, Jean-Francois, Bélair[17]

---

17. This translation is found in Bell's *Toussaint Louverture*, 39–41. To my knowledge this is the first rendering of the French original of the July 1792 letter in English.

This letter of July 1792 registers the just complaints that the masses had against imperial France and sets forth all the rights of the African people in Saint-Domingue; as it would be done eleven years later on December 31, 1803, when Louis Félix Boisrond-Tonnerre crafted the Declaration of Independence, which was shortly read by Dessalines on January 1, 1804 (Laurent Dubois Avengers *of the New World* 298). As a rhetoric of protest, the thrust of the document, however, is the radical demands of general liberty for all black slaves in the colony and equally the uncompromising affirmation of their humanity and equality with the civilized French. As a rhetoric of resistance, the letter responds militantly to oppression of racial slavery and the prevalent injustices of the colonial regime. But the language of the letter is crafted to reflect conclusively the experiences of the enslaved, and embodies the spirit of Enlightenment principles of political freedoms and rights; among which are natural rights, justice, truth, and the basic human equality. More importantly, the chief insurgents highlight the "Freedom Principle" which France symbolizes and employ almost the same rhetorical strategies of the French *Déclaration des droits de l'Homme et du Citoyen* of 1789 (*Avez vous oublié formellement jurée la déclaration des droits de l'hommes qui dit que les hommes naissent libres et égaux en droit et que les droits naturels sont la liberté, la propriété la sûreté et la résistance à l'oppression*: "Have you forgotten that you have formally vowed the declaration of the rights of man which says that men are born free, equal in their rights; that the natural rights include liberty, property, security and resistance to oppression?").

Observably, any form of protest is an automatic response or a counter-response to people, movements, or events. Rhetoric protest is structurally designed to persuade and motivate the hearer or recipient. For example, this letter was written against the backdrop of the systematic racialized violence and the hegemony of white supremacy of the colonial order. Its clear objective was to influence the French Assembly, Legislative and Constituent to take a decisive course of action which the senders effortlessly laid out in precise terms: (1) the general liberty for all men detained in slavery, (2) the general amnesty for the past, and (3) the guarantee of articles one and two, and other principles of justice assumed

---

Bell's English text, however, is incomplete; the author leaves a good portion of the letter untranslated. For substantial details, see Pauléus-Sannon, *Histoire de Toussaint L'Ouverture*, 3:35; Laurent, *Toussaint Louverture*, 68–72; Piquionne, "Lettre de Jean-François," 133–35.

in the correspondence (*La liberté général de tous les hommes détenus dans l'esclavage, l'amnistie général pour le passé, et la garantie de ses articles*).

The demands in the letter can be classified as rhetoric of desire accentuating the forceful demands of the general masses of slaves. Notably in the text, Jean-Francois, Biassou, and Toussaint expose France's paradox and hypocrisy concerning its claim of general liberty and equality for all. In one hand, France preaches a gospel of the civilized order, human rights, and the unconditional equality of all man; on the other hand, she denies those rights to Africans and maintains a rigorous structure of human servitude at Saint-Domingue and elsewhere in the Caribbean seas.[18] The French ambiguity could be explained in light of David Scott's striking phrase, "the tragedy of colonial Enlightenment"[19] and Césaire's lamentation "that Europe is unable to justify itself either before the bar of 'reason' or before the bar of 'conscience'"[20] on the colonial question. It is from this premise that the three interrogated the policies of the metropole and their overdue application in the French colonies.

Five bold strokes/questions form a dialectic progression have been observed: First, *Quel est cette loy qui dit que l'hommes noirs doit appartenir et être une propriété à l'homme blancs?*: "What is the law that says that the black man must belong to and be the property of the white man?" This particular rhetoric calls for a public debate and simultaneously anticipates the qualified answer: Yes, our skin color is black but we are your equals and ought to be free like you. Second, *Messieurs qui prétendez nous assujettir a l'esclavage n'avez vous pas, jurer de maintenir la constitution française dont vous êtes membres?*: "You Gentlemen who pretend to subject us to slavery—have you not sworn to uphold the French Constitution of which you are members?" The third question is in a form of rhetoric of intimidation. It follows a logical sequence: *Que ait elle c'ette respectable constitution?*: "What does it say, this respectable Constitution?" The second and third interrogations are the heart of the memo. They are the essence of the conversation, the real deal! After they have read this line, it must have been clear to the members of the French Assembly that those former slaves have studied the laws of the Metropole scrupulously. They quote them innerantly and even memorize the greatest maxim of the

---

18. Historians account for 480,000 African slaves in Saint-Domingue: Geggus, *Haitian Revolutionary Studies*; Dubois, *Avengers of the New World*; Fick, *Making of Haiti*.

19. Scott, *Conscripts of Modernity*, 170–208.

20. Césaire, *Discourse on Colonialism*, 31.

Declaration: *Les hommes naissent libres et égaux en droit:* "Men are born free, equal in their rights."

A well known story was told by a colonial historian, an eyewitness of the Saint-Domingue revolutionary war. Shortly after the general revolt of 1791, an insurgent was captured by a squad of white soldiers; as he attempted to flee by pleading his innocence, as one soldier reports, "when he saw that his fate was sealed," he started to "laugh, sing, and joke and jeered at us in mockery." At his execution, "he gave the signal himself and met death without fear or complaint." The slave captor who searched his body found "in one of his pockets pamphlets printed in France, filled with commonplaces about the Rights of man and the Sacred Revolution."[21] On the other hand, it must be noted that the slaves scarcely needed to be persuaded or reminded by bourgeois' political ideas of the legitimacy of their freedom and basic rights. Largely, when Thomas Jefferson spoke these historic and famous words: "We hold these truths to be self-evident" to the American public in 1776, he was in turn asserting certain undeniable facts that were universal, true, and sacred to all men. Creative human laws are only a witness to the natural right and human sameness. How can one defend self-evident principles? Assuredly, our judicial policies must protect them and guarantee those rights and liberties for all human beings.

The imperatives of human ontological equality, life, liberty, and resistance to oppression embedded in this letter exhibit in the most emphatic language the popular conviction and demands of the unfree slave population. It is evident that the slave masses judged that these rights which the French Declaration triumphs must be extended to them as individuals. So, their leaders, with the popular consent, penned this protest letter articulating implicitly these categories of the organized will of the people. By "the will of the people," I posit the notion of self-contained political actions of the masses, what Peter Hallward terms "a dialectical voluntarism."[22] The latter means the deliberate steps toward emancipation and the process of collective self-determination. Therefore, the "Gentlemen" of the French Assembly have been warned of the consequences of miscarrying injustice in the name of progress and reason, a threat that is articulated in the latter part of the text.

---

21. Dubois, *Avengers of the New World*, 102; Fick, *Making of Haiti*, 111; Parham, *My Odyssey*, 32–34.
22. Hallward, "Will of the People," 17.

Finally, the last two interrogations in the form of a rhetoric of intimidation state: *Quelle est sa loix fondamentale? Avez vous oublié que vous avez formellement jurée la déclaration des droits de l'hommes qui dit que les hommes naissent libres et égaux en droit et que les droits naturels sont la liberté, la propriété la sûreté et la résistance a l'oppression?*: "What is its fundamental law?"; "Have you forgotten that you have formally vowed the declaration of man which says that men are born free, equal in their rights; that the natural rights include liberty, property, security, and resistance to oppression?" These substantial concerns recapitulate the thesis of the letter and recast the fervent urgency of its rigorous requests. The most memorable line of the letter articulates a rhetoric of desire, the resolution of the slaves: *Ils sont résolu de vivre libres ou de mourir*: "They are resolved to live free or die." To put it in another way: *ils préfèrent de vivre libre que de vivre esclaves*: "They prefer to live free than living as slaves."

In summary, this eloquent statement embodied in human speech wages war against any form of human injustice or oppression. The vigor of the language employed therein constitutes perhaps the most succinct and compelling testimony of the Saint-Dominguan slave population's commitment to the ideals of liberty and equality and their total dedication to these principles. The meaning of freedom contested here is not presented merely as a function of space or people, be it France or French citizens; but how we concomitantly and deliberately pursue pure justice for all and uphold human dignity. In addition, the aspiration for liberty expressed in these pages of the letter is the paramount determination of the enslaved to get rid of slavery and live in a free society. As David Scott observes, "The problem of emancipation entailed. . . .The project of imagining and constructing a sustainable freedom with new forms of life"[23] for the Saint-Dominguan slaves. Consequently, this rhetoric of protest dated July 1792 could not be ignored by its recipients. Its indelible voice would not be silenced. The enslaved Africans were resolved to live free or die, such was their undivided commitment, an early testament of the inescapable inner drive for freedom. And this freedom was both sacrificial and determinative. The letters examined in the previous chapter and the current one show clearly how the African slave community at Saint-Domingue used the craft of writing to deliberately make known their longing for freedom and independence.

---

23. Scott, *Conscripts of Modernity*, 133.

CHAPTER THREE

Changing Western Historiography and Epistemology

Anténor Firmin, the Egyptian Question, and Afrocentric Imagination

WHILE THIS PRESENT CHAPTER is not concerned with freedom and independence in the context of the previous chapters examined above, it calls for intellectual reparations in the context of Western intellectual modern history and Black Atlantic thought and vindicative discourse. There is a sense to understand this chapter in terms of a clarion call for the intellectual freedom of the (black) mind and the decolonization of the (black) spirit, as Firmin himself a prominent black intellectual deliberately interrogates the narrative and logic of Western intellectual history and brilliantly acknowledges the contributions of Africa and people of African descent in ancient and modern civilizations. For Firmin, this call of freedom and determination means to let the black thinker speaks his mind freely and unapologetically by interrogating the narrative of erasure and alienation in Western history and by reclaiming the voice of black people in hum/global history.

Consequently, the present chapter examines Joseph Anténor Firmin's engagement with the racial situation in ancient Egypt. We are particularly interested in Firmin's confrontational claim of the Black African origin of the ancient Egyptian civilization. This analysis also considers Firmin's thought along the line of Afrocentric articulation of the historic contribution of the Kemetic culture to classical Greece and world civilizations, as well as his plea for the "formal recognition" of the achievement of the "Black race" in the intellectual development of the modern world. Ultimately, Firmin makes an urgent call for the revolution of the mind and for the transformation of the intellectual trajectories of Western historiography and African history.

In 1885, the nineteenth-century Haitian lawyer, statesman, antiracist intellectual, anthropologist, and Egyptologist Joseph Anténor Firmin (1850–1911) published his magisterial text, *De l'égalité des races humaines (Anthropologie positive)* (*The Equality of the Human Races*) in Paris in the form of an impassioned "scientific rebuttal" to Arthur de Gobineau's scientific racism and, particularly, against his central thesis of the ontological superiority of the Aryan-White race and the ontological inferiority of the Black race. Gobineau articulated his ideas on the subject of racial hierarchy and racial essentialism of the human races, and correspondingly the history and achievement of the white race in modernity in his controversial and unfortunate text, *Essai sur l'inégalité des races* (*An Essay on the Inequality of the Human Races*) (1853–1855).[1] For Gobineau, the history of the world in the strictest sense of the term is a racial accomplishment, the accomplishment of whiteness.[2] On the contrary, Firmin argued that the Aryan race does not name the conclusion of human history and the history of an achievement, which the French anthropologist and other proponents of white ideology and white supremacy celebrated. The Haitian intellectual also challenged Western racist attitudes toward Blacks and the logic of nineteenth century's scientific racism for ranking the Black race discriminately and deliberately in the lowest racial ladder of the racial hierarchy of the human races and in the metanarratives of human history. Ostensibly, Firmin anticipated Du Bois's 1903 perennial question: "What does it mean to be a problem?"[3] In the same line of thought, Firmin was deeply troubled about what Western Egyptologists had reformatted ancient Egyptian-African history to fit their ideological agenda and intellectual vision of world history.

---

1. An excellent and more recent translation of Gobineau's work in the English language is by Mosse, *Inequality of Human Races*.

2. African American theologian and public intellectual J. Kameron Carter writes brilliantly about the problem of European construction of history and the *anthropos*, and Western racially motivated theological discourse, *Race: A Theological Account*. Carter cogently argues that race is a theological problem in modern Western intellectual history.

3. See Du Bois, *Souls of Black Folk*.

Firmin's cogent response in his celebrated text not only interrogates Gobineau's racist biases but also the logic of other racists who had denied the intellectual and moral achievements of the African and Black people in the foundations of modern civilization and Western modernity. Firmin's intellectual curiosity and rigor weights the veracity of Western historiography, Western Egyptology, modernity's racial imagination, and the scientific enterprise of his time.[4] A major aspect of this present analysis is to explore precisely Firmin's Afrocentric imagination and sensibility championed by Molefi Asante—the most vocal proponent and poignant intellectual voice of Afrocentrism in modern times—in regard to the Nile Valley Civilizations. We will also study his argument about the African origin (or the Africanness) of the ancient Egyptian in comparison with other Black Atlantic writers who seem to exhibit an Afrocentric tendency and leaning. Consequently, this essay will apply some of the protocols of Afrocentric inquiry as delineated in Asante's theoretical and yet practical work, *Kemet, Afrocentricity and Knowledge, The Afrocentric Idea*, and other cognate texts.

Firmin posits that the Kemetic-Egyptian civilization was a Black civilization and that the Black race had made notable contributions to universal civilization, which are often undermined in Western scholarship. His revisionist exposés were motivated by a genuine desire to correct European perspective on African history and culture as well as to valorize Black achievement in human history. In so doing, the Haitian anthropologist-intellectual was concurrently deconstructing Western Egyptology and reshaping ancient Egyptian-African historical narrative. The general outline of the essay offers a succinct narrative of scholarly reflections on Firmin's text (part 1) and analyses the Afrocentric discourse (and Afrocentricism and Egyptocentrism) in order to situate Firmin's Afrocentric sensibility (part 2). We close the essay with Firmin's thoughtful engagement with the "Egyptian question," that is with the ideological interpretation of the history, life, and culture of ancient Egypt by Western Egyptologists.

Firmin and His Text: A Brief Assessment

Firmin's main objective in *The Equality of the Human Races* primary was first intended to dismantle De Gobineau's racist ideas—such as his

---

4. Firmin anticipates Cheikh Anta Diop, *Nations Negres et Culture*.

doctrine of the innate inferiority of the Black race and the innate superiority of the Aryan-White race—and to challenge the strident racist voices, dangerous ideologies and scientific racism of the nineteenth century.[5] His second objective was to underscore Black pride, the historic achievement and intellectual contributions of ancient Egypt and the people of African ancestry across time and space—such as the symbolic example of Haitians and African Americans[6]—in the metanarratives of human history. His third objective was to demonstrate that "white reason" was delinquent and inadequate. His fourth goal was to stress that "whiteness" was the central problem of modernity and the greatest threat to human flourishing and solidarity. Firmin's final goal was to challenge and destabilize Western arrogance and its claim of ontological superiority. Hence, in the book Firmin portrays himself simultaneously as an anti-racist, anti-colonial, and anti-imperial radical as well as an anti-white oppression and anti-white arrogance intellectual. Most importantly, Joseph Anténor Firmin presents himself as the Apostle of the undivided equality of all people.

In several chapters of *The Equality of the Human Races*, Firmin endeavors, with intellectual rigor, commitment, and scrupulous research, to analyze and debunk European construction of race and interrogate the logic of white supremacy. In the process, he attempts to offer a different epistemology than what was provided by European men of letters by highlighting the distinctive role Africa had played in the advancement

---

5. Firmin critically engaged a wide range of European anthropologists, philosophers, scientists, and Egyptologists. Some of his most conversational partners were Broca, *Bulletin de la Société d'Anthropologie* (1860), and *Histoire des progrès des études anthropologiques depuis la fondation de la société en 1859. Mémoires de la Société d'anthropologie de Paris, III* (Paris, 1869); Joseph Arthur de Gobineau, *Essai sur l'inégalité des Races Humaines*, 4 vols. (Paris, 1853-55); Julian J. Virey, *Histoire naturelle du genre humain* (1800); Paul Topinard, *Eléments d'anthropologie générale* (Paris, 1885); Auguste Comte, *Cours de philosophie positive* (1835); Charles Darwin, *On Origin of Species* (1859); Herbert Spencer, *Classification des sciences* (1872); Georg Hegel, Immanuel Kant, Jean-François Champollion, Jacques Ampère, Jean Louis Armand de Quatrefages de Bréau, etc.

6. Firmin argues for the significant impact of the Haitian Revolution in world history as well as appeals to Haiti's national history, and the intellectual evolution of Haitians and African Americans to refute the doctrine of the inequality of the races, 180-201, 203-24, 295-323. In a recent review of Firmin's work, Watson R. Denis states that "Firmin's work extends the nineteenth century Haitian political and historical thoughts, which defended the Haitian, independence, the equality of races, and the pride of Black achievements in world history" ("Review of *The Equality of the Human Races*," 327).

of human civilizations as well in the emergence of modernity, what we might phrase Black African particularity.[7]

The Equality of the Human Races is an apologetic text that showcases with clear arguments, intellectual meticulousness and lucidity the momentous contributions of ancient Egyptian civilization in the early developmental stages of classical Greek life and thought and ultimately in the birth of the Western world.[8] Yet, the reception of Anténor Firmin, his ideas, and his magnum opus as a pioneer work in modern anthropology and in modern Western intellectual history had been a disappointment. It was after sixty-three years after his death that prominent twentieth-century Haitian scholar and anthropologist, Jean Price-Mars, an intellectual heir of Firmin, produced the first full biography on him in the French language. Price-Mars's posthumous *Anténor Firmin* was released in the French language in 1978.[9] In the same way, the first English translation of *The Equality of the Human Races* was produced by the Haitian literary scholar Asselin Charles in 2002, some eighty-three years after its original publication.[10]

The gradually recent resurgence of scholarly interest in the Anglophone world indicates a renewed appreciation of the significance of Firmin's ideas in our postcolonial moment. It is possible to group recent scholarship on *The Equality of the Human Races* in five interrelated categories: the book's relation to the discipline of modern anthropology, race

---

7. The idea of Black contributions to modernity and world civilizations is well documented voluminously in the writings of other Black Atlantic writers such as Du Bois, *The Negro*, *The Gift of Black Folk*, and *The World and Africa*; Price-Mars, *Ainsi parla l'Oncle*; Diop, *African Origin of Civilization*, and *Civilization or Barbarism*.

8. In the final part of the essay, we will discuss Firmin's argument for Greek borrowings from Egyptian arts, mathematics, sciences, literature, rhetoric, philosophy, religion, and architecture.

9. Previous short studies on Firmin and the present text in evaluation in French include the following: Viaud, *La pesonnalite d'Antenor Firmin*; Pompilus, *Anténor Firmin par lui-même*; Firmin's biographer, Price-Mars highlights two important studies on Firmin: the first is by historian H. P. Sannon, which appeared in the Haitian review *Le Temps*, respectively on August 24 and 31, 1938; the second is by Seymour Pradel which was also published in the pages of *Le Temps*.

10. Asselin Charles, the incredible translator, reproduced, as he himself remarks, "in modern English Firmin's modulate French style" ("Note on the Translation," in Firmin, *Equality of the Human Races*, ix); Charles also mentions that Firmin's style is "at once lyrically poetic, scientifically technical, and passionately polemical"(ix). In this present essay, I will often refer to Charles' *tour de force* translation.

studies, Egyptology, history of ideas, and Africana studies.[11] According to Firmin's biographer, Price-Mars, Firmin "attacked without interruption the most diverse aspects of thorny problems of anthropology and the related disciplines in the science of man."[12] Afro-Jewish philosopher Lewis R. Gordon names *The Equality of the Human Races* a "classic in Africana philosophy, philosophical anthropology, and historical anthropology."[13] Anthropologist Carolyn Fluehr-Lobban claims that as a pioneering work on anthropology and a scientific project, *The Equality of the Human Races* was "a positive assertion of the potential of the anthropology objectivity to study human differences without the bias of biological and social ranking."[14]

Current studies on Firmin delineate a clear connection between the science of modern anthropology and the modern construction of race, as observed in *The Equality of the Human Races*. Lamentably, Kevin A. Yelvington remarks that "the Haitian anthropologist Antenor Firmin (1850–1911), whose writings on 'race' preceded those of Franz Boas and were in direct opposition to contemporaneous racist theorists like Gobineau,

---

11. It is good to point out here the religious element of the book had not been studied by scholars. Hence, religion is the sixth interrelated category.

12. Price-Mars, *Antenor Firmin*, 147–48.

13. Gordon, "Not Exactly Positivism," 1. Anténor Firmin was a complex intellectual, whose ideas on race, (Black) nationalism, and cosmopolitanism are debatable among scholars. Anthropologist Faye V. Harrison states that "Antenor's legacy in the 20th century was a vibrant school of *ethnologie* that documented and theorized the African-derived cultural heritage shaping Haiti's social-cultural landscape. This ethnological project aimed to vindicate Haiti and assert the first Black Republic's right to state and cultural sovereignty in the face of widespread international hostility and, most immediately, U.S. hegemony" ("Dismantling Anthropology's Domestic and International Peripheries," 91); Dash declares that Haitian nationalists had mistaken Firmin "as a precursor to the negritude movement" and that "the irony is that some elements of racial theorizing by the negritude writers are closer to the conception of racial difference promoted Joseph-Arthur de Gobineau whose ideas were famously contested by Firmin in his *De l'égalité des races humaines* (1885)" ("Nineteenth-Century Haiti," 47); contrary to Dash, Nicholls in his well-received book, underscores Firmin's nationalism and asserts that "Firmin was a formidable defender of Haitian independence and gathered around himself many young disciples" (*From Dessalines to Duvalier*, 125). In a recent article that compares the ideas of Jean Price-Mars and Anténor Firmin, Gerarde Magloire-Danton advances the idea that "Firmin's and Price-Mars's scholarship of commitment served to promote national self-definition, self-understanding" ("Antenor and Jean Price-Mars," 152).

14. Fluehr-Lobban, introduction to *The Equality of the Human Races*, xv. Fluehr-Lobban wrote the most comprehensive and lucid introduction to the book in the English language (xi–xlvi).

placed himself and his work squarely within a framework of diasporal exchanges but can nowhere be seen as an anthropological ancestor."[15] Faye V. Harrison, who has commented on the multiple legacies of Firmin, remarks that Firmin's robust *anthropologie positive* contested the scientific racism of Count Arthur de Gobineau (1853–55), whose ideas resonated with his contemporaries in metropolitan France and Anglo-North America.[16] Fluehr-Lobban clarifies that Firmin "developed a critical view of racial classifications and of race that foreshadowed much later constructions of race . . . [and the text] lies historically at the foundations of the birth of the disciplines of anthropology, yet it is unknown to the field."[17] Similarly, Gordon states that the absence of attention to Firmin's work in Western academic studies "is perhaps one of the great travesties of the impact of racism on the history of ideas."[18]

In his recent book on the relevance of Anténor Firmin for the twenty-first century, Haitian scholar and public intellectual Leslie Péan declares that "Firmin's powerful interventions struck the prevalent racist ideology of Black inferiority evoked by anthropologist 'scholars' to justify, on one hand, the enslavement of blacks, on the other hand, the division of Africa by whites at the Berlin Conference of 1885."[19] Complementarily, Watson R. Denis, in his interpretation of the significance of Firmin's work, reports that "Firmin arrived at the conclusion that the idea of the inequality of the human races was a European strategy to maintain the racial domination of Europe over the rest of the world, and by extension, to keep the political and economic exploitation among peoples and

---

15. Yelvington, "Anthropology of Afro-Latin America," 228; for excellent studies on the relationship between the discipline of anthropology and the problem of race and racism in American culture and in Western societies at large, see Baker, *From Savage to Negro*, and *Anthropology and the Racial Politics of Culture*; Stocking, *Race, Culture, and Evolution*; Benedict, *Patterns of Culture*; on the relationship between anthropology, colonialism, and the Enlightenment, see Harrison, *Decolonizing Anthropology*; Harris, *Rise of Anthropological Theory*; Duchet, *Anthropologie et histoire*.

16. Harrison, "Dismantling Anthropology's Domestic and International Peripheries," 91.

17. Fluehr-Lobban, "Anténor Firmin: Haitian Pioneer of Anthropology," 449.

18. Gordon, *Introduction to Africana Philosophy*, 58.

19. See, Péan, *Comprendre Anténor Firmin*; the French original reads as follows: "Les interventions de Firmin battent en brèche l'idéologie raciste de l'infériorité des Noirs évoquée par des 'savants' anthropologues pour justifier, d'une part, l'esclavage des Noirs et, d'autre part, le partage de l'Afrique par les Blancs lors de la Conférence de Berlin de 1885" (15–18).

races to justify the social domination within their respective societies."[20] Furthermore, historian Laurent Dubois writes:

> Firmin's work was largely ignored by European anthropology, which continued for decades to focus on racial differences and hierarchy. It would take another generation before a new set of thinkers, led by Frantz Boas in the United States, began to dismantle the racist "science" that Firmin had lambasted. And it took much longer yet for Firmin to begin to assume his rightful place in the history of anthropological thought. . . . In Haiti, however, Firmin's powerful attack on European racism gained him many admirers and established him as one of the country's most revered intellectuals.[21]

In the same line of reasoning, Fluehr-Lobban contends that Western scholars and scientists had consciously marginalized and ignored Firmin's work in its time because of its "antiracist themes and the use of anthropology in the assertion of human equality . . . no doubt because of its then revolutionary premise clearly stated in the title."[22]

Scholars have also commented on the contours of Firmin's ideas and the importance of *The Equality of the Human Races* for the field of Africana critical studies and theory, postcolonial studies, and cosmopolitanism. For example, Péan states that, in its publication in 1885, Firmin's work had quickly become a response to the problem of colonialism and its thinkers.[23] Fluehr-Lobban notes that Firmin's book articulates "early Pan-Africanist ideas as well as an analytical framework for what would become postcolonial studies."[24] Prominent African historian Theophile Obenga writes that Firmin "was a lawyer by profession, a Pan-Africanist by political choice."[25] Magloire-Danton substantiates that claim by affirming that

---

20. Deny, review of *The Equality of the Human Races*, 331.
21. Dubois, *Haiti: The Aftershocks of History*, 184.
22. Fluehr-Lobban, introduction to *The Equality of the Human Races*, xv.
23. Péan, *Anténor Firmin*, 15. In this sense, *The Equality of the Human Races* anticipates Aimé Césaire's anticolonial and revolutionary text, *Discours sur le colonialism* (*Discourse on Colonialism*).
24. Fluehr-Lobban, "Anténor Firmin," 449; it is my goal in this essay to demonstrate that *The Equality of the Human Races* also demonstrates early Afrocentric imaginations, and the text can be conceived as an expression of what we might call performative Afrocentrism.
25. Obenga, "Hommage à Antenor Firmin," 133.

Firmin's perspective methods encompass the three main elements of Pan-Africanist thought identified by Immanuel Geiss, which makes Firmin an early theoretician of the movement: the rejection of the postulate of race inequality, reference to the history of ancient Africa as proof that Africans were capable of civilization, and examples of illustrious individuals of African descent in diverse fields.[26]

J. Michael Dash in a recent article on the Black internationalism of Firmin presents him simultaneously as a universalist and cosmopolitan thinker. He also claims that not only Firmin had made the case for "crosscultural negotiations" and "post-territorial theorizing," he had also anticipated prominent Caribbean thinkers such as Edouard Glissant and Frantz Fanon.[27] Jean-Elie Gilles sees the competitive ideas of universalism, humanism, and nationalism intrinsic to Firmin's thought and intellectual development.[28] Gordon contends that the book "challenged what could be called colonial epistemology and intellectual dependency ... the presupposition was that black people could offer at most unreflective experience—data—for the proper purveyors of reason to assess or offer resources for study."[29] In other words, Firmin diagnosed the problem of what we might call "the crisis of Western reason" as well as sought to "demonstrate that Paul Broca and Arthur de Gobineau (among many others) were wrong and *how* they were wrong."[30]

Moreover, current studies on Firmin do not publicly distinguish him as a "formal Egyptologist" until a recent article was published in French by the African Egyptologist Theophile Obenga. Obenga offers linguist and rhetorical evidence from a careful study of Firmin's text that substantiates his thesis. He concludes that Firmin was an "Egyptologist ... one of the first among the Blacks of Africa and the Diaspora."[31] In addition, Obenga observes that "Antenor Firmin was strongly critical of racist theories of physical anthropology. He also defended the Africanness

---

26. Magloire-Danton, "Antenor and Jean Price-Mars," 156; Geiss, *Pan-African Movement*, 96.
27. Dash, "Nineteenth-Century Haiti," 44–53.
28. See Elie, "Patriotism, Humanism and Modernity."
29. Gordon, "Not Exactly Positivism," 2.
30. Gordon, "Not Exactly Positivism," 2–3.
31. Obenga, "Hommage à Anténor Firmin," 133.

of Pharaonic Egypt. The Egyptian question was an interesting historiography to know."[32]

This present essay expands on Obenga's thought by considering the relationship between Firmin's ideas to Afrocentrism as an intellectual project of revisionist history and his engagement with the Egyptian question. I am particularly interested in Firmin's Afrocentric imagination and his daring thesis of the Black origin and Africanness of ancient Egyptian civilization. In various ways, *The Equality of the Human Races* Firmin has clearly exhibited early manifestations of Afrocentrism and pre-Negritudist ideas. As previously noted in the valuable body of scholarship reviewed above, Firmin was a complex intellectual, whose ideas on the human nature, race, Negritude, Black pride, Black nationalism, postcolonialism, and cosmopolitanism can be interpreted as paradoxical and sometimes ambivalent. These ideas can be very challenging to us; yet, we must learn to wrestle with them and read Firmin more closely. While this current analysis is built upon current scholarship on Firmin, it seeks to fill many intellectual voids on Firmin studies.

The Afrocentric Discourse

In a recent article, Molefi Asante, the most representative figure of the Afrocentric school of thought in the Anglophone world, pays homage to Firmin when he writes, "When the Haitian intellectual Antenor Firmin in 1885 wrote his famous book, *The Equality of the Human Races*, he was defending all black people, those in the United States, Brazil, United Kingdom, and Nigeria, against racist assaults and bias commentary."[33] Asante's reflection on the meaning of Firmin and his work is pan-Africanist in leaning; it situates the Haitian intellectual in the tradition of Black Atlantic vindicationism and the anti-racist narrative in the history of ideas. The passage below succinctly summarizes Firmin's intellectual vision and bond between his ideas and the Afrocentric discourse:

> In examining the region of Ancient Kemet (currently referred to as "Ancient Egypt"—another discussion for another time),

---

32. Obenga, "Hommage à Anténor Firmin," 133. The French original translation is as follows, "*Antenor Firmin a vivement critiqué les théories racistes de l'Anthropologie physique. Il a aussi défend l'africanité de l'Egypte pharaonique. Cette question de l'Egypte pharaonique a toute une historiographie, intéressante à connaitre.*"

33. Asante, "Afrocentricity: Toward a New Understanding."

Firmin presents incontrovertible historical evidence supporting his and early writers' accounts that the inhabitants of the region were black, a term that over time has acquired greater social significance than in the past. In providing copious research on the region, particularly the journal entries of early visitors, Herodotus among them, Firmin soundly situates the origins of the peoples of the region in Upper Kemet/Egypt, i.e., in the interior of black Africa. Interestingly, his argument regarding the African/Black phenotype of the ancient Kemites/Egyptians predates assertions made by Afrocentric scholars by nearly a century. Such a position by a scholar from the 19th century, from Haiti no less, allows for the removal of defaming designations applied to today's Afrocentric scholars who are often viewed as scholarly extremists and historical revisionists.[34]

Firmin's affinity to and connection with Afrocentricism can be captured in five main ideas or concerns:

(1) The problem with Western Egyptology and historiography in constructing African history and culture,

(2) The conceptualization of an alternative epistemology grounded on African-Egyptian phenomena and achievement,

(3) The importance of ancient Egyptian history for understanding modern African history and the history of the Black race across time and space,

(4) The intellectual role and significance of ancient Egypt in the birth of classical Greece and Rome, and

(5) The Black race had played a singular role in universal civilization by bringing its distinct contributions.[35] What is then Afrocentrism? Where does it come from?

A critic has recently observed that Afrocentrism is "many things to many people."[36] For the sake of precision, we shall define Afrocentrism primarily as an ideology and a cultural, intellectual, and educational movement that stresses the African agency and perspective in the quest

---

34. KMT-Sisouvong, "Equality of the Human Races."

35. The last point is very important to understand Leopold Sedar Senghor's theoretical conceptualization of the Negritude (hence, "Senghorian Negritude"), Lewis has written intelligently on Senghorian Negritude, *Race, Culture, and Identity*, 50–54.

36. For example, Sundiata, "Afrocentrism: The Argument We're Really Having."

for values, knowledge, truth, and understanding. Like *The Equality of the Human Races*, Afrocentrism is an intellectual orientation that seeks to decenter the Eurocentric paradigm by shifting the geography of reason and the discourse of civilization to the significance of ancient Egypt in the birth of the modern world. Firmin and Afrocentrists would argue for the putative influence of ancient Egypt—which they contend was undeniably black—on the ancient Greek civilization. The Afrocentric paradigm articulates the cultural uniformity thesis of continental Africa and across the Black Diaspora; advocates of this school of thought valorize the African heritage and the continuity of African cultural traditions and values in the African Diaspora as well as the survivals of Egyptian civilization. The Afrocentric enterprise is chiefly concerned with the vexed question of the Black African origin of civilization and the blackness of Pharaonic Egypt. Yet, like Firmin their intellectual predecessor, Afrocentrists pursue the de-Europeanization of world history and the culture of modernity by promoting a wider openness to cultural relativism, alternative histories and worldviews.

Ama Mazama, a fervent advocate of this school of thought, suggests that Afrocentrism should be understood as a "paradigm."[37] Mazama relies heavily on Kuhn's work in her conceptualizing of Afrocentrism as a "scientific paradigm." While she subscribes to the cognitive aspect and the structural aspect of a paradigm as defined by Kuhn, she adds a third one: the functional aspect, which she describes as the notion that "knowledge can never be produced for the sake of it but always for the sake of our liberation, a paradigm must activate our consciousness to be of any use to us."[38] By inference, Afrocentrists are intellectual-activists. Mazama rejects Russell Adam's fourfold classification of Afrocentrism as defined below:

> The "Nile Valley" Afrocentrists (the "hard-liners" identified as espousing "pure Afrocentrism," and gathered around Molefi Asante); the Continental Afrocentrists, who do not pay any special attention to Kemet (Egypt), and the Afrocentric Infusionists, primarily concerned with making the African cultural and social experience a part of the curriculum; and the Social

---

37. Mazama, "Afrocentric Paradigm," 87–406; the concept of "scientific paradigm" is developed Kuhn's original work, *Structure of Scientific Revolutions*. The notion of Afrocentrism as a paradigm is also affirmed by Asante, more recently in his autobiography, *As I Run toward Africa*, 274.

38. Mazama, "Afrocentric Paradigm," 392.

Afrocentrists, for whom "African per se is more of a target of interest than inspiration."[39]

Accordingly, Firmin may be classified as a Nile Valley Afrocentrist. Firmin certainly used the ancient Egyptian civilization as a symbol of Black pride and to rebuke the prevalent doctrine of Black innate inferiority. For him, African achievement in history was a target for Black inspiration in the Diaspora. Mazama goes on to demarcate that Afrocentrism views "the European voice as just one among many and not necessarily the wisest one,"[40] acknowledging the existence of alternative epistemologies in the market of ideas and the realm of multiculturalism. The Africological methodological principles underscore that "the African experience must determine all inquiry, the spiritual is important and must be given its due place, immersion in the subject is necessary, holism is a must, intuition must be relied on, not everything is measurable because not everything that is significant is material, and the knowledge generated by the Afrocentric methodology must be liberating."[41] Mazama acknowledges that the methods employed by Africologists may vary, as they are connected with their particular subject of research; in the same line of thought, she avers the existence of a multiplicity or variety of Afrocentric theories in the world of ideas.

Afrocentrist moral philosopher Maulana Karenga does not affirm the paradigmatic status to Afrocentricity but rather construes the school of thought as a category. He sustains that Afrocentricity is "essentially a quality of perspective or approach rooted in the cultural image and human interest of African people."[42] Karenga insists that "the focus is on the cultural and human quality of African thought and practice rather than on thought and practice as an ideological conception and conduct." Nonetheless, critics of Afrocentrism state that the movement gives

39. Quoted in Mazama, "Afrocentric Paradigm," 389–90; also in Adams, "African American Studies and the State of the Art." Mazama characterizes Adam's definition of Afrocentrism as "intellectual bric-a-brac, dumped under the label *Afrocentricity*, is bound to dilute the meaning and the power of the Afrocentric idea as well as to create a great of confusion," 390.

40. Mazama, "Afrocentric Paradigm," 388.

41. Mazama, "Afrocentric Paradigm," 399–400.

42. Karenga, "Black Studies and the Problematic of a paradigm," 404; Karenga sharply differentiates the two terms: Afrocentrism and Afrocentricity. He notes that "Afrocentrism appears more often in ideological discourse between Afrocentric advocates and critics.... Afrocentricity is used in my work to stress its intellectual value as distinct from its ideological use" (*Introduction to Black Studies*, 35).

attention to the building pride in African American and Black diasporic communities, and stops short in analyzing interaction and transformation; it stresses more on race than on community, more on heritage than on exchange, and more unity than on variety.[43] As will be observed later in the essay, Firmin emphasizes direct links between Egypt and Ethiopia, and the shared cultural traditions and common religious practices between the two countries.

Critics of Afrocentrism also bring to the front the following challenges to the school of thought:

(1) Afrocentricity is presented as a dogma of authenticity rather than an orientation and methodology,

(2) It denies the reality and value of the diversity of perspectives and approaches within the disciplines of Black Studies,

(3) It promotes a static, monolithic and unreal concept of African culture which denies or diminishes its dynamic and diverse character,

(4) it overemphasizes the Continental African past at the expense of recognizing the African American past and present as central to and constitutive of African culture and the Afrocentric enterprise, and

(5) finally, Afrocentrism is unable to prove its utility in intellectual production beyond declaration of its presence and aspirations.[44]

The origin of the term "Afrocentrism" is unknown. African American historian William Jeremiah Moses credited W. E. B. Du Bois as probably the first writer to have used the concept of "Afrocentrism" as early as 1961 in a paper proposal entitled "Proposed plans for an Encyclopaedia Africana," whose objective was to be "unashamedly Afro-Centric, but not indifferent to the impact of the outside world."[45] Nonetheless, the cultural critic and most influential Afrocentrist scholar today Molefi Asante of Temple University would popularize Afrocentrism as a distinctive

---

43. Manning, *African Diaspora*, 7; in contrast to the Afrocentricity, "The Black Atlantic" model, popularized by Afro-British sociologist Gilroy (*Black Atlantic*), puts greater emphasis on the non-essentialist, hybrid, and creolized nature or character of the African Diapora as well as underscores the interaction and exchange between the people of the African ancestry and white people in North America.

44. These remarks are documented in Karenga, *Introduction to Black Studies*, 38–39.

45. Moses, *Afrotopia*, 2.

worldview in numerous path-breaking studies.⁴⁶ Asante defines Afrocentricity as a philosophy and program for social change. In Kemet, *Afrocentricity and Knowledge*, he writes, "The Afrocentric method seeks to transform human reality by ushering in a human openness to cultural pluralism which cannot exist without the unlocking of the minds for acceptance of an expansion of consciousness."⁴⁷ He continues by noting, "I seek to overthrow parochialism, provincialism, and narrow Wotanic visions of the world by demonstrating the usefulness of an Afrocentric approach to questions of knowledge."⁴⁸ Asante's objective is to inspire proponents of this school of thought "to put African ideals and values at the center of inquiry"⁴⁹ as well as to "allow the student of human culture investigating African phenomena to view the world from the standpoint of the African."⁵⁰ Both Asante and Firmin would construe the liberative project of Afrocentrism is its clear emphasis on emancipative epistemology and on the African as subject (that is African agency) rather than object in the overarching narrative of humanity.⁵¹ Afrocentrists employ rigorously the African cultural image as a tool to increase the self-esteem and consciousness of the people of African ancestry in the United States and in the African Diaspora.

In *The Afrocentric Idea*, Asante asserts that Afrocentricity "proposes a cultural reconstruction that incorporates the African perspective as a part of an entire human transformation, critical theory suggests a pathway."⁵² As he makes clearer, "The crystallization of this critical perspective I have named Afrocentricity, which means, literally, placing African ideals at the center of any analysis that involves African culture and behavior."⁵³ While Mazama is correct to affirm that "it is to Asante that we

46. See Asante, *Afrocentricity*; Asante, *Afrocentric Idea*; and Kemet, *Afrocentricity and Knowledge*.

47. Asante, *Kemet*, v.

48. Asante, *Kemet*, v–vi.

49. Asante, *Kemet*, 5.

50. Asante, *Kemet*, vi.

51. While the word "Afrocentrism" does not appear anywhere in Firmin's work, nonetheless, several tenets of the school of thought can be observed in Firmin's ideas and literary corpus. Elsewhere in *As I Run toward Africa*, Asante would write, "African agency is important in interpretation and analysis of African and African American life situations" (144).

52. Asante, *Afrocentric Idea*, 5.

53. Asante, *Afrocentric Idea*, 6.

owe the making of African epistemological relevance into an operational scientific,"[54] she only tells half of the truth when she also enunciates, "much like we owe Cheikh Anta Diop the making of the Black-ness of the ancient Egyptians into an operational scientific principle."[55] The problem with Mazama's assessment is her failure to acknowledge our considerable debt to Firmin as the first Black Egyptologist who revolutionized our understanding of the Black origin of the ancient Egypt and put the ancient Kemetic civilization at the center of African epistemological inquiry, as early as in the nineteenth century. Firmin was also among the first Black anthropologists and intellectuals to deconstruct Western Egyptology and decolonize Eurocentric perspective on African historiography. He reconstructed scientifically the African historical narrative from the source that is from classical Egyptian civilization. Consequently, both Asante and Diop are intellectual heirs of Anténor Firmin.

Afrocentrism and Egyptocentrism

Echoes of the Afrocentric ideology can be traced in the writings of both Anglophone and Francophone Black and non-Black writers in the nineteenth and twentieth-centuries.[56] To various degrees, the works of these writers exhibit explicitly both Afrocentric and Egyptocentric themes and ideologies. While the discourse of Afrocentrism seeks to link the cultural traditions and civilization of ancient Black Egypt to those of continental Black Africa and the Black Diaspora, the discourse of Egyptocentrism puts forth the idea that ancient Egypt was geographically and culturally African and that the flourishing civilization of Egypt was unquestionably Negroid. The thesis of the black African creation of ancient Egyptian civilization had been defended with intellectual force and brilliance relatively almost by all the aforementioned writers.

---

54. Mazama, "Afrocentric Paradigm," 394.

55. Mazama, "Afrocentric Paradigm," 394.

56. Anglophone writers include the following: Martin Delany, Alexander Crummell, Edward Wilmot Blyden, David Walker, W. E. B. Du Bois, Carter G. Woodson, Marcus Garvey, Frantz Boas, Melville Herskovits, George G. M. James, John Henrik Clarke, Yosef A. A. ben-Jochannan, Maulana Karenga, Kwame Nkrumah, Martin Bernal, etc. Francophone writers include the architects of the Negritude movement: Aimé Césaire, Leopold Sedar Senghor, Leon-Damas; and Cheikh Anta Diop, Theophile Obenga, Hannibal Price, Louis Joseph Janvier.

Egyptian antiquities were first discovered by scholars and scientists who accompanied Napoleon Bonaparte on a travelling campaign to Egypt in 1799.[57] These researchers described the Egyptians as having Negroid features including the high-status individuals in the Egyptian society and political order.[58] As Cheikh Anta Diop explains:

> Egyptologists were dumfounded with admiration for the past grandeur and perfection then discovered. They gradually recognized it as the most ancient civilization that had engendered all others. But, imperialism being what it is, is became increasingly "inadmissible to continue to accept the theory—evident until then—of a Negro Egypt. The birth of Egyptology was thus marked by the need to destroy the memory of a Negro Egypt at any cost and in all minds.[59]

Proslavery interest in Western societies had discredited the Black African origin of the ancient Egyptian civilization. In addition, Firmin had also reported that White racist scientists had denied the historic contribution of Black Egypt to the intellectual development of humanity to support the doctrine of racial inequality, the innate inferiority of the Black race and the enslavement of Blacks.[60] St. Clair Drake informs us that while White racists in the United States maintained that the extraordinary Egyptian civilization was debased by miscegenation with Negroes, black intellectuals and anti-racist writers used the Sphinx as a symbol of the Negro presence in Egypt.[61] For example, Edward Wilmot Blyden who himself immigrated to Liberia in 1851 wrote about the emblematic Egyptian Sphinx in this manner:

> Her [sic] features are decidedly that of the African or Negro type, with "expanded nostrils." If, then, the sphinx was placed here—looking out in majestic and mysterious silence over the empty plain where once stood the great city of Memphis in all its pride and glory, as an "emblematic representation of the King"—is not the inference clear as to the peculiar type of race to which that King belonged?[62]

57. See, Meyerson, *The Linguist and the Emperor*.
58. Drake, *Black Folk Here and There*, 132, 357.
59. Diop, *African Origin of Civilization*, 45.
60. Firmin, *Equality of the Human Races*, 379–91, 399–402.
61. Drake, *Black Folk Here and There*, 131–32.
62. Quoted in Skinner, "Restoration of African Identity," 33. Skinner writes, "But Blyden was not content to assert that human civilization began in Africa, that Africa civilized Greece, and that Greece civilized Europe" (34).

In *The Negro*, published in 1915, W. E. B. Du Bois wrote, "Egyptian civilization seems to have been African in its beginnings and in its main line of development . . . Egyptian monuments show distinctly Negro."[63] Two decades later after much research on the subject of the ancient Egypt, Du Bois published *Black Folk Then and Now* and stated that "in recent years, despite the work of exploration and interpretation in Egypt and Ethiopia, almost nothing is said of the Negro race. Yet that race was always prominent in the valley of the Nile."[64] In 1946, Du Bois would revisit the topic again and even included a chapter on "Egypt" in *The World and Africa*. Du Bois was more decisive to declare more strongly that "we conclude, therefore, that the Egyptians were Negroids, and not only that, but by tradition they believed themselves descended not from the whites or the yellows, but from the black peoples of the south."[65] As Drake once again remarks, "Egyptology thus became a crucial arena in the persisting struggle between antiblack racists and those black intellectuals who considered themselves to be vindicationists."[66]

Furthermore, the debate over the Black genesis of civilization and over the character of ancient Egypt and the idea that the ancient Greece had borrowed both cultural and intellectual resources from the black people of Egypt had also appeared in the pages of several important controversial texts.[67] It is noteworthy to underscore here it was the three-volume magisterial work of the white British and Cornell University historian Martin Bernal, under the provocative title *Black Athena*, that has gained the academic attention of the Afrocentric movement in the United States. The multivolume work was published by the Rutgers University Press,[68] and, as the author states, is "essentially concerned with the Egyptian and Semitic roles in the formation of Greece in the Middle

---

63. Du Bois, *The Negro*, 17.

64. Du Bois, *Black Folk Then and Now*, 135–36.

65. Bois, *The World and Africa*, 106.

66. Drake, *Black Folk Here and There*, 132.

67. For example, James, *Stolen Legacy*; Yosef Ben-Jochanan, *African Origins of the Major "Western Religions"*; *Black Man of the Nile and His Family*; and *Africa: Mother of Western Civilization*.

68. See the excellent three-volume work by Bernal bearing the general title; for counter responses to the Black Athena thesis, see Lefkowitz and Rogers, *Black Athena Revisited*; Berlinerblau, *Heresy in the University*; Bernal's response to his critics is documented in this text, Moore, *Black Athena Writes Back*.

and Late Bronze Age."⁶⁹ In this historical revisionism project, Bernal also sought to affirm Black agency in world history and in the making of world civilizations.

In these rigorous and learned studies, Bernal complemented and fortified the works of previous Afrocentrists and especially the Firminian thesis of Black genesis as will be observed in subsequent paragraphs, by establishing literary, archeological, and linguistic data of the substantial influence of ancient Egypt and Phoenician on Greek civilization. His well-developed thesis about the Egyptian question claimed for the African backgrounds of Attic civilization resulting in his rejection of the notion that Greek civilization was original and autonomous. Martin put forth the idea that Western historians "have not acknowledged the full extent of Greece's debt to Egypt and the Near East." He explained that this silence in Western historiography and modern intellectual history was chiefly due to eighteenth and nineteenth centuries' racism and anti-Semitism, and consequently, European scholars had dismissed the Phoenician and Egyptian influence on Greece.

Bernal declared that Greece had imported both Egyptian culture and language through the exchange with the Semitic people known as the Hyksos in the seventeenth and sixteen centuries BC. He agreed with Firmin and other Afrocentrists in many points: (1) that the Egyptians introduced civilization to Greeks, (2) the Hyksos brought to Greece Egyptian language and culture during the seventeenth and sixteenth centuries BC, (3) Classical Greek philosophers borrowed from Egyptian philosophy, (4) the Egyptian origins of many of the Greek heroes such as Socrates and Inachus, (5) the Roman poet and playwright Terrence was a Black African, and (6) Cleopatra had African ancestors.⁷⁰

69. Bernal, *Black Athena*, 1:22.

70. In response to Afrocentrist claims and reconstruction of modern history, see Schlesinger, *Disuniting of America*; Howe, *Afrocentrism*; Lefkowitz, *Not Out of Africa*. Throughout the book, Lefkowitz sustains the long standing tradition of the priority of Greece in the intellectual development of world civilizations. For her, Afrocentrism should be regarded as a mass of invented histories and traditions of Black achievements in world history. As she comments, "The Afrocentric myth of ancient history is a myth, and not history. . . . The ancient Egypt described by Afrocentrists is a fiction," xvi. She also adds that Afrocentric theories of history and culture are "based on false assumptions and faulty reasoning, and cannot be supported by time-tested methods of intellectual inquiry" (xv). Arguably, Lefkowitz is among the most powerful voices in academia who longs to see the end of liberal relativism and multicultural and pluralistic perspectives in American education. As she observes, "Teaching the myth of the Stolen Legacy as if it were history robs the ancient Greeks and their

Firmin, "The Egyptian Question" or the "White Problem"

Exclusively in chapter 9 in *The Equality of the Human Races*, with intellectual force, clarity, and brilliance, Firmin defends the Blackness of Pharaonic Egypt and the influence of Kemetic civilization on ancient Greece as well as the contributions of ancient Egypt to world civilizations. Foremost, Firmin indicates that the "Egyptian question" was both an intellectual and psychological crisis of Western Egyptology and nineteenth-century scholarship. This predicament clearly had to do with two basic factors: the origin, and the cultural identity (i.e., skin color) of the inhabitants of ancient Egypt. In turn, the Egyptian conundrum left an indelible mark on the mind and intellect of Western cynics in regard to the creators of the ancient Egyptian civilization. Subsequently, Firmin could write, "The Egyptian question . . . involves the most complex interests and absorbs the attention of the Ottoman world, the Slavic world, and the Germanic world, and the Latin world."[71] The Egyptian phenomenon was inevitably tied to the history and the achievement of a people in the history of ideas in the West in both eighteenth and nineteenth century, respectively.

Quoting the Spanish republican politician Emilio Castelar (1832–1899) in full, Firmin reiterates that the source of Egyptian civilization was he riddle of Western modernity, an epistemological watershed among the nations in the West:

> For the Turks, Egypt is but a part of their empire. For the Austrians, it is a line they respect because of their own possessions in the Black Sea and the Adriatic Sea. For the Italians, concerned with the security of their beautiful Sicily and aspiring to claim Malta and colonize Tripoli and Tunis, it is a border to be protected. For the great and powerful Germany, whose pride could not withstand the loss of its hegemony in the European world, Egypt is both a continental and extra-continental question. For Russia, which dreams of a Greek Bizantium in Europe and of

---

modern descendants of a heritage that rightly belongs to them" (126). It is interesting to note here in the last debate between Lefkowitz and Asante at the Smithsonian, the Wellesley classics scholar professes admittedly, "Molefi, everyone knows now that the ancient Egyptians were black"; in response, Asante said, "Mary, I wish you had read the accounts *before* you wrote your book." For more a detailed personal narrative of Afrocentrisim and its reception in the United States and beyond, see Asante, *As I Run toward Africa*, 159–60, 199–200, 241–42, 274–79, 302–10.

71. Firmin, *Equality of the Human Races*, 386.

land route to India through Asia, Egypt is a European question. For Spain, Portugal, and Holland, it is an important crossroads on the itinerary to the various islands and archipelagos still under their respective flags. For all of them, in this moment of horrible anxiety, Egypt is the preeminent question. All events pertaining to it can lead either to peace, which fosters work, trade, and freedom, or to implacable war, which spreads death, desolation, and sorrow in the world. But the Egyptian question is essentially an Anglo-French question.[72]

Ultimately, for Firmin, the Egyptian question was inescapably a "White problem." He sought to provide a plausible scientific rejoinder to the popular belief among European men of letters that "Blacks have no social history and so have never influenced the march of humanity."[73] Firmin professed that the white problem was the misrecognition that the Black race had contributed "its stone to the construction of the edifice."[74] Looking at the issue in a grand scale, Firmin informed us that white prejudice and Western anti-Africanism were deeply rooted in European racial solidarity and ethnic superiority, what he calls "Caucasian union"[75] and "the worst form of egocentrism."[76] Firmin described the logic of European solidary. First, he inferred that it was customary for Western scientists and scholars to scorn "everything that was not European."[77] In fact, he noted astutely, "all White European nations naturally tend to unite in order to dominate the rest of the world and the other human races. . . . It is more in order to paralyze the progress of a feared or resented rival than to support that people, whom in any case it only intends to exploit itself."[78] There is a sense to infer here that Firmin connected the Egyptian question with European "civilizing mission" and imperial hegemony and colonialism.

Firmin moves on to address Western construction of the ancient Egypt and the central claims (or the major tenets) of anthropologists and Egyptologists of his time: (1) That the ancient populations of Egypt

---

72. Firmin, *Equality of the Human Races*, 386; also in Emilio Castelar, *Las guerras de América y Egypto*, 120–21.
73. Firmin, *Equality of the Human Races*, 390.
74. Firmin, *Equality of the Human Races*, 390.
75. Firmin, *Equality of the Human Races*, 379.
76. Firmin, *Equality of the Human Races*, 383.
77. Firmin, *Equality of the Human Races*, 226.
78. Firmin, *Equality of the Human Races*, 382.

belonged to the White race,[79] (2) Westerners had severed the ancient Egyptians from the Ethiopian race and turned them into a branch of the Caucasian race,[80] (3) They also claimed that Egyptians felt great contempt for the other Black peoples of Africa,[81] (4) The Black African race did not create the ancient civilization that flourished on the shores of the Nile Valley,[82] (5) The Egyptians were not originated from Ethiopia,[83] (6) Egypt was all Asiatic,[84] (7) Gobineau claimed that a White people from Asia civilized the Egyptians,[85] (8) Egyptologists and anthropologists denied that the people living in the Nile banks were not Black,[86] and (9), finally, the Egyptians were gifted *dark-skinned Caucasians* descended from Ham, the son of Noah.[87] Firmin attempts to expose the various ways that European scholars had reformatted ancient Egyptian history for their own gain.

In the subsequent paragraphs, we allow Firmin to respond to those objections and directly engage the major tenets and assumptions of scholars and scientists of his time.

The Case for the Black Civilization in the Nile Valley

Firmin opens chapter 9 ("Egypt and Civilization") of the book with an excellent illustration, an elaborate syllogism:

> Truth is eternal. It must remain whole through time and space, otherwise it cannot be validated by logic.... When one asserts that the Black race is inferior to all others, one must prove that the fact is true now and was true in the past, that is, that not only is this the case today, but that things were never different in past history and that nothing happened in the past which could be in flagrant contradiction with the dogmatic views of the anthropologists or with the pretentiously self-assured conclusions of the scholars.[88]

79. Firmin, *Equality of the Human Races*, 229.
80. Firmin, *Equality of the Human Races*, 228.
81. Firmin, *Equality of the Human Races*, 235.
82. Firmin, *Equality of the Human Races*, 237.
83. Firmin, *Equality of the Human Races*, 237.
84. Firmin, *Equality of the Human Races*, 244.
85. Firmin, *Equality of the Human Races*, 232.
86. Firmin, *Equality of the Human Races*, 286.
87. Drake, *Black Folk Here and There*, 132.
88. Firmin, *Equality of the Human Races*, 225.

To express the matter a different way, the historical record of the past and the experience of Black people across time and space do not validate nor justify the position of white racists that blacks are inferior to whites. In the passage above, Firmin intends to surface historical accomplishments of the Black race in order to bear witness and dismiss white arrogance. Yet, his ultimate goal is concurrently to critique white supremacist ideology, challenge pseudo-scientific claims that are presented and proliferated as exclusive truth claims, and reconstruct African history and culture from the standpoint of classical Egypt and Black agency.

He pursues forward to articulate his major arguments. That the civilization of the ancient people of Egypt, which he calls by the original name "Kemet," "precedes all the others."[89] He advances the idea that the Black Egyptians "were unquestionably the initiators of the White nations of the West in science and the arts, had created alone, on the shores of the Nile . . . the most impressive social organization that a human population had ever built."[90] The Nile Valley civilization theory best explains the rise of the ancient Egyptian civilization, an idea that is relatively supported by all modern Egyptologists.[91] For example, Diop posits that "the Nile Valley was peopled by a progressive descent of the Black peoples from the region of the Great Lakes, the cradle of Homo *sapiens sapiens*."[92] J. D. Walker proclaims that,"the northern Nile Valley owes much to development in the Sahara and probably the Sudan. . . . Nilotic flora and fauna were well integrated into the belief and cultural systems, including writing."[93] Firmin identifies precisely the Hamites, "the inventors of geometry," as the people who lived on the shores of the Nile. He exclaims that they existed "more than three thousand years before the Christian era, when the European nations were still in a barbarous state, the Hamites who lived on the shores of the Nile had already been doing geometric computations, calculating the area of different types of surfaces."[94] Other power-

---

89. Firmin, *Equality of the Human Races*, 225–26.

90. Firmin, *Equality of the Human Races*, 226.

91. For a collection of fine essays on the topic, see Edwin, *Africa & Africans in Antiquity*.

92. Diop, *Civilization or Barbarism*, 103.

93. Walker, "Misrepresentation of Diop's Views," 81.

94. Firmin, *Equality of the Human Races*, 168; he also adds, "Besides the honor of having invented the science of numbers and surface measurement does not belong to the White race. The origin of mathematics goes back to Black Egypt, the land of the Pharaohs" (168).

ful African kingdoms and civilizations such as the Kushitic or Ethiopian emerged around the Nile Valley.[95]

The majority of Egyptologists in Firmin's era maintained that the people inhabited within the precincts of the Nile bank were not black and a people of different ethnic group and culture. Firmin strikes back by countering the prerogative of the ethnography of Egyptologists of the ancient peoples of the Region is not historically reliable. He thus points out that "the further back in antiquity we go the more we become convinced that all the peoples living on the shores of the Nile were of the same ethnological type."[96] To justify his position, the Haitian intellectual references an authoritative text in classical Greek literature, Aeschylus's drama, *Prometheus Bound*. He hence cites these famous lines:

> On the coast of Egypt, near the mouth and flood region of the Nile, there stands the city of Canope. There, by the sole touch of his caressing hand, Jupiter will restore your sanity.

> You will give birth to a son whose name will remind you of the god's touch, black Epaphus who will harvest his crops on all the plains irrigated by the Nile during its long journey.[97]

Admittedly, Firmin avers that scholars of his time often misread and debated the real meaning of the passage above. In his careful exegesis of the text, he interprets that the poet Aeschylus seeks to convey the message of the exodus of the Egyptian people who, according to Greek tradition, had journeyed from the farthest regions of equatorial African to the mouth of the Nile where they lay the first foundations of ancient civilization.[98] Accordingly, the "Black Epaphus," as mentioned in the text is the personification of the Egyptian people, was the bearer of civilization who would bring the light to all humanity. Pondering further upon these words, he makes the following pronouncement: "Should my interpretation of Prometheus Bound to be considered adequate proof that the Egyptians were a black race represented by Black Ephaphus who was to harvest all the plains irrigated by the Nile."[99] Asante remarks trenchantly that the Afrocentric discourse recognizes the cultural complex of the

---

95. Drake, *Black Folks Here and Then*, 129.
96. Firmin, *Equality of the Human Races*, 240.
97. Firmin, *Equality of the Human Races*, 247.
98. Firmin, *Equality of the Human Races*, 247–48.
99. Firmin, *Equality of the Human Races*, 248.

Nile Valley as "points of reference for an African perspective much the same way as Greece and Rome serve as reference points for the European world."[100]

Firmin continues with the conversation by asking a rhetorical question, how can "a race Europeans consider radically inferior, could produce a nation to which today's Europe owes everything, for Egypt is responsible for the original intellectual and moral achievements which constitute the foundations of modern civilization."[101] Firmin maintains that the vestiges of antiquity do testify that there was a period of history that Black people "were holding up the flame of early civilization."[102] Accordingly, if this first premise is attested as a truth claim, then, the theory of the inequality of the races is dismissed or rejected.

The Egyptians Called Their Land Kemet

We already referenced in the previous section that Firmin used the original name "Kemet," to identity the ancient Pharaonic Egypt. He continues by reporting that the Egyptians themselves called their land Kemet, meaning "the Black land of Egypt," or simply the "Black land."[103] He also adds, "As for their national name, the Egyptians called themselves *Khemi*, a word that means 'burnt face,' just like *AEthiopes*."[104] Firmin deploys the word *Retou* to denote the indigenous people of Egypt; as he notes, "We know, in fact, that the word *Retou* means nothing more than indigenous, a 'native of Egypt.'"[105] As a result, he could assert "that the ancient Egyptians, the true *Retous*, were Black Africans, just like the other Negroes," and that "they called themselves *Retou* . . . which seemed to distinguish them from the *Nahasi or Na'hasiou* (Negroes)."[106] At this point, Firmin does not give the impression that the Egyptians undermine their own Blackness and Africanness. In fact, before this particular observation, he clarifies the seemingly confusion this might bring to the readers:

100. Asante, *Afrocentric Idea*, 9.
101. Firmin, *Equality of the Human Races*, 227.
102. Firmin, *Equality of the Human Races*, 226.
103. Firmin, *Equality of the Human Races*, 226.
104. Firmin, *Equality of the Human Races*, 235.
105. Firmin, *Equality of the Human Races*, 235. It is good to note here the prominent Egyptologist Jean-Francois Champollion defines the Egyptian hieroglyphic word *Retous* as "real humans."
106. Firmin, *Equality of the Human Races*, 237, 234.

> The ancient Egyptians grouped together the Asiastics (*Aamou*) and the white-skinned peoples of the North (*Tamahou* or *Tahennou*). Isn't this division significant? Does it not suggest that they claimed for themselves the same origin as the other Black peoples of Africa and that, rightly or wrongly, they attributed a common origin of the White peoples of both Asia and Europe?[107]

Firmin expounds on his argument for the Black beginning of ancient Egypt by engaging another dimension in the Egyptian life and experience. He turns to the visual culture and the aesthetic character of Egyptian art, monuments, and paintings. He posits that "Egyptians artists seem to have taken particular care to distinguish themselves from Whites,"[108] and significantly, the Egyptians used the "black color to represent the principal deities as well as the Pharaohs."[109] By citing a quote from Champollion that "Egypt is all African and not in the least Asiatic,"[110] Firmin was dismissing the idea that external influences from Asia are the sole basis for the successes of Egyptian civilization and its intellectual development.

The Haitian Egyptologist strengthens his linguistic argument by appealing to an ancient authority in the Medieval era, Eustathius of Constantinople. He observes:

> Until the last years of the Middle Ages, then, scholars generally believed in the Negro origin of the *Retous* (In his Commentaries on *The Odyssey*, Eustathius of Constantinople comments on [a well-known phrase] asserting that the expression . . . was used to mean "to be burnt by the sun," that is, "to turn black, to turn brown.")[111]

Firmin's extrapolation based on linguistic data is confirmed by Obenga in the article we referenced earlier in the essay. Obenga shows systematically, through his close reading of Firmin's text and Firmin's usage of the Egyptian language, that the Haitian anthropologist was one of

---

107. Firmin, *Equality of the Human Races*, 234.

108. Firmin, *Equality of the Human Races*, 243; the famous monument of Sheikh-el-Balad is reproduced in Firmin, *Equality of the Human Races*, 242, and the painting of the well-known Egyptian couple as well, 245.

109. Firmin, *Equality of the Human Races*, 243.

110. Firmin, *Equality of the Human Races*, 244.

111. Firmin, *Equality of the Human Races*, 250; also, Fluehr-Lobban and Rhodes, *Race and Identity in the Nile Valley*, 108.

the earliest Black Egyptologists in the nineteenth century. Felicitously, he specifies that Firmin transcribes inerrantly Egyptian proper names—very close to the Egyptian language—a clear indication of his knowledge of ancient Egypt and familiarity with the Egyptian language.[112] For example, Firmin writes authentically the selected following Egyptian names:

1. *Ramses II or Ramesses II (Ri'mīsisu)*[113]
2. *Nahasi/Na'hasiou* (Negroes)[114]
3. *Tamahou or Tahennou* (White-skinned peoples of the North)[115]
4. *Aamou* (Asiatics)[116]
5. *Khemi*[117]
6. *Retous*[118]
7. *Kha-f-Ra (Cheops)*[119]
8. *Sheikh-el-Balad (Ka-aper)*[120]
9. *Rahotpou*[121]
10. *Nofrit*[122]

    112. Obenga, "Hommage à Anténor Firmin," 137.
    113. Firmin, *Equality of the Human Races*, 230–31.
    114. Firmin, *Equality of the Human Races*, 234.
    115. Firmin, *Equality of the Human Races*, 234.
    116. Firmin, *Equality of the Human Races*, 234.
    117. Firmin, *Equality of the Human Races*, 235.
    118. Firmin, *Equality of the Human Races*, 234, 237, 240–41, 250.
    119. This is one of the diorite statues of Cheops, a Fourth Dynasty king (Firmin, *Equality of the Human Races*, 241).
    120. Firmin, *Equality of the Human Races*, 242; Firmin includes the legendary wooden statue of a high dignitary, *Sheikh-el-Balad*, which Egyptologists call *dark red or brick red*. Sheikh-el-Balad is an Arabic title, which means "headman of the village." Nonetheless, his real and Egyptian name was *Ka-aper*. It is observed that Ka-aper was a high priest and lector at a Memphite temple, serving Menkaure (2490–72); for more information on Ka-aper, see Bunson, "Ka-aper Statue," in *Encyclopedia of Ancient Egypt*, 189–90.
    121. Firmin, *Equality of the Human Races*, 244; Firmin includes the famous two painted statues of *Rahotpou and Nofrit* from the Fifth or Sixth Dynasty era. They were discovered at Meidium. Firmin informs us that, in his time, these paintings were on exhibit at the Boulaq Museum. *Rahotpou*, the husband, is Black; his wife, *Nofrit*, is light-skinned.
    122. Firmin, *Equality of the Human Races*, 244. *Nofrit* was the wife of *Rahotpou*.

11. *Nofritari*[123]

12. *Medinat-Habu*[124]

13. *Ahmes*[125]

14. *Psamethik*[126]

15. *Piankhy Meri Amoun*[127]

In *Civilization or Barbarianism*, originally published in French in 1981, Cheikh Anta Diop would substantiate Firmin's position that Kemet was in fact an "African land" and connected with the rest of "Black Africa"; and that "Kemet gave birth to subsequent Black African societies such as Nubia, Kush, Meroe, and ancient Ghana."[128] In addition, Asante complements both Firmin and Diop when he writes, "The Africans called their land Kemet and it was designated 'the land of the Blacks.' This was quite appropriate inasmuch as the country had found its life from the emergence of civilization in Upper, that is, southern Egypt, where the people were often as black as the fertile soil that extended, on either side, the length of the Nile."[129] Troy D. Allen also observes, "Kemet provides us with a record of how Africans constructed their society before foreign influences had taken hold in Africa."[130] This same specialist on ancient Egyptian history sustains that the relationship between Kemet and Nubia

---

123. Firmin, *Equality of the Human Races*, 244. Queen Nofritari was Ethiopian who is always portrayed as a black-skinned woman. She was one of the great royal wives of Ramesses II the Great.

124. Firmin, *Equality of the Human Races*, 244. The title was given to the Mortuary Temple of Ramesses III.

125. Firmin, *Equality of the Human Races*, 249; *Ahmes* married Princess *Nofritari*.

126. Firmin, *Equality of the Human Races*, 249. Psamethik was a king of the Sais Dynasty, the twenty-sixth dynasty of Egypt (664–525 BC) during the Late Period.

127. Firmin, *Equality of the Human Races*, 250; Piankhy Meri Amoun was an Ethiopian king of Napata who had conquered the entire territory which extends from Thebes to the mouth of the Nile. He was also the founder of the XXVe Ethiopian dynasty (747–657 BCE); Obenga, "Hommage à Anténor Firmin," 138.

128. Allen, "Cheikh Anta Diop's Two Craddle Theory," 827.

129. Asante, *Kemet*, 50; he also declares, "The Kemetic heritage penetrates the literature, the orature, the pottery, the burial rituals, the procreative myths, and the modes of thought of Africa. It is the classical African civilizations themselves that given us so much organic contact with the history of ideas. The vivid example of the massive memorials to African genius, Karnak, the temples of the Valley of the Kings, the Pyramids, the major shrines" (47–48).

130. Allen, "Cheikh Anta Diop," 814.

(Ethiopia) is significant in studying the social organization of ancient Kemet. Nubia was egyptianized in all aspects of culture and that there had been uninterrupted contacts between the two nations and that both ancient Kemites and ancient Nubians-Ethiopians were of the same race.[131]

> We have already seen that temples were built all over Nubia by the Kings of the Eighteenth and Nineteenth Dynasties. Then towns important as religious, commercial and administrative centers grew around those temples. Nubia was entirely reorganized on purely Egyptian lines and a completely Egyptian system of administration was set up, entailing the presence of a considerable number of Egyptian scribes, priests, soldiers and artisans.[132]

As observed, Firmin cogently defended the blackness of ancient Egypt and delineated that there was a close relationship between ancient Kemet-Egypt and Ethiopia. Firmin establishes that close links between Egyptians and Ethiopians are important signals in finding the origin of the Egyptians. Firmin was particularly concerned to inquire about the skin color of the Ethiopians. Were the Egyptians black like the Egyptians? What was the nature of the relationship between the Egyptians and the Ethiopians? To what extent did the Egyptians and Ethiopians share similar cultural traditions and practices? How significant are those common customs in retracing the origin of the Egyptians?

The Egyptians Are the Descendants of the Ethiopians

Firmin debunks the predominant thesis of nineteenth-century European social scientists and anthropologists that the Egyptian people were a White race and that Egypt was not a part of Africa. Firmin also counters a major tenet of Western Egyptology the notion that the Ethiopians did not originate from Ethiopia. He does that by documenting scientific evidence ranging from the material culture in anthropology, archeology, linguistic (to a certain degree) and to religious practices as well as by offering the proof from the science of botany and fauna that links the Egyptian and Ethiopian peoples. He contends that Egypt was one of the colonies of Ethiopia and that the Ethiopians who migrated to Egypt created the great

---

131. Allen, "Cheikh Anta Diop," 821–22; for further studies on the topic, see Allen, *Ancient Egyptian Family*.

132. Quoted in Allen; also see Mokhtar, *General History of Africa*, 58.

pharaonic civilization. To express this idea another way, the Egyptians were the direct descendants of Ethiopians, a historical fact that attests to the origin of ancient Egyptian civilization. Consequently, in chapter 9 ("Egypt and Civilization"), Firmin's inquiry leads him to determine exactly the origin, cultural identity, and more importantly the "race" of the Ethiopian people and the nature of their relationships to the Egyptians.

Firmin underscores that there is no substantial historical nor scientific evidence that justifies classifying the ancient Egyptian race as Caucasian.[133] "Once we acknowledge the Ethiopian origin of the ancient civilizers of Egypt, he declares, we will necessarily acknowledge the innate capacity of all the races to develop their genius and their intelligence."[134]

Firmin remarks that the Egyptians had migrated from Ethiopia by following the flow of the Nile is an established belief among scholars and is well attested by the French philologist and man of letters Jean-Jacques Ampère in *Voyage en Égypte et en Nubie*. Ampère visited Egypt for scientific research and was influenced by the works of the "Father of Egyptology" Jean Francois Champollion.[135] In the referenced text, Ampère makes this striking observation about the peoples of the Nile Valley: "The farther one goes up the Nile, the more one finds physical similarities between the populations living today on the river's shores and the ancient race as it is portrayed on the old monuments and as its appearance has been preserved in the mummies."[136] As early as 1830, Ampère in *Heures de poésies* or *De l'Histoire de la poésie* had sustained the common racial identity and origin of the Egyptians and Ethiopians when he composed this poetic stand, which Firmin reproduced in his book:

> With their black tresses, the Nubian women
> Drapped in their flowing dresses
> Resemble the Egyptian maidens
> Whose portraits decorate the monuments.[137]

Ampère's understanding of the Egyptian-Ethiopian phenomenon and the close relationship between the two countries is communicated in his remarkable insight that the Ethiopians of the Nile Valley were

133. Firmin, *Equality of the Human Races*, 240.
134. Firmin, *Equality of the Human Races*, 237.
135. Firmin, *Equality of the Human Races*, 236; Ampère, *Voyage en Égypte*.
136. Cited in Firmin, *Equality of the Human Races*, 235; Ampère, *Voyage en Égypte*, 55.
137. Firmin, *Equality of the Human Races*, 226.

black just like the Egyptians. In this poetic note, he stresses the material culture exhibited in the common dress and visual painting, which the Egyptians and Ethiopians shared. Firmin also cites the French linguist Jean-François Champollion, who also visited Egypt and penned several influential works on the Egyptian civilization and language.[138] Champollion is prominently known as the founding "Father of Egyptology" who deciphered Egyptian hieroglyphs on the Rosetta Stone and published the first Egyptian grammar in the French language in 1822. From 1828 to 1830, he and a group of able scientists under the leadership of Emperor Napoleon conducted a scientific expedition in Egypt. Champollion, who had declared that the Egyptian and Ethiopian peoples were one and the same race and with common cultural and linguistic characteristics, also penned the following words about them:

> The ancient Egyptians belonged to a race of humans who resembled in every way the Kenuz or "Barabras," the current inhabitants of Nubia. The Copts found in Egypt today have none of the characteristic traits of the ancient Egyptian population. The Copts are the result of the anarchic métissage of all the different peoples that had successively dominated Egypt. It is wrong headed to try to find in these people the physical traits of the ancient race.[139]

In chapter 4 ("Monogenism and Pologyenism") in *The Equality of the Human Races*, Firmin like Diop rejects the theory of polygenism[140] but instead embraces the principle of monogenism as a theory explaining the origin of humanity; he offers additional historical and textual evidence from Roman literature supporting the long-standing tradition of the classical records which identify the people of Ethiopia as Black, and that the Egyptians were the direct descendants of the Ethiopians. He quotes a memorable line from the Roman poet Ovid in *Metamorphoses*, a mythico-historical poetic narrative describing the history of the world from the time of creation to the elevated divine status (that is his deification) of Julius Caesar of Rome:

---

138. Jean-François Champollion, *Précis du système hiéroglyphique des anciens Égyptiens*, and *Lettres écrites d'Égypte et de Nubie*.

139. Firmin, *Equality of the Human Races*, 228; Champollion, introduction to *Grammaire égyptienne*.

140. Lewis in his acclaimed intellectual history on the Caribbean contends that the notion of "the monogenist principle ... that is to say the unitary oneness of the human species" recapitulates Firmin's ideas (*Main Currents in Caribbean Thought*, 318).

Ovid, however, simply repeats an opinion shared by all the Ancients. The word Ethiopian itself (in Greek, *Aethiop* from *Aethein*, to burn, and *op*, face), which was already used by Homer, says it all. Long before Ovid, we find the same idea in the work of Thodectis of Phaselis, an ancient Greek tragedian who lived in the fourth century before Christ. Strabo attributes the following lines to him:[141]

Those to whom the burning sun comes too close in its course take on a soot-like complexion and their hair curls up, swells, and dries up in the heat.[142]

To continue, Firmin offers two basic reasons that explain the Ethiopian influence upon the Egyptian civilization and his reason to contradict and reject the unscientific claims of Egyptologists and anthropologists that the Ethiopians were uncivilized and barbarians. In other words, the Ethiopianization of Egypt is a historical attestation of the momentous of the peoples of Egypt and Ethiopia in world civilization. This position clearly affirms the dignity of the Ethiopian people. These two historical facts, he contends, would also support his suggestion that the *Retous* were a people of the same origin as the Ethiopians and the indigenous peoples of Sudanese Africa.[143] First, he mentions the historical Hyksos—a white race or a group of mixed Semitic-Asiatics—invasion of Egypt around 1720–1710 BCE. Second, he reports the mass migration from Egypt to Ethiopia.[144] When the Hyksos of West Asia annexed the land of Egypt, the Egyptians of the Delta region spontaneously withdrew themselves in the direction of Upper Egypt. It is there at the borders of the Thebes province they received military assistance and other substantial resources from the Ethiopians, their natural allies. Consequently, the Egyptians eventually overcame their invaders and removed them from their land. In fact, the Ethiopian civilization was at its peak in this time period to the

---

141. Firmin, *Equality of the Human Races*, 52; for the Greco-Roman regard toward Africa and Blacks, I suggest these excellent texts, Mudimbe, *Idea of Africa*, and *Invention of Africa*; and the exceptional works by Snowden, *Blacks in Antiquity*, and *Before Color Prejudice: The Ancient Views of Blacks*.

142. This is the English translation of the Greek quote; cited in Firmin, *Equality of the Human Races*, 52.

143. Firmin, *Equality of the Human Races*, 249–50.

144. Firmin, *Equality of the Human Races*, 248–49; for detailed historical study and information about the Hyksos people, see Bernal, *Black Athena*, vol. 2; Howe, *Afrocentrism*, 202–3; Leftkowitz, *Not Out of Africa*, 22–24.

point that an arranged marriage was performed between Princess *Nofritari* and *Ahmes* and in order to enact the alliance between Egypt and the king of Ethiopia.[145] To express this another way, the Hyksos were intruders whose cultural influence at the birth of the Egyptian civilization only came later in the game. They were not the original architects or makers of the Black Pharaonic Egypt.

Firmin's second historical reason to ascertain the common racial origin and identity of the people of Egypt and Ethiopia and to establish the priority of Ethiopia attests to the great migration already mentioned above. As he puts it, during the mass migration, "240,000 soldiers of the Egyptian army walked away in compact groups from Egypt into Ethiopia when the policies of the Sais Dynasty King *Psamethik* the First seemed to give too much access to the Greeks."[146] Firmin reinforces his position by referencing to an important historical period in Egyptian-Ethiopian history, in which more than a century before the restoration of the Sais Dynasty, King *Piankhy Meri Amoun*, the founder of the XXV Ethiopian dynasty, subjugated the entire territory which extends from Thebes to the Nile Valley. Moreover, he invites his readers to consider his judgment: "How else can we explain the destination of these Egyptian migrants if not by the fact that they shared a common racial identity with the people under whose flags they willingly gathered? Consciousness of race here superseded consciousness of nationality."[147]

Complementarily, Firmin showcases the shared cultural traditions and religious and spiritual practices between the Ethiopians and the Egyptians. He indicates that when scholars study African flora—including the papyrus and the *lebka* tree—and fauna—such as the ancient greyhound (*canis leporarius oegypticus*)—of classical Egypt, they soon realize that "most of the plants and animals the Egyptians used in their religious rituals or for their basic daily needs, originated in Ethiopia."[148] What did account for this common cultural tradition and shared practices between Egypt and Ethiopia? Firmin explains that these plants and animals were first used in Ethiopia and later transported to Egypt and raised there. He

---

145. Firmin, *Equality of the Human Races*, 249.

146. Firmin, *Equality of the Human Races*, 249. Firmin writes the Greeks were "a white people with an incompatible culture, who could not be integrated into the *Retou* national community."

147. Firmin, *Equality of the Human Races*, 249.

148. Firmin, *Equality of the Human Races*, 238.

was convinced that the Egyptians came from Ethiopia with their plants, livestock, and material and religious resources.

The Firminian logic is the sustaining argument that Egypt not only had close cultural links and relationships with Ethiopia but with the rest of the African populations with which Egypt shared thousands of similarities in terms of customs, popular religion, and language.[149] This judgment is further affirmed by Cesar Cantu and Ampere. Firmin quotes the latter below:

> Some objects used in Egyptian religious rituals are originally from Nubia. Two such items are the sweet marjoram (*origanum majorama*), a plant sacred to Isis, and the ibis, a bird which comes down to these lands only at the time of the Nile's flooding. . . . It was only in Nubia that Caillaud had seen the black ibis and the sacred scarab (*scarabeus ateuchus*), which was worshipped b the ancient Egyptians.[150]

Firmin was also persuaded that "the further back in antiquity we go the more we become convinced that all the peoples living on the shores of the Nile were of the same ethnological type."[151] He projected the idea of the cultural unity and shared identity and traditions[152] between the Egyptians and Ethiopians by citing another authority, the distinguished Greek historian and classical writer *Diodorus of Sicily*. By appealing to this canonical writer, Firmin was reiterating the commonly-held belief in antiquity among Greek and Roman writers about the true origin of the Egyptians:

> The Ethiopians claim that Egypt is one of their colonies. There are striking similarities between the customs and the laws of the two countries: kings are called gods; funerals are very elaborate rituals; the same writing systems are in use in Ethiopia and Egypt, and the knowledge of the sacred characters, which is the exclusive preserve of the Egyptian priests to be familiar to all Ethiopians.[153]

---

149. Firmin, *Equality of the Human Races*, 239–40.

150. Firmin, *Equality of the Human Races*, 239.

151. Firmin, *Equality of the Human Races*, 239–40.

152. The thesis of cultural unity and shared cultural customs across continental Black Africa is supported both by Diop and Afrocentrists like Asante.

153. Firmin, *Equality of the Human Races*, 236; *Diodorus of Sicily*, bk. 3, ch. 8.

Classics scholar Frank M. Snowden Jr. concurs that the Greeks and Romans used the generic term Ethiopian (*Aithiops, Aethiops*) to refer to "dark-and black-skinned people" who lived south of Egypt and on the southern fringes of northwest Africa.[154] He makes the following observation as depicted in the classical records as early as the second millennium:

> The Greeks and Romans . . . in detailed descriptions and striking realistic portraits have provided a very accurate and precise picture of the African peoples whom they described as Ethiopians. Ethiopians were black and flat-nosed in Xenophanes; black with the wooliest hair of all mankind in Herodotus; black, flat-nosed, and woolly-haired in Diodorus; and in the *Moretum* described with the detail and accuracy of later anthropological classifications of the so-called Negroid type.[155]

Substantially, Firmin cites G. M. Ollivier-Beauregard in *Des divinités égyptiennes*, a text that was published in 1866 before the rise of Egyptology and anthropology as academic disciplines in the West, to accentuate ancient Egyptian attitude toward white people: "From the most remote antiquity, the Egyptians customarily referred to the White nations by such expressions as 'cursed of Schet' or 'the plague of Schet.'"[156] This particular assertion is exploited here as a supportive evidence that the Egyptian had rejected the white identity as a people. As outlined in the preceding paragraphs, Firmin brilliantly offered strong opinions and convincing arguments to dismiss the common belief of the day that the ancient Egyptians were a White race. He also dismantled the traditional belief of his time that the ancient Kemetic-Egyptian civilization was the achievement of the White race, and the Egyptologist prerogative that "the classical civilizations of the Nile Valley were not possible without European input."[157]

Prominent Haitian intellectual-anthropologist Price-Mars reiterates in his 1928 masterpiece, A*insi Parla l'Oncle*, what Firmin had already established in 1885 that "Abyssinia [Ethiopia] was a center of civilization

---

154. Snowden, "Attitudes towards Blacks," 246; for an excellent study on the relationship between Africans, Greeks, and Romans and their view of Blacks in the classical period and records, see Snowden, *Blacks in Antiquity*; Mudimbe, *Idea of Africa*, 20–52.

155. Snowden, "Attitudes towards Blacks," 246–47.

156. Firmin, *Equality of the Human Races*, 139; Ollivier-Beauregard, *Les divinités égyptiennes*.

157. Asante, *Kemet*, 46.

in direct contact with Egypt? Its influence like that of Egypt extended far to the West over the peoples of eastern Sudan."[158] He accentuates that we must connect the Ethiopians with the ancient Egyptians.[159] In the text, Price-Mars elaborates on the wide-range spread and influence of ancient Ethiopian-Egyptian civilization upon the rest of continental Africa, which included the cultural and imperial centers of Songhai in the sixteenth century, the Askia dynasty, and that of Sudan in the domain of arts and sciences. For example, he concludes that the land of Songhai "bore the seeds of ancient Egypt."[160]

In our previous analysis, we have noted that the Black origin thesis of the ancient Egyptian civilization and the connection between Egypt and Ethiopia and their complementary roles in the civilizing process is substantially supported by Black Atlantic writers and intellectuals of the Vindicationist tradition, both in the Anglophone and Francophone worlds. The Black presence in Egypt and the Ethiopian-Egyptian connection is also supported by Count Constantin Volney (or Constantin François de Chasseboeuf). Volney was an influential French scholar, philosopher and historian who travelled to Egypt in 1782 and 1785 in the blossoming era of slavery and the slave trade in Western societies. He wrote the excellent work entitled *Voyage en Egypte et en Syrie* in 1787. It is to him that Firmin turns to confirm his provocative claim. The Haitian Egyptologist reproduces Volney's historic observation: "When I saw that characteristically Negro head, I remembered this remarkable passage in Herodotus where he sates, 'I believe that the Colchis are a colony of Egyptians because, like the latter, they have a black skin and wooly hair.'"[161] Firmin interprets the words of the French scholar to mean that "the Egyptians were true Negroes, of the same race as the natives of Africa."[162] Volney, who denounces European hypocrisy and racism toward blacks, also makes this striking declaration about white racism and Black slavery:

> Just think that this race of black men, today our slave and the object of our scorn, is the very race to which we owe our arts, sciences, and even the use of speech! Just imagine, finally, that it is in the midst of peoples who call themselves the greatest

---

158. Price-Mars, *Thus Spoke the Uncle*, 79.
159. Price-Mars, *Thus Spoke the Uncle.*, 63.
160. Price-Mars, *Thus Spoke the Uncle*, 67.
161. Firmin, *Equality of the Human Races*, 228.
162. Firmin, *Equality of the Human Races*, 228.

friends and humanity that one has approved the most barbarous slavery and questioned whether black men have the same kind of intelligence as Whites!¹⁶³

Firmin closes the pages of the chapter on "Egypt and Civilization" by restating his underlying thesis:

> It is time now to put an end to the dogma according to which the ancient Ethiopians were a bunch of barbarians unable to attain civilization simply because they were Black.... The population of Egypt was Black like the Ethiopians, and the inhabitants of Ethiopia were as civilized as the Egyptians.... The population of Egypt was Black like the Ethiopians, and the inhabitants of Ethiopia were as civilized as the Egyptians.... Egypt was a country of Negroes, of Black Africans. The Black race has preceded all other races in the construction of civilization. It is in the Black race that thought first emerged and human intelligence first awakened.... The Greeks paid homage to the ancient Egyptians; the Romans paid homage to the Greeks; and the whole of Europe salute them all!¹⁶⁴

The Indebtedness of Classical Greek to Ancient Egypt

In this division of the essay, we shall comment on Firmin's unapologetic position for the considerable impact of ancient Egypt on classical Greek. In chapter 6 ("Artificial Ranking of the Human Races") in *The Equality of the Human Races*, the anti-racist intellectual cross-examines and hence rejects the logic of the "systematic hierarchy among the human races," and the scientifically-derived racial categories and criteria used both by anthropologists and Egyptologists. In the opening words, he voices strong criticisms against the unreasonability of Gobineau's judgment, "the idea of an innate, original, profound, and permanent inequality among the races is one of the oldest and most widespread opinions in the world."¹⁶⁵ For Firmin, Gobineau's exaggerated and unsustainable claim—his ethnographic division of humanity into distinct races—cannot be justified or sustained on the basis of serious works of history and plausible scientific reason. He explains that the basis in classifying humanity as such and as

---

163. Quoted in Diop, *African Origin*, 27–28.

164. Firmin, *Equality of the Human Races*, 252.

165. Here, Firmin reproduces a quote by Gobineau, *De l'inégalité des races humaines*, 139; Gobineau, *De l'inégalité des races humaines*, 35.

an intellectual idea has its roots at the birth of ethnographic science and modernity's racial imagination.

Firmin contends that the concept of race assumed its definitive meaning only with the works of eighteenth-century naturalists, and race as a social construct is an invention of modern science.[166] The Haitian anthropologist reasons, as a reply to Gobineau's ideology of racial superiority, that it is not absolutely accurate to suggest that the idea of original inequality of the human races is one of the oldest and most widespread opinions.[167] The problem was not race but patriotic zeal. He thus writes, "Through history, civilized peoples, self-centered and proud, have always thought themselves superior to their neighbors. But there was been the least connection between this sense of superiority, which results from a narrow but highly respectable patriotism."[168] He explains further that scientists who have developed the doctrine of the inequality of the races and the superiority of one race over another race base their judgment upon four possible factors or criteria: intelligence, physical factors (physical anthropology)—which include height, muscular strength, proportion of the limbs, etc.—beauty, and morality.[169] After a thorough analysis of each individual proposal, Firmin bluntly dismisses all of those criteria of authenticity for maintaining white supremacy and hegemony, and the racist culture of Western societies. He judges that they do not have strong scientific foundation and that the arguments that sustain them are curious, ambivalent, unstable, and even contradictory.

The claim that bothered Firmin the most was the idea that the Black race had no history, as philosopher Georg Hegel had also reminded us that continental Africa was a place with no history. Firmin was uncomfortable with white claim of history—that is, history is the achievement of a race and a people, the Aryan myth and the triumph of white people in modern history. Also, he could not tolerate the thought of white denial that a Black population in Egypt could have produced the high intellectual culture and social development, which for him, "constitutes crucial arguments against the doctrine of the inequality of the races"[170] and

---

166. Firmin, *Equality of the Human Races*, 140.
167. Firmin, *Equality of the Human Races*, 140.
168. Firmin, *Equality of the Human Races*, 139.
169. Firmin, *Equality of the Human Races*, 147.
170. Firmin, *Equality of the Human Races*, 237.

counters the doctrine of "the innate inferiority of the Black race."[171] To illustrate the pervasiveness of the problem of whiteness and the preposterousness of white claim of black innate inferiority in Western thought, Firmin reproduces a passage from the French naturalist Armand de Quatrefages's book *L'espèce humaine*, published in 1877:

> The set of conditions that produced the different races has also brought about an actual inequality which is impossible to deny. But such is the penchant of the professional Negrophiles for hyperbole that they insist that the Negro was in the past, and much as he is, equal to the White man.
>
> Barth's discoveries have a verified something which could be doubted until then: the existence of a political history among Negroes. But this very fact serves to underscore more the absence of an intellectual history, which consists of a general progressive movement marked by literary, artistic, and architectural achievements. Left to tis own devices, the Negro race has produced nothing of the sort. The Black people, which have been classified among the Negro race in order to disguise the race's too obvious inferiority, are connected to it at best through crossbreeding cases in which the superior blood predominates.[172]

It is evident that both Gobineau and Quatrefage maintained a similar view on race and white supremacy in particular. Both of them had overlooked and undermined the long-established tradition of the Black origin of the Egyptians as maintained in the classical records and the indebtedness of classical Greek to ancient Egypt. Firmin was convinced by bringing careful attention to the triumph of the ancient Egyptian civilization in world history and by highlighting the manifold debt the Greco-Roman civilization, and ultimately Western civilization owes to ancient Egypt, he would be able to prove that the Black race was capable of grand and noble actions, capable especially of standing up to the White race.[173] Hence, it suffices for the Haitian anthropologist to once again revisit the classical records of ancient Greece and Rome in which prominent figures and writers of antiquity acknowledge deliberately and pay homage to Egypt.

Firmin cogently reasons that classical Greek civilization and culture owes its intellectual development to Africa and ancient Egypt. He

171. Firmin, *Equality of the Human Races*, 402.
172. Firmin, *Equality of the Human Races*, 154.
173. Firmin, *Equality of the Human Races*, 399.

presents forceful, sustainable, and systematic arguments to validate all of his points. First of all, he declares that, "Besides the honor of having invented the science of numbers and surface measurement does not belong to the White race. The origin of mathematics goes back to Black Egypt, the land of the Pharaohs."[174] Accordingly, the intelligence of Black Egyptians in creating the science of geometry required high level aptitude and critical thinking:

> All the scientists who researched the history of the exact sciences unanimously recognize the Egyptians as the inventors of geometry. More than three thousand years before the Christian era, when the European nations were still in a barbarous state, the Hamites who lived on the shores of the Nile had already been doing geometric computations, calculating the area of different types of surfaces.[175]

Second, he insists on Greece's borrowing from Egypt when he writes:

> Plato and Diogenes Laerces both recognize that arithmetic too originated in Egypt, which is quite logical, given that arithmetic calculations are indispensable in the solution of geometric problems. As with many other things, Greece, the first White Western nation to have attained a considerable of civilization indisputably owes to Egypt the first notions of mathematics.[176]

Third, Firmin denies Greek originality by attacking its intellectual foundations:

> The first Greek scientist to have concerned himself with mathematics with some brilliance was Thales of Miletus; he had acquired most of his knowledge in Egypt. In the sixth century, before the decline of her culture, Greece produced, for her greater glory, Pythagoras, who showed the most brilliant aptitudes for the sciences. We owe him the discovery of several properties of numbers, the proof of the value of the square of the hypotenuse, and several theorems. But are we not justified to ask whether he had achieved all this on his own, or simply transmitted to us the notions he had learned from the Egyptian priests, especially as he studied in their college in Thebes and lived in their country for twenty years?[177]

174. Firmin, *Equality of the Human Races*, 168.
175. Firmin, *Equality of the Human Races*, 168.
176. Firmin, *Equality of the Human Races*, 168.
177. Firmin, *Equality of the Human Races*, 168–69.

Fourth, he advances the idea that Plato, one of the intellectual giants of the Greek culture and thought, and Western civilization, studied in Egypt: "Plato, who practiced mathematics with great success and who is mainly responsible for giving them the prestige they continue to enjoy, was not satisfied with studying with the Pythagoreans; he went to Egypt, to the very source of the light."[178] Asante encapsulate the Firminian logic when pronounces these striking words: "Since Egypt preceded the civilizations of Greece and Rome in antiquity it is only natural that it would be the source of Greek knowledge, even names of towns and deities."[179] In this sense, it is Africa, to some extent, rather than Greece, that has made a lasting impact on Western societies.[180] By emphasizing the achievement of Egypt in Greece and Rome respectively in the intellectual, cultural, social, and historical sense, both Firmin and Asante came to a similar conclusion.

Some seventy-one years before Firmin would publish his groundbreaking and anti-racist text, the first postcolonial writer of postrevolutionary Haiti Pompée Valentin baron de Vastey, the secretary and publicist to King Henry Christophe, published *Le système colonial dévoilé* (*The Colonial System Unveiled*) in 1814. Vastey, in many ways, echoes Afrocentric sensibility and condemns the colonial system and slavery as an inhuman institution. In this manifesto, anticipating Firmin's work, the royal apologist articulates anti-racist, anti-colonial, and anti-Western oppression sentiments. Vastey brings to surface that "Danaus and Cecrops brought agriculture, enlightenment (*les lumières*), and the arts of the Egyptians to Greece."[181] Like Firmin, he accentuates the tremendous impact of Egypt in the emergence of Greece and Rome as nations, and insists that both countries "had received these goods/benefits from Egypt,"[182] that is the Egyptians brought with them to Greece and Rome "the arts, the commerce, and the navigation system."[183]

178. Firmin, *Equality of the Human Races*, 169.

179. Asante, *Kemet*, 100.

180. Asante, *Kemet*, 47.

181. Baron de Vastey, *Le système colonial dévoilé* (Cap-Henry: Roux, 1814), 19; the French text reads as such: "*Danaus et Cécrops apportèrent l'agriculture, les lumières et les arts des égyptiens dans la Grèce.*"

182. Vastey, *Le système colonial dévoilé*, 19. Greece and Rome "avaient reçus ces bienfaits de l'Egypte."

183. Vastey, *Le système colonial dévoilé*, 19. The Egyptians "*apportent avec eux les lumières, les arts, le commerce et la navigation.*"

Finally, with his critical and brilliant mind, Firmin proposes two basic reasons why Western scholars had failed to give credit to the Egyptians for all their accomplishments in world history. The first reason is that the Egyptians "had a language with a rather sophisticated grammar but also with a writing system that was so complicated and so difficult that scientific and literary documents in the language remained incomprehensible for centuries."[184] The second reason he reports is that "Egyptian achievements in mathematics have not been recognized, one which worsens the effects of the first, the exclusionary mindset of the priest, the principal depositories of science."[185] To express this concern another way, the second problem had to do explicitly with what we might call the "epistemic apartheid" which explains the "epistemic crisis" in Egyptian cultural and intellectual history. Egyptian priests who were supposed to teach the common people about the art of wisdom and science limited their scientific knowledge and findings or discoveries to a limited few in the population. As Firmin reports, "Egyptian priests made a mystery out of all their scientific acquisitions and taught them only in a restricted milieu, to a small number of pupils, training a close elite who would have the total monopoly of the esoteric doctrine."[186] In spite of these shortcomings in Egyptian history, Firmin find comfort as he ponders upon the enduring impact of ancient Egyptian civilization upon the life and culture of classical Greece and Rome, and by extension the entire Western civilization:

> Nevertheless, Egypt was considered the fount of science, so much so that it was in Alexandria that the Greeks went to develop their aptitudes for mathematics, producing such famous figures as Euclid, Archimedes, Appollonius of Perga, and so many other bright stars in the Alexandria Pleiades. Now that the human mind has entered a mature stage, as indicated by the conscientiously critical approach to phenomena that has become the norm, we wonder whether it is not possible that unknown scientists of the ancient Egyptian race helped to light the first sparks of science in the immortal city founded by Alexander the Great. Whether the answer is affirmative or not, it

---

184. Firmin, *Equality of the Human Races*, 169; he also remarks, "We may assume that during all the long period when the meaning of the hieroglyphs remained obscure, as mysterious as the Sphinx in this mysterious Egypt, most of these documents disappeared forever with the secrets the contained."

185. Firmin, *Equality of the Human Races*, 169.

186. Firmin, *Equality of the Human Races*, 169.

remains a fact of history that the Black race of Egypt was the first to cultivate the abstract notions of arithmetic and to formulate the first calculations.[187]

Diop and Firmin: The Legacy Continues

In the final division of the essay, we shall briefly comment on the legacy of Diop in relation to Firmin's work. In his seminal text, Firmin has not succeeded o explore profoundly the linguistic link between ancient Egypt and the rest of continental Black Africa. In 1954, the brilliant and highly respected Senegalese historian, anthropologist, physicist, and philosopher Cheikh Anta Diop would fill the gap by establishing in his epoch-making book *Nations nègres et culture* the decisive and impressive linguistic connection between Egypt and several countries in Black Africa. Diop articulates a coherent theory of common linguistic roots of African languages he studies as well as the theory of Black genesis of ancient Egypt, as his intellectual predecessor had achieved.

Diop repudiates the racially-based scientific theories and dangerous ideologies propagated by European Egyptologists, anthropologists, archeologists, linguistics, and historians. In September 1956 at the First International Congress of Black Writers and Artists, Diop pronounces these words to his predominantly Black audience:

> We have come to discover that the ancient Pharaonic Egyptian civilization was undoubtedly a Negro civilization. To defend this thesis, anthropological, ethnological, linguistic, historical, and cultural arguments have been provided. To judge their validity, it suffices to refer to *Nations nègres et culture*.[188]

Likewise, in the footsteps of Firmin, in the English translation of *Civilization or Barbarism: An Authentic Anthropology*, Diop would rehearse and sustain the Firminian thesis that "ancient Egypt was a distinct African nation and was not historically or culturally a part of Asia or Europe"[189] as some scholars had traditionally maintained. The Black origin of ancient Egypt, according to Diop, was critical for the reconstitution of African history and the future of the whole continent. Consequently, he would write in *The African Origin of Civilization*: "Ancient Egypt was a

---

187. Firmin, *Equality of the Human Races*, 170.
188. Diop, *Nations nègres et culture*, ix.
189. Diop, *Civilization or Barbarism*, xvi.

Negro civilization. The history of Black Africa will remain suspended in air and cannot be written correctly until African historians dare to connect it with the history of Egypt."[190] Diop describes with more precision and clarity the significant contributions of the Black race in the making of modernity:

> The ancient Egyptians were Negroes. The moral fruit of their civilization is to be counted among the assets of the Black world. Instead of presenting itself to history as an insolvent debtor, the Black world is the very initiator of the "western" civilization flaunted before our eyes today. Pythagorean mathematics, the theory of the four elements of Thales of Miletus, Epicurean materialism, Platonic idealism, Judaism, Islam, and modern science are rooted in Egyptian cosmogony and science. One needs only to mediate on Osiris, the redeemer-god, who sacrifices himself, dies, and is resurrected to save mankind, a figure essentially identifiable with Christ.[191]

The Significance of Firmin in the Twenty-First Century

The problem of scientific racism and the exclusion of Black people of ancient Egypt and the people of African ancestry from the metanarratives of human history and world civilizations are central points to the vindicationist discourse of Anténor Firmin's *The Equality of the Human Races*. As a result, Firmin attempted to shift the geography of reason—that was then Eurocentric—and decenter the Westernization of epistemology and human history. He found Western historiography and its treatment of African history and culture deficient, and assessed the scientific enterprise and vision of Western scholarship as racist and unscientific. For Firmin, the problem of whiteness (or the Aryan myth) was a major crisis of modernity, which was deeply rooted in the racist culture in Western societies and white supremacist ideology. The second problem of modernity was Black recognition, and the fear and averseness of Western scholars and scientists to acknowledge and valorize the substantial contributions of the Black race in the intellectual development of world civilizations and cultures. As Asante has rightly observed, European scholars and Egyptologists had tripped "Africa of its productive and generative

---

190. Diop, *African Origin of Civilization*, xiv.
191. Diop, *African Origin of Civilization*, xiv.

subjectivity."[192] For Firmin, ancient Egypt, for a better word, the Kemetic civilization was a master symbol of black achievement in world history. As he has also argued, by the virtue of the Haitian Revolution, the Haitian people are a symbol of Black equality and intelligence in human history.

Firmin's book is significant in the twenty-first century for its direct and indirect engagement with important and critical issues of our time, both academic and practical; these include ethnic and postcolonial studies, critical race theory, the discipline of modern anthropology and history of ideas, and the practical effects of racism and discrimination in society . As long as whiteness remains a dominant problem in the modern world and our postcolonial moment, the necessity to read Firmin will become inevitable. Firmin refused to judge people based on their social rank, wealth, much less of the color of their skin; rather, he championed the dignity of every individual.[193] As he himself writes at the end of his book, "All men are brothers . . . once they acknowledge they are equal, the races will be able to support and love one another. . . . That human beings everywhere are endowed with the same qualities and defects, without distinctions based on color or anatomical shape. The races are equal."[194] It was Jean Metellus who reminds us that "Firmin deserves to be included not only among the pantheon of great Haitians, not only among the great Blacks of the world, but also among the first representatives of universalism."[195]

The Equality of the Human Races will remain an important text to consult from time to time as long as the onerous burden of race and white supremacy and arrogance, Western hegemony, neocolonial imperialism, and racism continue to exist and threaten human existence, and hinder the furtherance of peoples and nations in the twenty-first-century culture.

In sum, for Firmin, the heritage of ancient Egypt belongs to all humanity regardless of one's geography, race, gender, culture, and ethnicity. The significance of Firmin in the twenty-first century is what he exactly represents and what he does not represent in the history of ideas. Joseph Anténor Firmin is the Haitian intellectual par excellence and the fervent defender of the equality of the human races. Such legacy will never die!

192. Asante, *Kemet*, 116.
193. Pean, *Comprendre Antenor Firmin*, 303.
194. Firmin, *Equality of the Human Races*, 448–50.
195. Quoted in Pean, *Antenor Firmin*, 19. The French original reads: "*Firmin mérite de figurer non seulement parmi la panoplie des grands haïtiens, non seulement parmi les grands negres du monde, mais parmi les premiers représentants de l'universalisme.*"

PART II

Faith, Secularism, and the Problem of Change

CHAPTER FOUR

Revolution of the Mind: Religion, Marxist Humanism, and Development

An Analysis of Roumain's Religious Feeling and Marxist Rhetoric

BOTH ANTÉNOR FIRMIN AND Jacques Roumain articulate a robust secularist worldview in their work; nonetheless, it is a secularism that acknowledges the place of theism in human history and modernity. Firmin places emphasis on the imperative of intellectual reparations leading to a radical change in Western modern intellectual history and African ancestry. For him, a radical change of the Western mind toward the African past would enhance our attitude toward the African people and the people of African ancestry in the Black Diaspora. Nonetheless, while the previous chapter did not address Firmin's secularism, this present chapter examines the place of secularism, religion, and development in the thought of Roumain. What unites Roumain and Firmin is their emphasis on the freedom of the mind and the freedom of action.

Jacques Roumain was one of the most influential public intellectuals and writers in twentieth-century Haiti and in the Black Atlantic world. He was a founding member of the literary and cultural movement known as Haitian *indigénisme*, which rejected the hegemony of French-Western values and culture in Haiti and reacted against the imperial culture of the American military occupation (1915–1934) in the Caribbean country. As an anti-imperialist and Marxist writer and a critic of Western colonialism and hegemonic domination in the world, Roumain advocated strongly for the decolonization of the peoples and countries in the developing world and championed the liberation and human rights of the oppressed. In 1934, he founded the *Parti Communiste Haitien* (PCH—the Haitian Communist Party) and spread the gospel of Marxism and Socialism through his prolific writings. In his various publications, he analyzed issues pertaining to the relationship between Haiti's oppressed underclass peasants, the working class, and the ruling Elite group minority. From a Marxist social theory, Roumain wrote about religion, social development, and the role of the oppressed people in history as agents of their own liberation. He relentlessly addressed the global problem of the capitalist world and its exploitation of those living in the darker side of modernity.

This chapter investigates the intersections of religion, social transformation, and Marxist social theory in the thought of Jacques Roumain. It argues that Roumain's radical perspective on religion, development, and his critiques of institutionalized Christianity were substantially influenced by a Marxist conception of historical materialism and secular humanist approach to faith and human progress. Roumain rejects Christianity for its ineffective role in society in fostering social change. This essay also contends that Roumain's rejection of religious supernaturalism and divine intervention in human affairs and history was shaped by his non-theistic humanism and secular worldview on faith. Ultimately, the essay demonstrates that Roumain believes that only through effective human solidarity and collaboration can serious social transformation and real human freedom take place. He downplays the potential role of religion to deal adequately with the ambiguities of life in this world. Roumain holds that man was the measure of all things and his own agent of liberation. Consequently, individuals themselves must cooperate and unite in order to alter the social order toward a fruitful life of peace, harmony, and freedom.

The chapter is divided in three parts. The first explores Roumain's orientation to Marxism, Socialism, and Communism as a writer and activist-intellectual. The second part studies his Marxist-inspired religious rhetoric and scientific realism, and their relationship to human progress in his well-known debates with the French Catholic priest-theologian Joseph Foisset. Finally, we conclude the essay by looking at the relationship between religion and social development, and collective liberation in Roumain's well-known novel, *Gouverneurs de la rosée* (*Masters of the Dew*).

Toward a Marxist and Communist Orientation and Aesthetic

As a creative writer and freedom fighter, Roumain's only English biographer Carolyn Fowler states that "Jacques Roumain shared a vision of the function of art as the articulation of a people's condition, as a reflection of the culture which that people develops to cope creatively and to express their hope for the fulfillment of universal human aspirations."[1] Roumain has exercised an enormous influence on Haitian literature, Caribbean writers, and on the young generation of poets and intellectuals associated with the Haitian Renaissance from the time of the American Occupation in Haiti to the growing post-occupation generation of Haitian writers.

He was particularly committed to the welfare of Haitian "peasantariat" and the "universal" proletariat, and the betterment of humanity.[2] Roumain was interested in the religious expression and sensibility of people as well as the function of religion in culture and society. He used his writings as political interventions for social renovation and emancipative action. He was not only deeply concerned about the everyday experience of the black masses in Haiti, and the world's poor, but how these groups of individuals repeatedly confronted some of the most egregious evils of modern times and the man-made social oppressions, abuses, and exploitations. His engagement with faith is documented in several of his works.

At the beginning of 1932, the French Marxist writer Tristan Rémy requested biographical information about Jacques Roumain for a

---

1. Fowler, "Shared Vision of Langston Hughes and Jacques Roumain," 88.

2. I am thankful to an unnamed reviewer of this present essay who made an important observation about my use of the "peasant" terminology here: "In the Western tradition of Marxism, writers like Eric Hobsbawm have called the peasant 'prepolitical' and 'premodern,' unable to effectively confront capitalist modernity in the same manner as the urban, industrial proletariat. But in other, non-Western manifestations of Marxist thought, scholars have suggested that the peasant's agency in capitalist modernity is far more potent. Still others, especially in African studies, have coined the term 'peasantariat' to conjure the hybrid nature of peasant and working-class consciousness in the developing world"; because of the scope of this piece, it is impossible for me to explore various schools of thought (i.e., the Subaltern Studies group) associated with these various terminologies and concepts as well as their historical contexts. The interested reader would find the following studies on the these critical issues helpful: Guha, *Elementary Aspects of Peasant Insurgency*, and *Subaltern Studies Reader*; Guha et al., *Selected Subaltern Studies*; Spivak, *Critique of Postcolonial Reason*; Chakrabart, *Rethinking Working Class*, and *Habitations of Modernity*.

forthcoming article. Rémy was a champion of proletarian literature in France in the 1930s and a contributor to the newly launched socialist and political review *Monde*. In his response letter, Roumain confesses to Rémy that he was a committed Marxist and revolutionary Communist and was interested in proletarian literature. As a member of the Haitian high class, Roumain, who has renounced his wealth and well-regarded social status, divulged his anti-Haitian bourgeois sentiment and commitment to the (cause of) Haitian underclass peasants. Unapologetically, he declares:

> *Je suis communiste. Non militant pour l'instant, parce que les cadres d'une lutte politique n'existent pas encore en Haïti. Je m'applique à préparer....*
>
> *Fils de grands propriétaires terriens, j'ai renié mes origines bourgeoisies. J'ai beaucoup vécu avec les paysans. Je connais leur vie, leur mentalité, leur réligion—ce mélange étonnant de catholicisme et de vaudou.*
>
> *Je ne considère pas le prolétariat paysan comme une valeur sentimentale. Le paysan haïtien est notre seul producteur et il ne produit que pour être exploité, de la manière la plus effroyable, par une minorité ... politicienne qui s'intitule l'Elite. Toutes mes publications ont combattu cette prétendue élite.*
>
> *Je travaille au renouvellement de notre littérature par l'étude de notre très riche folklore.... J'estime que notre littérature doit être nègre et largement prolétarienne.*
>
> *Je travaille également au rapprochement des écrivains nègres de tous les pays.*[3]

[I am a Communist. Not a militant one for the moment, because the cadres of a political struggle do not yet exist in Haiti. I am applying myself to this end....

The son of owners of great land holdings, I have disavowed my bourgeois origins. I have lived a lot among the peasants. I know their life, mentality, religion—that surprising fusion of Catholicism and Vodou.

I do not regard the peasant proletariat as a sentimental value. The Haitian peasant is our only producer, and he only produces only to be exploited, in the most gruesome manner, by a minority ... of politicians known as the Elite. All of my publications have fought against this so-called elite.

---

3. Roumain, "Lettre à Tristan Rémy," in *Jacques Roumain: Œuvres Complètes*, 639. The letter is dated 1932.

I am working for the renewal of our literature through the study of our rich folklore . . . I believe that our literature must be *Negro* and largely proletarian. I am working equally for the bringing together of Negro writers of all countries.]

Roumain's idea for the country's new course in literature is a marriage of his Marxist-Communist politics and proletarian-peasant literature. Unlike many Western Marxist intellectuals at that time who had suppressed race for class, Roumain's race and class consciousness are blended and one. He writes, "I believe that our literature must be *Negro* and largely proletarian." His Pan-Africanist and transnationalist vision in the establishment of a new literary ethos in Haiti is attested in this declaration: "I am working equally for the bringing together of Negro writers of all countries." Yet, the emphasis on the "proletarianist turn" in literature reveals his cross-racial, trans-cultural, and global sensibility. David Nichols remarks that Roumain seeks to associate

> the interests of the Haitian masses with those of the proletariat in metropolitan countries, accepting the Soviet line on this matter. . . . The Russian revolution had created a new proletarian front throughout the world, extending from the proletarians of the West, through the Russian revolution, to the oppressed peoples of the East.[4]

Furthermore, in a critical essay entitled "Analyse schématique" which he wrote in 1934, Roumain examined the Haitian condition from a Marxist perspective. He criticizes the Haitian bourgeoisie class and the political charlatans for exploiting Haitian peasants and the working class, and for misusing their material production and resources for their own profit. He brings to surface the dilemma of social classes, the problem of color and economic oppression, and the abuse of power, which substantially accounted for Haiti's underdevelopment and the poor living condition of the majority in the island. He declares, "*Il s'agit, on le voit, d'une oppression économique qui se traduit socialement et politiquement. Donc la base objective du problème est bien la lutte des classes*"[5] ("As we might observe, the phenomenon is that of economic oppression, which is translated socially and politically. Thus, the fundamental problem is indisputably of a class struggle"). In diagnosing the Haitian problem,

---

4. Nicholls, *From Dessalines to Duvalier*, 173.

5. Roumain, "Analyse schématique," in *Jacques Roumain: Oeuvres Complètes*, 778–80; also quoted also in Nicholls, *From Dessalines to Duvalier*, 183.

Roumain's basic contention is the underlying fact that the issue of class struggle and economic exploitation of the common people by the middle class bourgeoisie and the minority elite has had significant effects and repercussions on the social and political life in Haiti. Alex Dupuy insightfully points out that

> the U.S. military occupation set the stage for renewed conflicts between the mulatto bourgeoisie and the black bourgeoisie and middle class to control the state after the departure of the Marines in 1934. Those struggles culminated in the victory of the nationalist black middle class in alliance with the black bourgeoisie.... The Duvalier regime did not seek to transform the class structure of Haiti or to eliminate the economic dominance of the mulatto and expatriate bourgeoisie. Rather, it monopolized political power for the black middle class allied to the black bourgeoisie as a counterweight to the mulatto and expatriate bourgeoisies' economic dominance.[6]

Roumain proceeds to expound on the dynamics of imperialism and class oppression in the Haitian experience. In general terms, he insists that imperialism has played a decisive role in orchestrating social and economic inequality and structural oppression in Third-Word societies: *"De plus en plus, elle lie étroitement la notion de la lutte anti-impérialiste à celle de la lutte des classes."*[7] ("Increasingly, it closely binds the notion of anti-imperialist struggle to that of the class struggle."). Michel-Rolph Trouillot affirms that "instability is inherent in the social structure of peripheral capitalism."[8] He also makes a critical observation that we feel is noteworthy in understanding Roumain's central argument here:

> It [instability] stems from the very dependency that characterizes these societies and "disarticulates" to varying degrees the social organism. Societies on the periphery of the capitalist world economy are of necessity outward-looking, if only because they are economically dependent on capitalist centers. Yet states are inherently inward-looking: they exercise primary control over a definite territory and derive their momentum from the dynamics of coercion and consent within that space.... The peripheral capitalist state is often a colonial legacy, the result of a political

---

6. Dupuy, *Haiti in the World Economy*, 208.

7. Jacques Roumain, "L'Ecroulement du mythe nationaliste," in *Jacques Roumain: Œuvre Complètes*, 655.

8. Trouillot, *Haiti State Against Nation*, 22.

"independence" built upon the remains of a power structure imposed from outside.[9]

Dupuy takes the matter back to "the concept of plantation economy in describing a particular form of dependency and underdevelopment and the internal organization and dynamics of that type of economy."[10] Like Trouillot, he underscores that "the extroverted and unintegrated structures of the peripheral and dependent economies created during the colonial period, however, are necessary but not sufficient to explain why some countries like Haiti failed to develop both the capital and consumer goods sectors, after independence."[11] Roumain knew that the theory of dependent development which explains Haiti's underdevelopment and the economic struggle of the country's working class and the underclass peasants was both an internal and external crisis. It is the historical fact that "foreign capital dominates and directs this process of development, but in alliance with the national state and local capital."[12] Consequently, for Roumain, in order to have a self-sustaining and self-determining Haiti, it is necessary for Haitian nationalists to enter a double fight against the internal and external ruthless capitalism: "*C'est combattre le Capitalisme étranger ou indigène, c'est combattre à outrance la bourgeoisie haïtienne et les politiciens bourgeois, valets de l'impérialisme, exploiteurs cruels des ouvriers et paysans*"[13] ("To fight against foreign or native Capitalism is equally to fight to the point the Haitian bourgeoisie and bourgeois politicians, the servants of imperialism and cruel exploiters of workers and peasants"). The root of the Haitian problem is both local and global, as he stresses, "*Le fait concret est celui-ci: un prolétariat noir, une petite bourgeoisie en majorité noir, est opprimé impitoyablement par une infime minorité, la bourgeoisie (mulâtre en sa majorité) et prolétarisé par la grosse industrie internationale*"[14] ("The concrete fact is this: a black proletariat, a petty bourgeoisie in a black majority, is ruthlessly oppressed by a tiny minority, the bourgeoisie (mulatto in its majority) and proletarianized by the international heavy industry/corporation"). Therefore, it is not

---

9. Trouillot, *Haiti State Against Nation*, 22–23.
10. Dupuy, *Haiti in the World Economy*, 3.
11. Dupuy, *Haiti in the World Economy*, 6–7.
12. Dupuy, *Haiti in the World Economy*, 3.
13. Roumain, "L'Ecroulement du mythe nationaliste," 655.
14. Roumain, "L'Ecroulement du mythe nationaliste," 656.

enough to fight global imperialism and international capitalism; it is a clarion call to resist all forms and modalities of human oppression.

Next, Roumain would describe exactly the contributive role of the Haitian Communist Party in diagnosing, scrutinizing, and analyzing this national (and global) crisis scientifically and scrupulously. He affirms that the predicament might have already aggrieved psychologically some blacks and undermined their dignity. However, the problem is beyond race, and that the denigrated and exploited majority black Haitians should rather view race as the handmaid of class and economic greed. Roumain does in fact hold that the predicament of race and color in Haiti is sourced in class hierarchy, economic inequality, and the (mis-)distribution of wealth:

> Le P.C.H. pose le problème scientifiquement sans nier aucunement le bienfondé des réactions psychologiques des noirs blessés dans leur dignité.... Mais le devoir du P.C.H., parti d'ailleurs à 98% noir puisque c'est un parti ouvrier, et ou la question de couleur est vidée systématiquement de con contenu épidermique et placée sur le terrain de la lutte des classes, est de mettre en garde le prolétariat, la petite bourgeoisie pauvre et les travailleurs intellectuels noirs contre les politiciens bourgeois noirs qui voudraient exploiter à leur profit leurs colères justifiés.[15]

> [The PCH (Partie Communiste Haitien / Haitian Communist Party) investigates the problem scientifically, without denying the valid basis for the psychological reaction of the blacks, whose dignity had been wounded.... But the duty of the PCP—after all, it is a party composed of 98 percent Blacks, a worker's party in which the color question is systematically relieved of its epidemic content and placed on the terrain of class struggle—is to warn the proletariat, the poor lower middle-class and the black intellectual workers against the black middle-class politicians who would like to exploit for their own profit by justifying their anger.]

Almost at the end of the essay, he thunders: "*CONTRE LA SOLIDARITE BOURGEOISIE-CAPITALISE NOIRE, MULATRE ET BLANCHE: FRONT PROLETARIEN SANS DISTINCTION DE COULEUR!*"[16] ("AGAINST SOLIDARITY [WITH] THE BLACK BOURGEOISIE-CAPITALIST, MULATTO AND WHITE: PROLETARIAN FRONT

15. Roumain, "L'Ecroulement du mythe nationaliste," 656.
16. Roumain, "L'Ecroulement du mythe nationaliste," 656.

REGARDLESS OF COLOR!"). Roumain's anti-bourgeois sentiments and his efforts to directly confront the bourgeois class in Haiti and to address publicly this crisis are restated in this declaration: "All of my publications have fought against this so-called elite." The anti-bourgeois standing can be traced to the embraced tenets of the surrealist movement, which began as an intellectual force in post-World War I Paris, by André Breton, Paul Elouard, and Benjamin Péret. The movement was a reaction to oppressive capitalism, colonial imperialism, and Western cultural hegemony in the world. As observed, Roumain sought to bridge the gap between Surrealism, Marxism, and Black radical tradition. European surrealists and Black surrealists who have drawn their aspirations from "Freud and Marx while remaining critical of Marxism . . . explicitly called for the overthrow of bourgeois culture, identified with anticolonial movements in Africa and Asia."[17] "As a generalized revolt against the very foundations of Western civilization and its morality, surrealism was drawn immediately towards non-Western cultures, and issues of colonialism soon impinged upon the surrealists' thinking."[18] Surrealism provided black radicals the critical tool for intellectual expression, the spiritual reflection to reevaluate their own black culture, and ultimately a means to combat black oppression and suffering.

In the same line of relationship between Black Surrealism and Black Marxism, most of the Black intellectuals in the 1930s–1960s associated with Black Internationalism embraced the promising ideas of a Marxist-Surrealist/Communist ideology. As Roumain, they maintained that these ideas could counter the oppressive weight of the Euro-American capitalist-exploitative structures against the Third-World working class people and peasants. On the other hand, as the eminent Black Marxist writer Richard Wright reminds us, "Marxism is but the starting point. No theory of life can take the place of life."[19]

Black Marxists in the twentieth century held to an anti-bourgeois ideology and believed that the doctrine (Marxism) was potentially liberative to blacks, the economically disadvantaged, and those living in the margins of society.[20] Cedric Robinson, who has written the most provoca-

---

17. Robinson, *Black Marxism*, xii.

18. Richardson and Fijalkowski, *Refusal of the Shadow*, 3. Both Richardson and Fijalkowski comment on the widespread influence of Surrealism and Marxism on Negritude and Caribbean intellectuals in the twentieth century.

19. Quoted in Robinson, *Black Marxism*, 299.

20. Among the more prominent Black internationalists and radical Marxists in

tive text on Black Marxism, states that the notion of class solidarity was of substantial importance both practically and theoretically to Black Marxist intellectuals. "It provided a category of political activity through which the diverse social elements of the revolutionary movement—ethnics and nationalities, workers and intellectuals—could be reconciled, transcending their several particular interests."[21] Valerie Klaussen asserts that Third International Communism, Black Marxism and Socialism offered Black internationalists and "West Indian intellectuals models of liberation of the colonies and neo-colonies of Africa, Asia, and the Americas as the first step toward worldwide working-class revolution."[22] In other words, Black Atlantic intellectuals "saw in communism a genuine universalism that insisted that modernity make good on its philosophical premises and promises."[23] Such Marxist and Communist leanings can also be detected in Roumain's radical poem, "*Bois d' ébène.*"[24] In that poem, Roumain calls for collective mobility and global revolution among all races and across different working class groups:

> Garde rouge de la Chine soviétique ouvrier allemand de la prison de Moabit indio des Amériques / Nous rebâtirons....
>
> Ouvrier blanc de Detroit péon noir d'Alabama/peuple innombrable des galères capitalistes le destin nous dresse épaule contre épaule et reniant l'antique maléfice des tabous du sang nous foulons les décombres de nos solitudes . . . / Nous briserons la

---

Black Atlantic thought in the twentieth century are Etienne Léro, René Ménil, W. E. B. Du Bois, Richard Wright, Langston Hughes, Claude McKay, C. L. R. James, Aimé Césaire, Jacques Stephen Alexis, Rene Dépestre, etc.; for a recent and detailed treatment on the relationship between black international intellectuals during the interwar period, see Banner-Haley, *From Du Bois to Obama*, 12–31; Stephens, *Black Empire*, 35–55, 129–268; James, *Holding Aloft the Banner of Ethiopia*, 101–21, 185–94, 232–57; Robinson, *Black Marxism*, 175–306; Robinson has written the most comprehensive study on Black Marxism and its genesis in the Black Atlantic world.

21. Robinson, *Black Marxism*, 218.

22. Klaussen, *Migrant Revolutions*, 102.

23. Klaussen, *Migrant Revolutions*, 102.

24. Other black intellectuals and postcolonial theorists such as Frantz Fanon had explored the prospects and pitfalls of Black Marxism and its cognates; in the chapter called "On National Culture" in his famous book *The Wretched of the Earth*, Fanon makes this insightful observation: "Negro and African-Negro culture broke up into different entities because the men who wished to incarnate these cultures realized that every culture is first and foremost national, and that the problems which kept Richard Wright or Langston Hughes on the alert were fundamentally different from those which might confront Leopold Senghor or Jomo Kenyatta" (216).

mâchoire des volcans / ffirmant les cordillères / et la plaine sera l'esplanade d'aurore où rassembler nos forces écartelées /par la ruse de nos maîtres / comme la contradiction des traits.[25]

[Red Guard of soviet China German worker in the prison of Moabite Indian of the Americas / We will rebuild . . . / White worker of Detroit black peon of Alabama/innumerable people of the capitalist gallery / fate ties us up shoulder to shoulder / dispelling the ancient evil spell of the taboos of blood / we walk on the rubble of our solitudes / we will break the jaw of volcanoes affirming the cordilleras / and the plain will be the esplanade of / dawn where to gather our quartered forces / by the trick of our masters as contradicting features.]

and the international solidarity and unity of the oppressed people:

Nous proclamons l'unité de la souffrance / et de la révolte de tous les peuples sur toute la surface de la terre / et nous brassons le mortier des temps fraternel / dans la poussière des idoles.[26]

[We proclaim the unity of suffering / and of revolt of all the peoples on all the surface of the earth / and we mix the mortar of fraternal times in / the dust of the idols.]

For Roumain, liberation of the oppressed must begin with a genuine solidarity with them by affirming their right to exist and think, to express themselves freely and act liberatively, and ultimately the right to a human life.[27] Roumain's vision is cross-cultural, interracial, and transnational; the mention of international laborers in China, Germany, India, North America, and the Americas is indicative of his global perspective and cosmopolitan humanism. As he affirms, the goal is to dispel "the ancient evil spell of the taboos of blood." Perceptibly in the abovementioned poetic verses, Roumain projected that proletarian revolution would engender new forms of life and breathe the fresh air of freedom for the globally oppressed humanity. He suggested that working class individuals should be self-determined and plan their own revolution. The world's workers and underclass people are the sole creators of their destiny whose actualization is rooted in group effort because their "fate ties us up shoulder to shoulder."

25. Roumain, *Bois d'ébène*, 23–24.
26. Roumain, *Bois d'ébène*, 24.
27. See Gutierrez, *Power of the Poor in History*.

From this perspective, we can presume that collective liberation is the attempt to reorder overbearing social dynamics and end the social evils menacing their existence. On the other hand, mass solidarity would necessitate the genesis of new forms for the future. The immediacy of that act would call for radical recreation. Acting alone is not ideal; cooperative participation is urgent in the process of breaking the bonds and chains of universal dominations and oppressive structures. The oppressed have resolved to "break the jaw of volcanoes." This viewpoint also insists that the working class, the oppressed people of the world, and the universal proletariat must divide in order to unite; demolish to rebuild. After all, they are "the protagonist[s] of their own liberation."[28] Roumain upheld that all variegated aspects of orchestrated-human tyranny and suffering must be eradicated for the reconstruction of the desired democratic and fair society. This is significant in grasping Roumain's vision of history and human agency, and the correlation of literature and society.

From this same Marxist position, Roumain saw the economic problem as the determining factor in human history and the history of ideas; he believed that it is social reality that determines human consciousness, and oppressive social structures must be reversed.[29] History is rationally depicted in a progressive state through a series of class struggles between the exploited masses and the rich in society, and it has been moving in such a way that it has affected thought, human existence, economy, and human relations. As already noted in the previous analysis, Roumain rejected the capitalistic misuse of the poor and their resources by the wealthy and mainstream corporate institutions. José Míguez Bonino, who rejects capitalist projects of developmentalism and forms of production remarks about its regressive and inhuman nature:

> Capitalism creates in the dependent countries (perhaps not only in them) a form of human existence characterized by artificiality, selfishness, the inhuman and dehumanizing pursuit of success measured in terms of prestige and money, and the resignation of responsibility for the world and for one's neighbor.... Insofar as this sham culture kills in the people even the awareness of their own condition of dependence and exploitation, it destroys the very core of their humanity: the decision to stand up and

---

28. Gutierrez, *Theology of Liberation*, 307.
29. Nicholls, *From Dessalines to Duvalier*, 175–76.

become agents of their own history, the will to conceive and realize an authentic historical project.[30]

Robinson establishes that "the historical dialectic identified the industrial worker—the proletariat—as the negation of capitalist society; the force produced by capitalism that could finally destroy it. Capitalism pitted one class, the bourgeoisie, against another, the proletariat."[31] As Ernest Mandel has consistently argued in his works, "Capitalism is a system that produces and reproduces exploitation, oppression, social injustice, inequality, poverty, hunger, violence and alienation.... It shows itself in the mutilation of human life, of human nature, and of the human potential for freedom, joy and solidarity."[32]

Using protest literature as an activist tool and intellectual force, Jacques Roumain fought for a just social order, the economic justice and social stability of the wretched of the earth. For the militant Marxist Roumain, the Hegelian dialectics of lordship and bondage were social and ideological structures that imputed meanings to world history. In the same line of thought, he sustained that class and race were intertwined in the human dilemma; he argued that blacks have been the victims of both racial and class injustice. This is clearly articulated in his Marxist study of the black condition in the Southern United States and his thought on cultural racism and black lynching in America are documented in *Griefs de l'homme noir* (1939). He contends that "racial prejudice was used as a divisive tool by the Southern ruling classes to ensure that the poor whites and the blacks did not unify and change the order of things."[33] With precision, he comments on the class problem in North America and the economic exploitation of poor blacks and whites:

> The lyncher is also a victim of the lynching. The mobs that pursue the human "game" are composed of poor whites whose material condition is hardly better than that of the blacks. They labour under the illusion of white superiority and think they have something in common with the ruling classes. Colour prejudice is a divisive tool among the workers of the South,

---

30. Bonino, *Doing Theology in a Revolutionary Situation*, 31.
31. Robinson, *Black Marxism*, 233.
32. Lowy, "Ernest Mandel's Revolutionary Humanism," 26.
33. Dash, introduction to *Masters of the Dew*, 7–8.

whose common revolt could shake the established economic structure.³⁴

What Roumain is articulating here is the Marxist materialist position that race is essentially unreal, and that it is a smokescreen for the material exploitation of class. Orthodox Marxism reduces race to epiphenomena, as an ideological obfuscation. As Marxists have argued over the years, Marxism, as a critique of the capitalist world, was inevitable. Nonetheless, they would ultimately realize that it was an internal critique. The epistemological nature of historical materialism took bourgeois society on its own terms, presuming the primacy of economic forces and structures in human dynamics and histories. As it follows, the historical evolution from feudalism of the bourgeoisie as a class arguably served as an archetypal model for the rise of the proletariat as a negation of capitalist society.³⁵

Scientific Marxism and the Logic/Illogic of Faith

Roumain's confrontation with the issues of class, race, and economic oppression in Haiti as well as the hard life condition of Haitian working-class people and the country's peasants are addressed elsewhere in his writings.³⁶ For example, in the well-known controversial Church-state sponsored anti-superstition campaign against the Vodou religion in 1941–1942,³⁷ Roumain had engaged publicly in a series of controversial debates with the French Catholic priest-theologian, Joseph Foisset, who grounded his position in the Christian worldview and conservative theology. Foisset approved the assault and the persecution of the adherents of the Vodou faith. The hotly contested written exchanges—a total of fourteen published articles or more—between these two engaging interlocutors, which appeared in the pages of the nation's Catholic newspaper, *La Phalange*, and the widely-read newspaper, *Le Nouvelliste*. The on-going

34. Quoted in Dash, introduction to *Masters of the Dew*, 8.
35. Robinson, *Black Marxism*, 233.
36. See, Roumain, *La Montagne ensorcelée* (The Enchanted Mountain), and *Analyse schématique* (The Schematic Analysis).
37. For a recent and brilliant work on the relationship between the Vodou faith and Haitian laws since the country's inception, see Ramsey, *The Spirits and the Law*; other helpful works treating this subject matter in relationship to the greater Haitian culture and society are Hurbon, *Le barbare imaginaire*, and *Comprendre Haïti*; Price-Mars, *Ainsi parla l'Oncle*; Lescot, *Avant l'oubli*; Peters, *La Croix contre l'asson*.

correspondence began on March 30, 1942, and continued until July 31, 1942. David Nichols observes that the Roman Catholic Church in Haiti was "largely dominated by European clergy, and was regarded as the principal weapon employed by the Francophile mulatto elite for maintaining the predominance of western culture in Haiti and for defending their own superior position."[38] Roumain's position, grounded in secular humanism and Marxism, was that the peasants should not be persecuted and their religious expression—as a philosophy of life—should not be underestimated. He posits that "Catholicism was no better for the peasants than Vaudou."[39] Vodou spirituality, for Roumain, "should rather be viewed as the peasant dependence on the supernatural in order to explain his world, and consequently would only disappear when the peasant was provided with a scientific explanation of his reality. In the face of economic progress and enlightenment, the peasant would be more able to understand his world and control it."[40]

Furthermore, this far-reaching claim by the author, we suppose, is nothing but a radically anti-religious feeling; however, we should not conclude quickly that this assertion represents Roumain's general characterization of the Vodou religion or his overall religious sensibility. His religious vision is more complex than what he articulated in those sentences above. His religious discourse is ambivalent at times. For example, Roumain had written a series of careful and rigorous scholarly essays on the Vodou faith and publicly presented an apologetic defense of the Vodou religion against Foisset's classification of the Religion as superstitious nonsense and scandalous practice. Other Haitian nationalists and intellectuals (i.e., Jean Price-Mars, Carl Brouard, Francois Duvalier, Louis Diaquoi, Lorimer Denis, etc.) and the cultural and nationalist movement known as *Les Griots* in the period and after Roumain had written favorably about Vodou, were sympathetic toward the popular religion, and even affirmed and praised the liberating force and revolutionary potential of Vodou in the time of the Haitian Revolution and subsequently in the anti-imperial struggle against the American military Occupation (1915–1934). (However, it is unclear to what extent Roumain's writings on the subject may have inspired affirmation of Vodou in revolutionary thinkers. Price-Mars's 1928 book, *Ainsi parla l'oncle*, did in fact change

38. Nichols, *From Dessalines to Duvalier*, 172.

39. Roumain, *Masters of the Dew*, 8. There are varied spellings of Vodou, throughout this paper, I will be using the term "Vodou," except when quoting others.

40. Roumain, *Masters of the Dew*, 8.

and directly influence Haitian intellectuals' perspective and prejudice about the Vodou religion and Haiti's derived-African traditions and practices.) For example, during the Occupation, the guerilla army called "*les cacos*" used the power of Vodou sorcery and magic to resist the American empire and to regain national sovereignty. Roumain was particularly concerned about Vodou as a cultural symbol and signifier contributing to a better understanding of the Haitian experience and history. It is in this manner, for the most part, that he engages the religion in his creative works. The evidence that he had written about the liberating presence of the Vodou religion in achieving national independence, or the faith's emancipative aspect as a causal effect leading to the Haitian freedom is totally absent in Roumain's writings. What remains indecisive and paradoxical in Roumain's thought on religion is the inevitable proof that he had written both positively and negatively about the religion of Haitian peasants. Perhaps, we should construe this particular engagement with faith as a critical reflection on religion and its role in the social fabric.

Moreover, Roumain would write cogently and fearlessly against the nationwide anti-Vodou campaign which the Catholic Church officially initiated in 1941. The goal of the struggle against the so-called "fetishism and superstition . . . aimed at pressuring Haitians to renounce Vodou."[41] In the paragraph below, Roumain exposes the possible relationship between religion and terror (or violence) as related to the campaign:

> *L'essentiel n'est pas d'amener un paysan à renoncer, à rejeter la croyance en Hogoun-St.-Jacques. Il s'agit avant tout de changer complètement sa conception du monde. L'élément de coercition morale qui a été mis en jeu dans la campagne antisuperstitieuse: c'est la peur. La peur du refus des sacrements de l'Eglise. . . . Il faut naturellement débarrasser la masse haïtienne de ses entraves mystiques. Mais on ne triomphera pas de ses croyances par la violence ou en la menaçant de l'enfer. Ce n'est pas la hache du bourreau, la flamme du bûcher, les autodafés qui ont détruit la sorcellerie. C'est le progrès de la science, le développement continu de la culture humaine, une connaissance chaque jour plus approfondie de la structure de l'Univers.*[42]

[The key is not to lead a peasant to renounce and reject the belief in Hogoun-St.-Jacques (a combined name for Vodou spirits or

---

41. Dubois, *Haiti: The Aftershocks of History*, 307.

42. Roumain, "A propos de la campagne 'anti-superstitieuse,'" in *Jacques Roumain: Œuvres Complètes*, 750.

divinities). Above all, it is a question of completely changing his conception of the world. The element of moral coercion that has been employed in the anti-superstitious campaign: It is fear. The fear of refusal of the Sacraments of the Church. . . . Naturally, we must get rid of the Haitian masses of their mystical impediments. But we will not triumph over these beliefs by violence or by the threat of Hell. It is not the executioner's axe, the flame of the pyre, the auto-da-fes which destroyed sorcery. It is the progress of science, the continuous development of human culture, a growing and deeper understanding of the structure of the universe on a daily basis.]

In this analysis, Roumain bluntly condemns the campaign for its deliberate censoring of the religious freedom of Haitian peasants and for undermining the democratic vision of religious tolerance and pluralism. He rejects the psychological subordination of religion in the process of inciting fear in people and in promulgating violence through strict dogmas and dangerous ideologies. The problem here with religion and the Catholic hierarchy in particular is deeply rooted in a psychological and philosophical understanding and misunderstanding of the world as well as in the misapprehension of the richness of various religious traditions and spiritual practices. The Catholic Church (along with Protestant Christianity) had exercised ferociously religious xenophobia and cultural hostility against Vodou practitioners. Therefore, it is reasonable to infer that bad religious practices or behaviors clearly promote and sustain social alienation and social exclusion. As historian Laurent Dubois comments on the problem:

> The campaign left permanent scars on the Haitian landscape. In many communities, ancient trees were considered holy by those who practiced Vodou, understood to be a kind of home for some of the *lwa*; to eliminate such sites of worship, Catholic priests ordered these trees to be chopped down. . . . The Protestants often saw Catholicism and Vodou as twin enemies . . . one Baptist missionary declared that "The Roman Catholic Church in Haiti is a bastard production of Voodoo-ism, witchcraft, and other African heathenish cults with a gloss of Roman Catholicism." Catholics, for their part, returned the favor, portraying the Protestants as a spiritual menace and accusing them of doing "Satan's work" in Haiti.[43]

---

43. Dubois, *Haiti: The Aftershocks of History*, 307.

122   REVOLUTIONARY CHANGE AND DEMOCRATIC RELIGION

As observed above, the impossibility of tolerating competing religious traditions and divergent theological beliefs in the Haitian society in the period discussed had generated substantial conflict and tension between the people was a remarkable event. In another instance in the debates, Roumain launches another critique at imperial Christianity in the project of Western conquest, colonization, and the project of civilization. He speaks assiduously of the functional use of civil religion, and in particular of the hegemonic power of Christianity in land acquisition and social control. He underscores Christianity role (or support of) in subjugating weak peoples, pacifying them, and conquering less-powerful nations. He moves on to restate directly from Friedrick Engels:

> *On ne peut se contenter de déclarer que la religion qui conquit l'Empire romain et qui depuis 1.800 ans règne sur une importante partie du monde civilisé est une absurdité cuisinée par des imposteurs. Pour le comprendre, il est nécessaire de savoir expliquer son origine et son développement dans ces conditions historiques où elle naquit et atteignit la domination.*[44]

> [One cannot simply declare that the religion that had conquered the Roman empire, and, since 1800 years dominated by far the larger part of the civilized world, is fraud or just plain nonsensical. To understand it, it is necessary to know its origin and development from the historical conditions under which it arose and reached its dominating position.][45]

Clearly, the undeniable power of religion in the making of Western civilization is attested; the intimate dynamic between religion and domination and the project of invasion is also affirmed. To return to our conversation about Roumain's engagement with Vodou and Catholicism, it is important to attest here that he was not an advocate of a particular religious system such as the folk religion of Vodou or Catholic Christianity. What he articulated in the second part of the paragraph above—his comment on the Vodou religion—is a standard Marxist anti-religious rhetoric and scientific orientation to faith. The only difference is that the Catholic Church is both powerful and a promoter of ignorance, whereas the folk religion of Vodou is just superstition.[46] It is evident that Roumain

---

44. Dubois, *Haiti: The Aftershocks of History*, 765.

45. Niebuhr, *Karl Marx and Friedrich Engels on Religion*, 195.

46. Several writers have investigated the ambivalent role of the Vodou religion in the anti-colonial struggle and anti-slavery struggle in the context of the Haitian

sought to supplant both forms of religion with another system of authority, namely "scientific Marxism."

> Ce qu'il faut mener en Haïti, ce n'est pas une campagne anti-superstitieuse, mais une campagne anti-misère. Avec l'école, l'hygiène, un standard de vie plus élevé, le paysan aura accès à cette culture et à cette vie décente qu'on ne peut lui refuser, si on ne veut pas que ce pays tout entier périsse, et qui lui permettront de surmonter des survivances religieuses enracinées dans sa misère, son ignorance, son exploitation séculaires. . . . Si l'on veut changer la mentalité religieuse archaïque de notre paysan, il faut l'éduquer. Et on ne peut l'éduquer sans transformer, en même temps, sa condition matérielle.[47]

> [What is necessary to be carried out in Haiti is not an anti-superstitious campaign, but an anti-misery campaign. With school, hygiene, a higher standard of living, the peasant will have access to that culture and that decent life which one cannot refuse him if one does not want the whole country to perish, and which will permit him to overcome religious survivals rooted in his misery, ignorance, and secular exploitation. . . . If one wants to change the archaic religious mentality of our peasants, we must educate them. And one cannot educate them unless their material conditions are transformed.]

Like all religious traditions, the Vodou faith is a false consciousness, and Roumain believed religion of any tradition will be ultimately replaced by scientific progress. By applying Marxist theoretical analysis to Vodou as a reflection of the material process and of the mode of production, Roumain was positing that "this ideological superstructure reacts on historical development and often even determines the form" ("*cette superstructure idéologique rétroagit sur le développement historique et souvent même en détermine LA FORME*").[48] Furthermore, Roumain's vision of social development, sourced in secular humanism, compels him to question the nature of the social work of Catholic Christianity in

---

Revolution; generally speaking, the Vodou faith is depicted as a form of resistance to orthodox Catholicism and to the American occupation in Haiti (1915–1934), see Laguerre, *Voodoo and Politics in Haiti*; Ramsey, *The Spirits and the Law*; Hurbon, *Dieu dans le vaudou haïtien*; Bellegarde-Smith and Michel, *Haitian Vodou*, and *Vodou in Haitian Life and Culture*; Joseph, "Rhetoric of Prayer," "Prophetic Religion, Violence and Black Freedom," and "Memory, the Spirit of the Revolution, and Slave Religion."

47. Roumain, "Réplique au Révérend," 751.
48. Roumain, "Réplique au Révérend," 783.

Haiti. He holds that the Catholic Church must engage socially the life and experience of the Haitian people by doing acts of kindness and human liberation. In the same line of thought, Roumain is also stressing the progressive meaning and persistence of religion in society. His impression of religion here is that of a social institution that should be actively participate in the social transformation of the Haitian civil society by engaging responsibly and constructively in social justice issues.

In respect to the social vision of the Catholic Church in the Haitian culture, Roumain believes that the Church should be (or should had been) an instrument of social change and practical democracy, a catalyst of hope and human success. He also holds that the Church should never had been an initiator or a mediator of social ills and evils, but rather should had been engaged intentionally in solving social problems such as the project of educating peasants, the creation of schools, hospitals, and jobs in Haiti's rural communities would lessen the country's poverty. For the social activist, the mark of true religion and faith in action constitutes a serious commitment to alleviating harassing social ills such as the problems of hunger, poverty, class systems, globalization, global and local economy, education, environmental justice, healthcare, human rights, etc.[49]

On one hand, Roumain was articulating an orthodox Marxist perspective on religion and social development; on the other hand, he was advocating the "direct and open use of the Church's human and material resources to promote social change toward some form of democratic socialism."[50] He also interpreted the role of religion in society functionally, that is, religion should contribute to the good and progress of society; that genuine faith should also be "an active liberation from all forms of oppression: spiritual, social, racial, cultural, economic, and political."[51] Roumain's articulation of the place of religion in the civic order sandwiched with his Marxist social theory is a clarion call for transforming individuals' material condition toward total freedom from exploitation, corruption, and oppression—which would also involve "a more and

---

49. For a useful book that comments on the relationship between religion and social justice issues, see Cannon, *Social Justice Handbook*. The book is written from a Christian perspective.

50. Smith, *Emergence of Liberation Theology*, 51.

51. Smith, *Emergence of Liberation Theology*, 51–52.

human dignified life, the creation of a new man, the abolition of injustice, a new society, a truly human existence, a free life, and a dynamic liberty."[52]

Additionally, Roumain was suggesting that democratic socialism was the alternative to oppressive capitalism, participatory socialism-communism the alternative to poverty and social inequality and injustice. The democratic socialist vision of a cooperative democratic commonwealth has thus defined his moral vision of and understanding of the ethics of religion and the functional character of religion in society. This particular viewpoint emphasizes an ideology of centralized collectivism, and, from this perspective, "socialism meant economic nationalization . . . and the very act of collectivization [in Fabian socialism] marked progress toward the desired 'socialist' order of rationalized economic planning" for the good society.[53]

Roumain's understanding of the intersections of faith, scientific reason, and social development deserve further reflections. As we have observed above, he rejected the instrumental use of religion to inspire terror and violence in society. He embraced a secular humanist perspective on faith and history, which will be demonstrated in subsequent paragraphs.

In response to Foisset who unapologetically holds to a conception of life and history from a purely theistic Christian perspective in rejection for a scientific explanation of the world, Roumain contends that science can't be a method of violence *("La science ne peut être une méthode de violence, meme verbale . . .")*[54] as it might be the case for religion. Roumain challenges Foisset's belief system by maintaining the conviction that history, which offers a scientific explanation and method for understanding the world and human existence, has currency over (divine) revelation, and that faith and reason are incompatible. He moves on to clarify that his debate with the Catholic priest lies in two fundamentally opposing poles or two contradictory views: the collision between faith and reason, and the irreconcilability of history and revelation. Joseph Foisset the priest-theologian relies heavily on a metaphysical conception of reality; whereas, Jacques Roumain the anthropologist-scholar depends distinctively on a scientific-philosophical outset of the world, chiefly the theoretical concept of dialectical materialism. Further, the Haitian intellectual

---

52. Quoted in Smith, *Emergence of Liberation Theology*, 46.
53. Dorrien, *Soul in Society*, 287.
54. Roumain, "Réplique au Révérend Père Foisset," 765.

deploys a series of dialectics as he recapitulates for the reader what is at stake in his polemic with Foisset:

> *La controverse se meut sur deux plans fondamentalement distincts qui ne se touchent que par leur contradiction: celui de la Révélation et celui de l'Histoire. D'un côté: la croyance est une vérité divine, éternelle, immutable; de l'autre: une analyse rationaliste de la naissance, de la maturité et du dépérissement d'un phénomène social. D'une part: le cadre rigide du dogme, l'effusion mystique; de l'autre: une recherche qui n'emprunte qu'aux faits et à la froide raison.*[55]

> [The debate is driven by two basically distinct levels which are underscored only by their contradiction: that of Revelation and that of History. On one side: the belief in a divine, eternal, immutable truth; on the other: the rationalist analysis of the birth, maturity and decline of a social phenomenon. On the one hand: the rigid framework of the dogma, mystical effusion; on the other: a search that sustains only by facts and prudent reason.]

Roumain presupposes that science and religion are not complementary, and that history and revelation "use different languages and methods and ask and answer different questions."[56] He is also claiming that science and theology do not interact on common ground; they are in conflict and do not integrate.[57] While he concurs with the reality that *"une conception religieuse peut survivre malgré les progrès de la science"*[58] ("a conception of religion can survive despite scientific progress"), he reasons theoretically that *"le sentiment religieux, tout respectable qu'il est, n'a rien de stimulant pour l'esprit scientifique. . . . L'Histoire ne connaît pas de miracle"*[59] ("the religious sentiment, while it is respectable, is not a stimulus for the scientific spirit. . . . History knows no miracle"). We might infer that for the author science does not need religion for its survival; religion, however, is almost absurd without the scientific life. In this vein, the scientific method draws a fine line of demarcation between science and nonscience—miracles by nature violate the laws of physics—and the

---

55. Roumain, "Réplique au Révérend Père Foisset," 766.
56. Moreland, *Christianity and the Nature of Science*, 12.
57. Moreland, *Christianity and the Nature of Science*, 12.
58. Roumain, "Réplique Finale," 774.
59. Roumain, "Réplique Finale," 773, 783.

belief that science rules out religion by definition.⁶⁰ These daring declarations might incline one to rightly conclude that Jacques Roumain was anti-faith. While Roumain discusses the potentiality of religion in society to produce estrangement between people of various faith traditions, he was not anti-clerical but was practically against oppressive anticlericalism, religious authoritarianism, and any faith that deliberately promotes disharmony and between individuals and divides people—as both Protestant and Catholic Christianity had generated a great divide in the Haitian nation and alienated Haitians from each other in the period of the brutal anti-superstitious and Vodou campaigns.⁶¹

Roumain was not anti-religion but rather he respects all religions, as he affirms to Foisset: "*Je respecte la religion, toutes les religions*" ("I respect religion, in fact all religions").⁶² He was neither anti-Catholic nor Protestant. As a self-described modest and passionate seeker of truth (to be certain, he was a religious agnostic), he was against all forms of religious repressions and hierarchies.⁶³ He confesses that he equally admires both the Bible and Friedrich Engels's 1878 (*Anti-Dühring* or) *Herr Eugen Dühring's Revolution in Science*, a seminal text to the intellectual conception, development, and theoretical articulation of the Marxist doctrine.⁶⁴

Besides, Roumain confesses that he was not a Christian; he was neither an "atheist Marxist" as Jean-Pierre Makoutabut-Mboukou wrongly asserts.⁶⁵ He had strong affinities for Christianity and deep respect for it when the religion is used correctly and effectively to alleviate human suffering and to embolden people to resist oppression. Christianity is good and liberating presence for Roumain, when it can be used instrumentally to animate inclusive hope and support freedom causes. He was also drawn to and inspired by the moral teachings of Jesus Christ. In response to Foisset, he expresses this conviction:

> *Bien que non-croyant, j'ai écrit pour mon fils et je lui ai lu Une Vie du Christ parce que, à l'époque, c'était le meilleur moyen de*

60. Moreland, *Christianity and the Nature of Science*, 13–18.

61. Roumain, "Réplique Finale," 791.

62. Roumain, "Réplique Finale," 787.

63. He writes, "*Je ne suis qu'un modeste et passionnéé chercheur de vérité*" (Roumain, "Réplique Finale," 777).

64. Roumain, "Réplique au Révérend Père Foisset," 765; he also writes, "*J'ai une sorte d'admiration passionnée pour la Bible. La Bible et l'Anti-Dühring, pour des raisons différentes, sont mes livres de chevet.*"

65. Makoutabut-Mboukou, *Jacques Roumain*, 115, 529.

> *lui enseigner le respect et l'amour du people, la haine des exploiteurs, la dignité de la pauvreté, la nécessité de la fin du monde de l'oppression, de la misère, de l'ignorance.*[66]

> [Although as a non-believer, I wrote for my son and read to him a *Life of Christ*, for, at the time, it was the best means of teaching him respect and love for people, hatred of exploiters, the dignity of poverty, the necessity of ending world's oppression and misery, ignorance.]

Roumain's Christ is a revolutionary figure, the liberator of the oppressed. The eminent Haitian intellectual learned much from the founder of Christianity whom he believed has called for the end of world oppression and the vindication of the exploited poor and the outcast in the world.

Roumain encourages the likelihood of religious tolerance objectively when he declares: "*Nous croyons à la vertu de la tolérance. Nous entendons nous maintenir dans les limites d'une sévère objectivité*"[67] ("We believe in the virtue of tolerance. We intend to keep within the limits of strict objectivity"). Yet, he avows that he would not substitute the liberty of expression and the dignity of conscience/thought/reason for the sake of being objective and broad-minded at the expense of scientific evidence.[68] Suggesting the wide inconsistency between science and metaphysics when they merge, he contends that the inevitable will happen: the collapse of the scientific reason ("*Quand elles se mêlent, c'est qu'il a eu un effondrement de la raison scientifique*").[69] Despite his radical secular humanism and scientific realism, as ambiguous and brilliant they appear, Roumain does not embrace fully the totality of the scientific enterprise nor does he uncritically subscribe to the so-called "scientific imperialism"[70] in the world of ideas. (At this point, the critical reader may be interesting to find out how does Roumain's criticism of scientific imperialism coexist with his belief that science is incapable of leading to violence. Evidently,

---

66. Roumain, "Réplique Finale," 787.

67. Roumain, "Réplique Finale," 787.

68. Roumain, "Réplique Finale," 766. This is implied in the statement: "*Cependant la tolérance ne saurait signifier un sacrifice de la liberté et de la dignité de pensée. Chaque fois que l'évidence scientifique me forcera à dire: e pur si muove! je le ferai.*"

69. Roumain, "Réplique Finale," 773.

70. For studies on this topic, see Kuhn, *Structure of Scientific Revolutions*; Gould, *Structure of Evolutionary Theory*; Dawkins, *Selfish Gene*.

this is a potential blind spot of Roumain or in his thinking.) In fact, he acknowledges the transitory nature of science and defines it merely as a method, a mode of inquiry, which could lead to relative truths and objective realities. Accordingly, science can also guide humanity to progressive knowledge and the understanding of human relations and interactions, and the complexity of life and the cosmos:

> La science est une méthode d'investigation et de connaissance progressive du monde. Elle a un caractère transitoire, relative, approximatif; elle va de l'ignorance à la connaissance selon une courbe ascendante d'erreurs et de vérités relatives vers une appréciation de plus en plus exacte de la réalité objective. Mais ce relativisme ne nous conduit pas au scepticisme, à l'idéalisme philosophique: chaque parcelle de vérité scientifique relative contient un élément de la vérité absolue qui est égale à la somme des vérifiés relatives en voie de développements.[71]

[Science is a method of inquiry and of progressive knowledge of the world. It is transitory, relative, and approximate; it goes from ignorance to knowledge according to an ascending curve of errors and of truths relative towards an increasingly exact appreciation of objective reality. But this relativism does not lead us to skepticism or philosophical idealism; every piece of scientific truth contains an element relative to the absolute truth equal to the sum of the verified evidence, in view of scientific development.]

He restates his position or conviction in a clearer statement, "*C'est la distinction dialectique entre l'absolue et relative verité qui donne à la science son caractère vivant et progressif*" ("It is the dialectical distinction between the absolute and relative truth which gives science its living and progressive character"). As to a theoretical definition of religion, Roumain defines religious ideas (or religion as a concept) as the representation of the world, what the Germans call a comprehensive view of worldview and intellectual evolution, dependent rigidly on material evolution ("*Les conceptions religieuses, cette représentation du monde que les Allemands appellent: Weltanschauung et l'évolution intellectuelle, dépendent étroitement de l'évolution matérielle*").[72]

Roumain's Marxist analysis here may be taken as the absolute rejection of religious metaphysics or spiritual supernaturalism; as he goes on

71. Roumain, "Réplique Finale," 773.
72. Roumain, "Réplique Finale," 760.

clarify himself further, "*La métaphysique n'est qu'une sorte d'appendicite idéologique*"[73] ("Metaphysis is only a kind of ideological appendix"). We might take the liberty to name this perspective on religion "radical agnosticism." More directly and indirectly, the Haitian intellectual makes the unsettled but brilliant declaration that "religious fanaticism or anticlericalism is the frantic expression of ignorance and stupidity" ("*le fanatisme religieux ou anticlérical est l'expression frénétique de l'ignorance et de la sottise*").[74] At this point, such claim should not surprise the reader. It is good to point out here that Roumain's criticism targets both religious fanaticism and fanatical repression of religious institution like the Haitian clergy. It is wrong to assume that Roumain conceives anticlericism as a form of religious fanaticism. The reader should understand Roumain's statement above within the Protestant-Catholic tensions of the period.

Roumain's Marxist critiques of Foisset's religious framework and of Christianity in particular may be summarized in this supportive statement, "The Christian negation of what is and the transformation of prevailing realities are impotent, incorrect, and ill-informed."[75] His Marxist criticism of religion needs not be construed entirely anti-clerical to the institution; he seeks to improve religion as a human system and social institution. As Cornell West encapsulates the view of critics such as that of Roumain:

> They are impotent because they locate ultimate power in a transcendent God who seems to work most effectively beyond history rather than in history, given the historical evidence so far. They are incorrect in that the very positing of such power and such an almighty Being is intellectually unjustifiable and theoretically indefensible. They are ill-informed because they possess highly limited analytical tools and scientific understanding of power and wealth in the prevailing social realties to be negated and transformed.[76]

The difficulty with Roumain's point of view is his unrelenting faith in the scientific enterprise and exclusive commitment to the world of reason, which are by-products of intellectual modernity. Roumain's ostensible naivety about violence and scientific imperialism is a shortcoming

---

73. Roumain, "Réplique Finale," 774.
74. Roumain, "Réplique Finale," 765.
75. West, *Prophesy Deliverance!*, 95.
76. West, *Prophesy Deliverance!*, 96.

of his understanding of the nature and workings of science and religion, and, correspondingly of the close dynamics between the two. Roumain does not explore adequately the potential use of violence in both systems. Religion and science are constructed human systems in which the possibility for good and bad are inherent in both. For example, both science and religion have been used strategically in the enslavement of Africans in the New World, in the Western "civilization mission" in Africa, in Hitler's extermination of six million Jews during the Holocaust moment, and, likewise, in the European annihilation of the native population in North America as well as in the rest of continental America.

West informs us that an intellectual shift in modern science as well as in the theoretical study of religion in modern European intellectual history. According to him, while modern political theorists and philosophers were primarily concerned about the nature of science and its relationship to culture or society, modern theologians and religious scholars were gripped with the epistemic status of religious and theological beliefs. Many thinkers in the West have accentuated the philosophical origins of modernity; yet, they questioned its religious or theological foundations in the emergence of modernity in the West.[77] For example, West informs that religion was a response to modernity which is noticeable in the American pragmatic religious tradition of Charles Peirce and William James. The pragmatic approach to faith insists that "religious beliefs were in the same spectrum as any other beliefs—always linked to experience."[78] There is a sense to locate the religious imagination of Jacques Roumain in this American tradition, the phenomenological view of religion.

In addition, Roumain did not disregard the pivotal role of religion in the formation of the self and cultural identity in modern Western societies. Yet like the American religious pragmatics, he interrogates the inadequacy of religion to offer a plausible response to life's greatest challenges and to the omnipresence of the problem of evil and human suffering in the world. As in the case of Haitian Vodou, he does critique certain aspects of it as a possible a problem to social development and a hindrance to human flourishing in his native country. Roumain has

77. For careful and critical studies on this important topic, see Gillespie, *Theological Origins of Modernity*; Taylor, *Secular Age*; Lilla, *Stillborn God*; Asad, *Formations of the Secular*.

78. West, *Keeping Faith*, 121; interested readers should explore William James's 1902 masterpiece, *Varieties of Religious Experience*.

undermined the power and possibility of religious beliefs for critical scientific epistemology and inquiry, and elevated the prominence of science in the project of human development. He gives more credence to scientific reason and culture in the pursuit of truth; religion was only peripheral in his project of social development. Philosopher and cultural critic Cornell West reminds us that there is not ultimate triumph in the spheres of science and religion. He draws a practical balance between Christianity and science, faith and reason when he writes:

> Every penultimate court of appeal—every human conception of rationality, objectivity, and scientificity—is surreptitiously linked to a particular description or theory of the self, the world, and God. Therefore the spheres of science, art, and religion do not possess privileged access to ultimate truth and reality.[79]

Truth is not a property reserved idiosyncratically for scientific theories or scientific methods which might yield to absolute predictions and trustworthy explanations of the human nature, the complexity of human existence, the absurdity of life, and human history. To embrace such a perspective is to fall prey to a narrow positivism.[80] It is also to disregard or refuse to acknowledge the existence of multiple competing and contradictory scientific models and conflicting religious and theological perspectives. In the same line of thought, truth should not be conceived as an attribute aligned exclusively to religious traditions and to the scientific enterprise. To embrace such a point-of-view is to deny the cultural relativistic contexts of faith and to demean the significance of religious pluralism in our postmodern culture. Therefore, there is not a transcendental standard—a theory-neutral, portrayal-independent, description-free criterion—which enables us to choose the true theory, portrayal, and description... for truth can neither be reduced to the domains of science, art, and religion... we must acknowledge our finitude and fallenness as human beings and our inability to give life full meaning.[81]

Science and religion as cultural and intellectual resources can only lead us to various stages of knowledge toward an objective and relativistic understanding of the absolute and reality.[82] We should point out at various instances in the conversation Roumain commits the sin of

---

79. West, *Keeping Faith*, 121.
80. West, *Keeping Faith*, 97.
81. West, *Keeping Faith*, 97.
82. Roumain, "Réplique au Révérend Père Foisset," 774.

self-contradiction. Yet, he would acknowledge the limits of the scientific project when he sustains that *"la connaissance est un modeste, pénible et patient tâtonnement de l'erreur à la vérité"*[83] ("knowledge is a modest, patient and painful trial/groping of error to truth"). Nonetheless, the phrase "groping of error to truth," signals undoubtedly Roumain's acceptance of the theory of scientific progressivism and historical progress in the Hegelian sense. To elaborate on this point, the thoughtful Roumain comments briefly on various instances in modern Western history in which (pseudo-)scientific racism and destructive ideologies were used to support fascism and anti-Semitism, and generated wars and suffering across the nations:

> *La philosophie de l'histoire raciste et mythologique du fasciste Rosenberg, la pensée apocalyptique d'Oswald Spengler . . . sont l'expression d'une agonie sociale. . . . L'offensive anti-scientifique à des raisons historico-politiques que nous démontrons: l'intuitivisme bergsonien, la philosophie existentielle de Heidegger, la métaphysique du désespoir de Kierkegaard, les élucubrations de Gabriel Marcel, Gilson, etc., ont les relations les plus évidentes avec l'idéologie fasciste.*[84]

> [The history of philosophy of racism and the myth of fascist Rosenberg, the apocalyptic thinking of Oswald Spengler . . . are expressions of social agony. . . . The anti-scientific offensive to historico-political reasons that we have demonstrated: the intuitionism of Bergson, the existential philosophy of Heidegger, the metaphysics of despair of Kiekegaard, the wild imaginings of Gabriel Marcel, Gilson, etc., have relationships with the most obvious fascist ideology.]

Roumain moves on to draw a direct correlation between the human nature, social existence, and social development, and the significant intersections of the intellect, the emergence of ideas, worldviews, and institutions as modes of material and intellectual productions in the history of human culture and experience:

> *C'est en transformant la nature que l'homme évolue intellectuellement; son existence sociale détermine sa conscience. En dernière instance, c'est le mode de production qui modèle l'histoire. La*

---

83. Roumain, "Réplique Finale," 787.

84. Roumain, "Réplique Finale," 786; Roumain, "Réplique au Révérend Père Foisset," 774.

> *religion, la philosophie, la morale, le droit, l'organisation politique, ne sont que le reflet de ce processus matériel. A son tour, cette superstructure idéologique rétroagit sur le développement historique et souvent même en détermine LA FORME.*[85]

> [It is by transforming the nature that man evolves intellectually; his social existence determines his conscience. Ultimately, it is the mode of production which models history. Religion, philosophy, morality, law, political organization, is only the reflection of this material process. In turn, this ideological superstructure retroacts upon the historical development and often determines the FORM.]

In *The German Ideology* (1846), Marx posits that "it is not the consciousness of men that determines their existence, but their social existence that determines their consciousness." In the paragraph above, Roumain does not separate material forces of production and social relations as some have done. His materialist theory of history and social development sustains an intimate relationship between these two phenomena. Having been influenced by a Marxian-Hegelian view of history, society, and the human nature, Roumain insists that materialism best explains social and historical change in society as well as the evolution of the individual in society. The implication of this Marxist-Hegelian framework and social constructionist outlook is that individuals must continue aggressively and purposefully striving to alter the human condition for a better and promising future world. The work of humanity never ends! Roumain concludes his long debates with the Catholic theologian-priest by reiterating his conviction and by attempting to refocus the attention of the Christian priest to "earthly" and more immediate and dire needs of humanity. Roumain was also very keen of the critically sensitive issues of life facing peoples and nations globally:

> *Mais il y a des problèmes, tels que le chômage, la guerre, la lutte anti-fasciste, la liberté, la justice, le droit à une vie décente pour toute l'humanité, qui sont des problèmes TERRESTRES, que les hommes aux religions et aux philosophies les plus variées peuvent ensemble, sincèrement, essayer de résoudre. . . . Si telle est aussi votre opinion, je suis heureux et je considère comme un honneur de vous tendre une main loyale.*[86]

---

85. Roumain, "Réplique Finale," 783.
86. Roumain, "Réplique Finale," 792.

[But there are problems, such as unemployment, war, the antifascist struggle, freedom, justice, the right to a decent life for all people, which are "EARTHLY" problems that men of the most diverse religions and philosophies can attempt together to resolve.... If such is also your opinion, I am happy and I consider it an honor to extend a loyal hand.]

For the Haitian intellectual, religion should give considerable attention to the everyday life experience of individuals, and that social development should take into account the various social relations and forces of production. Jacques Roumain was not particularly concerned about the abstract dimension or theories of religion but on what religion can and should do to improve the human condition and to make the world a better place.

Religion, Marxist Communism, and Social Progress

In this last part of the chapter, I want to draw my final reflections on Jacques Roumain's posthumous Marxist-Communist novel *Gouverneurs de la rosée*. In *Masters of the Dew*, Roumain constructs an inspired-religious narrative that registers the religious experience of Haitian peasants as well as the survival of a peasant village in Haiti. The Vodou faith in the story serves as an emblem of cultural representation, national patrimony, and a vehicle for national solidarity within the sphere of Haitian rural population. Through the practice of the neo-African religion and spirituality, Roumain establishes that the communal interest formed the basis for cultural identity and ancestral affiliation. (Yet, his hermeneutics of suspicion of faith and feeling about the peasant religion will be quickly noted below). In one of the scenes in the novel, Roumain recounts a peculiar moment in a Vodou ceremony, in which the adherents summoned *Legba*, the African deity of the crossroads and the God of communication. The authorial interest here seems to convey the significance of ancestral religious traditions in peasant life and culture. He goes on to make this striking observation about the communal ritual and participation in the working of ancestral spirits:

The women's voices shot up very high cracking the thick mass of song:

> *Legba-se! Legba!*
> *Blood has been drawn!*
> *Blood! Abobo!*
> *Mighty Legba!*
> *Seven Legba kataroulos!*
> *Mighty Legba!*
> *Alegba-se!*
> *You and me!*
> *Ago ye!*[87]

> *Legba, show us how!*
> *Alegba-se, it's you and me!*
> *It's you and me, Kataroulo,*
> *Mighty Legba, it's you and me!*[88]

The omniscient narrator openly expresses the sensorial opacity of the religious experience in peasant life:

> Now the sacrifice to Legba was over. The Master of the Roads had gone back to his native Guinea by that mysterious path which *loas* [spirits] tread. Nevertheless, the fete [party] went on. The peasants forgot their troubles. Dancing and drinking anesthetized them—swept away their shipwrecked souls to drown in those regions of unreality and danger where the fierce of the African gods lay in wait.[89]

As one reads closely the above passage, it is probable that Roumain was articulating a similar sentiment about religion as his intellectual predecessors Karl Marx and Sigmund Freud. Marx declares that "religion is the sigh of the oppressed creature, the sentiment of a heartless world, and the soul of soulless conditions."[90] Freud professes that "religious ideas have arisen from the same need as have all other achievements of civilization: from the necessity of defending oneself against the crushing

87. Roumain, *Masters of the Dew*, 71.
88. Roumain, *Masters of the Dew*, 67.
89. Roumain, *Masters of the Dew*, 71–72.
90. Quoted in Kunin and Miles-Watson, "Karl Marx," in *Theories of Religion*, 69.

superior force of nature."[91] He draws an intimate connection between religious practice and the subconscious, an idea that can be seen in the Roumain's text. The illusory delight and frightened joy in the guise of religious performance are notable in the aforementioned passage of the novel; religious happiness and spiritual affections fill the heart of the worshippers, or as Marx tells us "The abolition of religion as the *illusory* happiness of the people is the demand for their *real* happiness."[92] This is exactly what Roumain meant to convey in this thought-provoking declaration: "The peasant forgot their troubles. . . . Dancing and drinking anesthetized them."

In the well-crafted passage which we have reproduced above, Roumain seeks to suggest the idea and the possibility of religion as being an instrument of domination, and as a worldview and ideology that could be candidly adapted to human oppression. This particular position on the religious experience is further amplified in the subsequent scene in the story in which religion is described positionally and deliberately as a powerful psychic force: "When dawn came over the sleepless plain, the drums were still beating like a heart that never tires."[93] Also, the narrator emphasizes paradoxically the psychological dimension of religious bliss and the religious experience of the hero of the story: "Manuel let himself go in the upsurge of the dance, but a strange sadness crept into his soul. . . . He caught his mother's eye and thought he saw tears shining there."[94] There seems to be a spiritual void that suffused Manuel's religious life with a sense of meaningless or in the words of Freud, religious beliefs are depicted here as "illusions, fulfillments of the oldest, strongest and most urgent wishes of mankind . . . our fears of the dangers of life."[95] This haunting void was probably the result of a series of powerful historical events including the effects of Manuel's former life as an exile in Cuba, the hegemony of Western capitalism in the island, the politics of globalization, economic oppression, and the post-effects of the American military occupation in Haiti. The novel seems to indicate that these were destructive forces added to human suffering in the island; they violently tore Manuel's soul and the peasant community at large, and this human

---

91. Freud, *Future of an Illusion*, 30.
92. Kunin and Miles-Watson, *Theories of Religion*, 69.
93. Roumain, *Masters of the Dew*, 71–72.
94. Roumain, *Masters of the Dew*, 71–72.
95. Robinson, *Black Marxism*, 301; Freud, *Future of an Illusion*, 30.

emptiness which must be satisfied is more powerful than religion itself. The phenomenon is without meaning; in the quoted passage above in the novel, the peasant consciousness is set adrift into religious terror and the condition of being is alienation and confusion in the religious world of the peasants.[96]

Furthermore, Roumain's complementary reflections on the lives and experiences of the Haitian working class and peasants provide substantial evidence of his radical vision of the masses and relentless social activism. *Masters of the Dew* is a peasant-proletarian novel that portrays the spiritual and aesthetic character of Haitian peasants, their life and culture, and the importance of collaborative labor in a rural village called Fonds Rouge. The account is an exposition on the struggles, fears, dreams, communal organization, and the self-determination of a Haitian rural community near Port-au-Prince, the country's capital. Manuel, the hero of the story who had returned to his native land after a fifteen-year period of exile in Cuba working in the depressing sugarcane industry, strives to keep his native villagers from starvation during a terrific drought. Valerie Kaussen describes the novel as Roumain's attempt to rewrite "the peasantry's misery by recasting the rural classes' demands in the worldwide Marxist project of decolonization and anti-racism."[97] The displaced peasant (Manuel) is the agent of revolution; as a migrant laborer, he calls for a collective movement that would be pan-Caribbean, transnational, cross-cultural, and even global in implications.[98]

In the narrative, Roumain inspires a new consciousness to the Haitian peasants; an example of such is communicated through an exchange between Manuel and the character Laurélien. By telling his own story, Manuel relates to the community's plight and identifies with the struggles of the people. Through the lips of the protagonist, Roumain emphasizes that the underprivileged and humiliated peasants were the pillars of Haitian society and the cultural and material resources of the country. He seeks to persuade them to see themselves for what they are: the Haitian peasants are the historical agents of their own freedom, and without them, the country will not go forward:

> Here, we've got to struggle hard with life, and what does it get us? We don't even have enough to fill our bellies, and we've no rights

---

96. Robinson, *Black Marxism*, 301.
97. Klaussen, *Migrant Revolutions*, 102.
98. Klaussen, *Migrant Revolutions*, 102.

at all against the crookedness of the authorities. The justice of the peace, the rural police, the surveyors, the food speculators live on us like fleas. I spent a month in prison with a bunch of thieves and assassins, just because I went in town without shoes. And where could I have gotten money to buy them, I ask you, brother? What are we, us peasants? Barefooted Negroes, scorned and maltreated.[99]

Manuel seeks to inspire the suffering community-villagers to think critically about their common condition, their worth and human dignity. His objective, however, is to foster a revolutionary consciousness in the peasants toward social change. The necessity for a new orientation in the mind and collective self-understanding becomes clearest in the paragraph below:

> What are we? Since that's your question, I'm going to answer you. We're *this country*, and it wouldn't be a thing without us, nothing at all. Who does the planting? Who does the watering? Who does the harvesting? Coffee, cotton, rice, sugar cane, cacao, corn, bananas, vegetables, and all the fruits, who's going to grow them if we don't? Yet with all that, we're poor, that true. We're out of luck, that's true. We're miserable, that true. But do you know why, brother? Because of our ignorance.[100]

Manuel as the frontrunner of peasant emancipation wishes to mobilize the community and bring them together toward a shared purpose. Human solidarity and the active participation of every peasant are assumed in the pursuit of adequate water, which will result in collective emancipation:

> If he found water, everyone's help would be needed. It wouldn't be a small matter to bring it down to the plain. They would have to organize a great *coumbite* [cooperative labor] of all the peasants. Thus the water would bring them together again. . . . With the new plants, with the fruit-and-corn-laden fields, the earth overflowing with simple fecund life, a brotherly community would be reborn.[101]

Without appeal to transcendence or divine providence, Manuel accentuates the paramount importance of communal collaboration and

---

99. Roumain, *Masters of the Dew*, 74.
100. Roumain, *Masters of the Dew*, 75.
101. Roumain, *Masters of the Dew*, 80.

alliance, the necessity of cooperative labor and mutual interdependence, and the sense of fraternity they must together muster as a community at risk:

> All peasants are equals, Manuel said. They're all one single family. That's why they call each other "brother," "cousin," "brother-in-law." One needs the other. One perishes without the other's help. That's the lesson of the *coumbite*. This spring that I've found needs the help of all the peasants of Fonds Rouge. Don't say no. It's life that gives order. When life commands, we've got to answer, "Present!"[102]

As Kaussen observes,

> In *Gouverneurs de la rosée*, the Haitian peasants' agricultural labor is a form of this productive and future-oriented interaction between humans and nature, between subject and object.... The *coumbite* is connected to international socialism through the allegorical relationship that Roumain creates between the rural work collective and *huelga* or labor strike, in Cuba.... In the *coumbite*, Roumain thus finds a figure for Haitian modernity and for a revolutionary consciousness that is both rural and cosmopolitanism, traditional and future oriented.[103]

Kaussen's observation substantially underscores an important aspect of the novel; nonetheless, she fails miserably to engage the religious ethos and dimension of the work, a critical factor which for the author (Roumain) is vital in understanding Haitian modernity and the revolutionary consciousness, which Kaussen engages more fully in her careful reading of the text. I am suggesting that Roumain's religious (Marxist agnosticism) and humanistic leanings are probably revealed in the lips of the hero of the story, Manuel. Roumain through Manuel also discloses his own tension with the role of religion in the project of social progress, and the possibility that the religious life and practice might hinder scientific reasoning and social betterment. This sentiment is explicit in another instance in the plot in which Manuel's anti-religious feeling is voiced in a gathering Vodou ceremony: "I have respect for our traditional customs but the blood of a cock or a goat cannot change the seasons."[104] This blunt rejection of (ancestral) religious traditions and practices presupposes the

---

102. Roumain, *Masters of the Dew*, 149–50.
103. Klaussen, *Migrant Revolutions*, 129–30.
104. Roumain, *Masters of the Dew*, 78.

notion that the need for supernatural intervention in the existential contexts of Haitian peasants and, to a larger degree in the variegated experiences of human life and interaction is unnecessary.

For the protagonist, the Vodou religion is unable to provide earthly salvation; it is up to individual men and women in the village to work collaboratively to put an end to their shared misery. While Manuel might agree about the possibility of religion in providing "the language or grammar for making sense of the world in life affirming ways";[105] in this particular declaration, however, he expresses his definite trust not in religion but on the inherent human virtue and human goodness to alter the course of life for better. The Vodou religion for Manuel does not appear liberating in nature; it seems to me that Manuel wants us to believe "it robs adherents of valuable hopes and comforts."[106] Roumain like the protagonist of his novel avoids full commitment to religious conservatism and metaphysical transcendence.

The call for unity and camaraderie among the peasants is accentuated in Manuel's words, as he seeks to instill hope. The hero believes in a bright future for the community:

> We don't know yet what a force we are, what a single force—all the peasants, all the Negroes of plan and hill, all united. Some day [sic], when we get wise to that, we'll rise up from one end of the country to the other. Then we'll call a General Assembly of the Masters of the Dew, a great big *coumbite* of farmers, and we'll clear out poverty and plant a new life.[107]

Through the project of *coumbite*, Haitian peasants would be able to express "self determination, freedom from plantation labor, and the liberty to pursue unalienated forms of ownership and work.[108] Their openness to inquiry would easily incorporate the activism and social reform marked by persistent humanism and communism.[109] This particular passage reveals the impossibility of (divine) providence because the entire narrative ideologically highlights the supremacy of self-autonomy and human reason. The religious ethos of *Masters of the Dew* is the underpinning (secular) humanistic assumption that God is not working

---

105. Pinn, *Varieties of African American Religious Experience*, 184.
106. Pinn, *Varieties of African American Religious Experience*, 184.
107. Pinn, *Varieties of African American Religious Experience*, 74–75.
108. Klaussen, *Migrant Revolutions*, 130.
109. Pinn, *Varieties of African American religious Experience*, 159.

actively behind the scene. This basic supposition is also revealed in the introductory words of the novel. Délira (Manuel's mother) complaints about the severe drought in the countryside and the painful living condition of the peasants; in these powerful words, she communicates her hurt to her wistful husband Bienaimé and eventually to her son:

> The drought's overtaken us, everything's wasting away, animals, plants, every living human. The wind doesn't push the clouds along any more. . . . Look at the swirls of dust on the savanna. From sunup to sunset, not a single bead of rain in the whole sky. Can it be that the Good Lord has forsaken us? . . . But there isn't any mercy for the poor.[110]

In his response, the non-theist protagonist (Manuel) of the novel disallows the prospect of divine providence and penetration in the plot of the peasants. He dismisses or discounts the probability of the Christian God or the deities of the Vodou religion to actualize the ultimate social change desperately needed in the community:

> Resignation won't get us anywhere. . . . Resignation is treacherous. It's just the same as discouragement. It breaks your arms. You keep on expecting miracles and providence, with your rosary in your hand, without doing a thing. You pray for rain, you pray for a harvest, you recite the prayers of the saints and the *loas*.[111]

Manuel's disregard for theistic orientation to life, history, and social development should be understood as a radical declaration for what eminent religious scholar Anthony Pinn phrases "the end of God-talk." This particular posture articulates an alternate means of centering. Roumain's Marxist-humanistic enterprise rejects "the symbol of God[s] as a human safeguard, a mechanism for protecting signs and symbols because of the ontological burden they bear . . . we [humans] have constructed the conceptual arrangements of this world and we must alone bear responsibility for this framing of life."[112] Manuel continues by asserting that man is his own "Master," and it is he who gives life meaning not the Christian God or the African gods:

---

110. Roumain, *Masters of the Dew*, 44, 54.
111. Roumain, *Masters of the Dew*, 44, 54.
112. Pinn, *End of God-Talk*, 6.

But providence—take my word for it—is a man's determination
not to accept misfortune, to overcome the earth's bad will every
day, to bend the whims of the water to your needs. Then the
earth will call you, "Dear Master." The water will call you, "Dear
Master." And there's no providence but hard work, no miracles
but the fruit of your hands.[113]

The nontheistic orientation of Manuel as a robust system of life providing meaning and purpose is further enunciated below. Manuel's humanistic outlook anticipates the divine farewell or the death of God movement in the 1960s or what the German philosopher and religious critic Friedrich Nietzsche had termed *"Gott ist tot"* ("God is dead").[114] Pinn's discerning remark below is useful in elucidating the religious ethos and sensibility of *Masters of the Dew*:

[The] God-symbol [/religion] as an organizing framework for
viewing and living life in relation to . . . has run its course, and
it is no longer capable of doing the heavy lifting required for the
contemporary world. God is a matter of human need and desire,
schizophrenia of theological kind. . . . Death of God theology
is a eulogy. It is a eulogy because the discourse involves both a
passing and a call/celebration of life left behind.[115]

The end of the novel culminates in Manuel's sacrificial death and his presentation as a Christ figure for the salvation of the peasant community. In explaining Manuel's wishes before his death, Délira declares to the assembled peasants at the funeral:

Here's what Manuel, my boy, told me. "You've offered sacrifices
to the *loas*, you've offered the blood of chickens and young goats
to make the rain fall. All that has been useless. Because what
counts is the sacrifice of a man, the blood of a man." . . . It's
customary to sing mourning with hymns for the dead, but he,
Manuel had chosen a hymn for the living—the chant of the

---

113. Roumain, *Masters of the Dew*, 54.
114. In Nietsche, *Thus Spoke Zarathustra*, 125, Friedrich Nietzsche announces:

God is dead. God remains dead. And we have killed him. How shall we comfort ourselves, the murderers of all murderers? What was holiest and mightiest of all that the world has yet owned has bled to death under our knives: who will wipe this blood off us? What water is there for us to clean ourselves? What festivals of atonement, what sacred games shall we have to invent? Is not the greatness of this deed too great for us? Must we ourselves not become gods simply to appear worthy of it?

115. Pinn, *End of God-Talk*, 5.

coumbite, the chant of the soil, of the water, the plants, of friendship between peasants, because he wanted his death to be the beginning of life for you.[116]

Manuel's last words through the lips of his mother are problematic in the sense that they consciously designate that there is an experience of loss and absence, the loss and absence of African gods or spirits, sustaining the viewpoint that the religious experience is meaningless, and that religious traditions, symbols and rituals are but rubbish avatars. In all of these things, Manuel avoids the "God-talk" rhetoric but rather focuses on the human-centered dialogue and the projection of ideal of human values. The definitive goal is to create together without the participation of the divine a flourishing future world and to cultivate a life worth living in the moment—the non-theistic existence and culture.[117] Nonetheless, Manuel the peasant-hero in *Masters of the Dew* is a type of Christ, a messianic figure in black face:[118] "You've done your duty, you've fulfilled your mission, Manuel. Life's going to start all over in Fonds Rouge."[119]

As a way to recapitulate, like his intellectual predecessors Karl Marx, Friedrich Engels, Vladimir Lenin, and Fredrick Nietzsche, Jacques Roumain was obsessed with the potential character of modern science and human reason to stimulate social development. For Roumain, modern science as a tool of analysis (not religion) might offer better solutions to social ills in this age of technology and scientific revolution.[120] Roumain was preoccupied with the social character of rationality and social theory, and especially the impact of modern science on culture and the world of ideas in his understanding of human progress and social development. He employed religion as a concept and religious discourse played a pivotal role in his conception of the good society. Religious rhetoric and vocabularies and social theory are used instrumentally as political tools in Roumain's articulation of an ethics of human solidarity and a politics

---

116. Roumain, *Masters of the Dew*, 181–82.

117. Pinn, *Varieties of African American Religious Experience*, 154–85.

118. For the concept of a "Christ-Noir" ("Black Christ") and the relationship between Christ and black suffering, and the liberation of the oppressed of the world in Roumain's writings, see my forthcoming article, "The 'Christ-Noir' and the Liberation of '*Les Damnés de la Terre*': Perspective on Jacques Roumain's Radical Activism and Liberation Theology."

119. Pinn, *Varieties of African American Religious Experience*, 153.

120. For a powerful analysis on the intersections of sociology, philosophy, and history and provocative response to the notion of scientific reason and linear progress.

of social transformation. Roumain deployed all sorts of intellectual resources and the best of human ingenuity in his efforts to communicate and affect what may be called "the permanent good of the whole people" in the Haitian civil society and in other worlds. As political theorist Cornelius B. Pratt observes, "The common good, as a communication ethic, transcends the values and interests of any single group"[121] or social class. Roumain rejects "the notion of redemptive suffering and the idea that suffering understood as good or redemption is a dangerous idea."[122] In other words, the humanist Jacques Roumain and the protagonist Manuel maintain that "humanity has no choice but to continue seeking progress."[123] The legacy of Jacques Roumain as a committed social communist, revolutionary Marxist, freedom fighter, agnostic humanist, and radical writer should be celebrated and esteemed, and his works continue to inspire and speak to us today in meaningful and liberative ways.

---

121. Pratt, "Managing Sustainable Development," 942.
122. Pinn, *Varieties of African American Religious Experience*, 185.
123. Pinn, *Varieties of African American Religious Experience*, 185.

CHAPTER FIVE

Democratic Faith as Religious Freedom

The Possibility of Christian-Vodouist Dialogue in Hurbon and Fils-Aimé

IN THE PREVIOUS CHAPTER, we examine Roumain's preoccupation with the idea of social change and the place of religion in contributing to that end. It is clear that Roumain does not trust any religion, especially the Vodou religion, in effecting radical transformation in the Haitian society. He puts his trust in the God that fails the Haitian people that is socialist Marxism. Roumain envisions the emancipation of the Haitian people from abject poverty and their wretched spiritual condition exclusively through the lens of Marxism and socialist communism. He rejects Vodou as a contributing force in alleviating Haitian suffering and restoring the Haitian mind. For him, a radical change of the mind is necessary as the Haitian people are making their way through modernity and modernization. What remains an intellectual ambivalence in Haitian thought and in the writings of Roumain correspondingly is the possibility of Vodou as a problem in Haiti's progress into modernity. Roumain undermines the spiritual comfort religion provides to its adherents, and even jettisons the possibility of the Vodou religion as a provider of an alternative way of thinking about human existence, community, and dealing with the problem of pain and theodicy in this world. Vodou, however, in its own way, does contribute to a kind of radical change that is often undermined in Haitian and Western history and literature.

    This present chapter examines the work of two prominent progressive Haitian theologians: Laënnec Hurbon, a Catholic theologian and former priest, and Jean Fils-Aimé, a Protestant theologian and former pastor in Montreal, and their interaction with the Vodou religion. Both thinkers have written prolifically about the three major religious expressions in Haiti and the enduring religious conflict between Protestantism, Catholicism, and Vodou in the Caribbean nation. The history of relations between Christianity—both Protestant and Catholic—and Vodou in Haiti is marked by a high degree of combativeness, hostility, and discomfort.

To resolve the religious tension between Haitian Vodou and Haitian Christianity, Hurbon has suggested a frank ecumenical dialogue between Vodou, Catholicism, and Protestantism, and carefully demonstrated the legitimation of Vodou in the Haitian experience and life. In the same line of thought, Fils-Aimé has recommended an interreligious dialogue between the two religious traditions, and brilliantly argues for the inculturation of the Vodou faith in Haitian Protestantism and culture. Both thinkers call for a reconceptualization of faith in the Haitian society and project to understand democratic faith as religious freedom.

Through their work, both thinkers continue to campaign for more religious tolerance, pluralism, and religious inclusivism in the Haitian society. I am suggesting that the Catholic theologian Laënnec Hurbon in his classic work *Dieu dans le vaudou haïtien* (1972) has inaugurated what we phrase the Christian-Vodouist compromissory tradition. Following the footsteps of Hurbon, Fils-Aimé in his controversial and learned work *Vodou, je me souviens*, published in 2007, has done for Haitian Protestantism what Hurbon has achieved for Haitian Catholicism—pushing forward the idea of the inculturation of Voudou culture and practices in Protestant Christianity in Haiti—within the framework of a Protestant-Vodouist compromissory tradition. Equally, in this chapter, we are concerned with the role of both religions in effecting radical change—spiritual, economic, political, social, etc.—in the Haitian society. This chapter demonstrates how many Haitian Protestant pastors and leaders do not view Vodou as a catalyst of change in the Haitian society; rather, for them, the Vodou religion has enslaved the Haitian people since the genesis of the Haitian nation.

Introduction

The Haitian experience in religion is full of complexity and ambivalence. Haitian Christianity is divided in two main branches: Catholicism and Protestantism. The three major religions practiced in Haiti are Roman

Catholicism, Protestantism, and Vodou. Recent studies have indicated that among 60 percent to 70 percent of people who have claimed Catholicism as an adopted faith, 80 percent of them are active Vodouists.[1] Haitians are also Muslims, Buddhists, even in the minority. Equally, there has always been Haitians who profess theism, agnosticism, theistic humanism, non-theistic humanism, and even atheism such as the great contemporary Haitian novelist and public intellectual Lyonel Trouillot. The religious experience of the Haitian people is not monolithic, but heterogeneous.

Briefly, we define religion as "that which provides orientation or direction to human life, for life in the world, together with motivation for living and acting in accordance with this orientation—that is, would gain, and gradually formulate, a sense of the *meaning of* human existence."[2] As Anthony Pinn has remarked, "Through the ritual structures and symbolic sources provided in various religions, human give their thought and actions meaning. Therefore, religion at its core is a process of meaning-making."[3] There are various factors that determine the religious life and foster the various religious ideas of a people. These might include internal factors such as spiritual depression, skepticism, fear; external forces might include certain historical events such as the birth of a child, the death of an important family member, family separation in the case of divorce, war, racism, new life experiences, psychological adjustment, moral struggle against sin, evil, human suffering, etc.[4] We should remember that the role of religion in society is not static. As society changes and people face new challenges, religions evolve with the society and the religious experience of the people also modify and acquire new meanings.

The first enslaved Africans who were shipped to the island of Hispanola in 1510[5] and the periods thereafter during the colonial moments of the Spaniards, the French, and the English brought with them religious traditions, values, "unwritten literature, systems of worship, and

---

1. Fontus, *Les églises protestantes en Haiti*, 63.
2. Pinn, *Varieties of African American Religious Experience*, 3.
3. Pinn, *Varieties of African American Religious Experience*, 3.
4. Mays, *The Negro's God*, 14–18.
5. Hurbon, *Voodoo: Truth and Fantasy*, 19. The author writes, "In 1503, the first cargo of slaves from Africa landed, brought in to replace native workers who showed the slightest distinction to work in the mines. Then in 1517 Charles V authorized the importation of fifteen thousand black slaves. The first small contingent of French travelers to settle the island of Tortuga, situate north of Haiti, landed in 1629."

a particularized African attitude toward nature and the supernatural."[6] "Most of the African peoples were represented in Saint-Domingue. But, of the three largest groups—the Sudanese, Guineans and Bantus—the one that carried the greatest influence was the Fon tribe of Dahomey, combined with the Yoruba of Nigeria, which provided the unifying basis for the ensemble of cultural practices transplanted to the island by the slaves"[7] The slaves were fervent Christians, Muslims, and practitioners of African traditional religions.[8] Historian John Thornton points out that "much of the philosophy that underlies the 'syncretic' or 'mixed' religious cults of the New World can be traced to African Christianity, and even much of the action taken by American clergy to suppress some types of religious practice among slaves came from African Christianity."[9]

Generally, the Haitian experience in religion can be summarized in six broad historical epochs or periods: from the arrival of first African slaves to the island of Saint-Domingue in 1510 to the founding of the nation of Haiti in 1804 (first epoch: slavery: 1510–1803); the Great Schism of 1804–1860 (second epoch: post-slavery to the Concordat, 1804–1860); from the signing of the Concordat in 1860 to the end of the American Occupation in Haiti (third epoch: from Concordat to the American occupation, 1860–1934); from the post-Occupation generation to the end of the presidency of Jean-Claude Duvalier (fourth epoch: post-Occupation to Duvalier, 1934–1986); from the end of the Duvalier regime to the presidential election of Jean-Bertrand Aristide (fifth epoch: from Duvalier to the triumph of the Lavalas-Liberation Theology movement, 1986–1996); from the end of Aristide to the (post) earthquake of January 12, 2010 (sixth period: post-earthquake to the present, 2010 to the present). Each one of these periods redefines the religious ethos in Haiti.

6. Courtlander, "Vodun in Haitian Culture," 2.

7. Hurbon, *Voodoo: Truth and Fantasy*, 20.

8. Garrigus, in an important article "'New Christians' / 'New Whites,'" 317, 320, reports the presence of a small community of Sephardic Jews who immigrated to the island of Saint-Domingue in the early eighteenth century. Garrigus does not say whether the African slaves embraced Judaism as an adopted faith. Several Jews in the colony, however, converted to Christianity, such was the case of the prominent Michel Lopez Depas, a medical doctor from an important Bordeaux Sephardic family. Garrigus also discusses about Jewish families.

9. Thornton, "On the Trail of Voodoo," 262.

The Catholic Christian Tradition and the Vodouphobic Discourse

The Catholic tradition in Saint-Domingue Haiti began with the missionary activities of colonial missionaries and Catholic priests who were commissioned to Christianize and civilize the enslaved African population in the French colony. Colonial missionary Christianity in the island was a failure, resulting in a few African converts to the Christian faith. Religious scholar and anthropologist Remy Bastien has suggested two chief reasons leading to the unsuccessful mission of Christianity in Haiti: Christianity's inability "to provide the Africans with a satisfactory religious life, and the resistance of the African to his lot, and his will to preserve as much of his cultural possible."[10] He adds:

> The French colonists were known for their lack of religiosity. Elsewhere religious teaching was frowned upon by the masters and, at least before Abolition, the ministers found little incentive to include the slaves among their flocks. . . . Meager as it was, the presence of Christianity was enough to impress the slaves. They borrowed elements form its ritual and dogma and blended them with their own African heritage. They syncretized Afro-religions of the New World simultaneously practiced both Vodoun and Catholicism, with surprising ease at times. While the economic system of the dominant Europeans created tensions, antagonism, and violence, the religious system of the slaves successfully created a workable pattern of coexistence. Religious coexistence, however, did not exclude resistance on the political plane.[11]

On the other hand, the Christian tradition in Haiti is also linked to Afrophobia and Vodouphobia. Colonial administrators outlawed Vodou immediately in the mid-1600s.[12] Gerarde Magloire-Danton explains that "since the period of slavery in Haiti to the middle of the twentieth century, Vodou remained synonymous with barbarism and was associated with bloody ritualistic practices and cannibalism in Euro-American narrative and scientific discourse."[13] Most Catholic priests who served as missionaries in the island of Saint-Domingue equated Vodou and African

---

10. Bastien, "Vodoun and Politics in Haiti," 41.
11. Bastien, "Vodoun and Politics in Haiti," 41.
12. Greene, *Catholic Church in Haiti*, 82.
13. Magloire, "Antenor Firmin and Jean Price-Mars," 161.

beliefs with sorcery, paganism, superstitious, even Satanism. In other words, Vodou was not considered a religion!

Father Jean-Baptiste Labat, a seventeenth-century missionary who reported with great details about the religious life of the Africans, in *Voyage aux Isles de l'Amerique*, equates Vodou with sorcery and magic. As he asserts, "Before baptizing the adults, it is necessary to mark out those who filled the role of sorcerer in their country, for whatever promises they make they will rarely abandon them."[14]

Correspondingly, the colonial historian Moreau de Saint-Remy in *Description topographique, physique, civile, politique et historique de la patrie francaise de l'Isle de Saint-Domingue* (1797) describes Vodou ceremony, ritual or dance "as a kind of Bacchanlia [that gave way to] a disgusting prostitution."[15] Hurbon summarizes aptly that

> as far as the Europeans at the beginning of the 18th century were concerned, African religions did not exist. The worship of Indian and Africans in Hispaniola could be explained only as Satanism.... Until the 18th century, the earliest descriptions of voodoo were dominated by stereotypes of a religion considered as snake-worshipping, diabolical and barbarous.[16]

The goal of the colonial (Catholic) church was to manage slavery and not to abolish it.[17] "Church records and historical journals show that the Church did not oppose slavery in Haiti. Some in the church even justified it on the basis that it gave slaves the opportunity to become Christian.... The best indication of Church acceptance of slavery is that priests owned slaves."[18]

Evidently, the Vodouphobic discourse was developed in colonial time as a way to justify the institution of slavery and the desire to civilize the Africans to Western worldview and lifestyle. In the twentieth century, Vodouphobic continues to be an intellectual discourse with the advent of American evangelicalism in Haiti during the American Occupation (1914-1934). In Fact, the post-Occupation era had brought more zealous American missionaries in the country with the view to eradicate Vodou and "save Haiti for Christ." In addition, the number of American

---

14. Quoted in Hurbon, *Voodoo: Truth and Fantasy*, 29.
15. Hurbon, *Voodoo*, 29.
16. Hurbon, *Voodoo*, 29.
17. Greene, *Catholic Church in Haiti*, 75.
18. Greene, *Catholic Church in Haiti*, 77.

evangelical missionaries escalated following the earthquake of January 2010 that had devastated Haiti—giving the evangelical narrative that the earthquake was a punishment by God.

Vodou still remains a very present reality in the Haitian society; similarly, both expressions of Christianity—Catholicism and Protestant—continue to be a crucial element in the Haitian experience with religion. Unfortunately, there have been many misunderstandings and conflicts in the past between these two religious traditions. These conflicts have created a lot of suffering among Haitians and harmed the country. (However, I believe that a pacific cohabitation between the two is possible in this era of religious pluralism and tolerance.)[19] Catholicism, for example, has been recognized as the state religion by a number of Constitutions of the country such as the Constitutions of 1801, 1806, 1816, etc. In March 28, 1860, the Haitian government Fabre Nicolas Geffrard signed a Concordat with Rome that made Catholicism the official religion of the Haitian state.

One of the major goals of the church, which was also the goal of the state, was to eradicate Vodou from the Haitian soil. Vodou was considered superstition, fetishism, idolatry and the main obstacle to modernization and Christian evangelization of the Haitian people. It is in this social and historical context that several major campaigns were organized jointly by the Church and the State to exterminate Vodou and Vodouizan. Over five anti-voodoo campaigns have therefore been organized (1864, 1896, 1912, 1925–1930, 1940–1941). During these campaigns, Vodou temples were searched and seized, and religious objects were destroyed and burned, etc.[20]

The Protestant/Christian Tradition

The first Protestant missionaries came to Haiti during the presidencies of Henri Christophe and Alexandre Petion. These missionaries came from the United States and England, and the Haitian people warmly welcomed them to their native land. The Quaker missionaries Etienne de Grellet and John Hancok first landed in Les Cayes in 1816. The English missionaries John Brown and James Catts (Haiti's first Protestant historian) also arrived about the same year. Brown and Catts established the "first

---

19. Francois, "Vaudou et catholicisme," 2.
20. François, "Vaudou et catholicisme," 2.

Protestant church in Port-au-Prince in 1817."²¹ The city of Cap-Haitien received two new Methodist missionaries: Harvey and Jones; King Henri Christophe cordially welcomed them. Moreover, Ann Greene informs us that

> the American Baptists sent Thomas Paul, a black minister from Massachusetts, to Cap-Haitien in 1823. Welcomed by President Boyer, he established some congregations before departing six months later. With time, the Baptists, Methodists, Pentecostals, Seventh Day Adventists, Episcopalians, and others have established roots in Haiti, settled, spread out, undergone many schisms, and produced numerous denominations.²²

In addition, the African American Episcopal Church minister Joseph Theodore Holly, who immigrated in Haiti in the 1860s, was instrumental in spreading Protestant Christianity in the Caribbean island. Rev. Holly became the first Episcopal Bishop in Haiti in 1874 and established "the Orthodox Apostolic Church—the country's first national church, and also the first church founded under Anglican auspices outside English-speaking countries."²³ In short, "Protestants were regarded as ethical, economically astute, and upwardly mobile. The government sought them out because of their reputation for honesty. . . . It became clear to the Church that Protestantism was attractive, not only to the uncommitted and Voodoo practitioners, but to Catholics and was turning into a threat to church membership and privilege."²⁴ In their early evangelistic endeavors, Protestant missionaries experienced minimal success in the Caribbean nation for many important factors.

> First, they were demanding and strait-laced. In addition, they faced hostility from the Church and sometimes from governments. Finally, they had to confront an historic Haitian bias for things French. Protestantism required followers to renounce other forms of worship. Converts were required to throw away symbols belonging to the Catholic and Voodoo religions. . . . The church in Haiti had reached its nadir by mid-century. It lacked power, authority, personnel, and scope—being almost exclusively urban. The Protestants were focusing their attention

---

21. Greene, *Catholic Church in Haiti*, 91.
22. Greene, *Catholic Church in Haiti*, 91.
23. Dubois, *Haiti: The Aftershocks of History*, 155.
24. Greene, *Catholic Church in Haiti*, 91.

on the cities also, so Voodoo went largely unchallenged in the countryside.[25]

Protestant denominations founded new churches and a few religious schools in Haiti. But, Protestant Christianity has failed to address the social question and the plot of Haitian poor, the peasant, and underclass. The mission of these protestant groups and missionaries can be described as a threefold perspective: (1) to evangelize the Haitian people and to win the Haitian soul for Christ, (2) to transform Haiti into a Christian nation, and (3) to eradicate Vodou from the Haitian soil. Like their Catholic counterparts, Protestant missionaries constructed an anti-vodouphobic discourse whose central premise was the rehabilitation and redemption of the Haitian people and their lost souls.

In Haiti's Protestant circle, a number of influential Haitian theologians (Jules Casseus, Mario Valcin, Lauture Magloire, Jean Duthene Joseph, etc.) and prominent Protestant leaders and pastors still maintain the belief that Vodou is primarily responsible for Haiti's underdevelopment and is an obstacle to modernity and democratic progress. According to these thinkers, Vodou has contributed enormously to the spiritual decline of the Caribbean nation.[26] By contrast, they interpret the central role of Haitian Protestantism as providing moral and spiritual guidance to the Haitian people. Haitian Protestantism does not play a social role in the Haitian society as to improving the Haitian condition and the life of more than 85 percent of the country's population who live in dire poverty. Haitian Protestantism rejects the social vision of Christianity.

Prominent Haitian theologian and the president of Université Chrétienne du Nord d'Haiti (UCNH) Jules Casseus in his important work, *Toward a Contextual Theology*, argues that the religion of Vodou and its worldview creates a narrative of fear among the Haitian people and contributes to Haiti's moral decline, unscientific thinking, and collective psychosis and low self-esteem.

> First, there is the Voodoo mentality, a pseudo-scientific way of thinking, a mentality where the people are dominated by fear, divisions, lack of confidence. For 60% to 70 % of the Haitian population and a good number of so called alphabetized people, almost everything that happens which has not being understood

---

25. Greene, *Catholic Church in Haiti*, 91–92.

26. Fils-Aimé, *Vodou, je me souviens*, 47; Casseus, *Quelle Eglise Quelle libération?*, 65; Valcin, "Development and Implementation of a Training Program," 65.

is a "mystery" that only the spirits are able to explain. Sickness, premature death, accidents, drought, inundation . . . are the work of the spirits, when they are angry or sent by wicked people. They are not simple [phenomena]; it is only through magic and the traditional religion of Voodoo that one can find the true explanation.[27]

Casseus's thought on the subject is conflicting. While religious worldview could alter one's vision of the world, what he describes above, as it pertains to Haiti's illiterate population, has to do with the lack of education not a religious or Vodou problem. At least, he has failed to make the connection between religion and education. What he calls "Voodoo mentality" is viewed as a psychological barrier for understanding the reality of natural illnesses and the importance of physical and psychological wellness. Further, according to Casseus, there have been two major curses in Haitian history and life: analphabetism and the Vodou religion; as he proclaims: "Analphabetism is, together with Voodoo, a curse to the Haitian society."[28] He calls for the overcoming of "this serious handicap if we want to see a new Haitian people in a new Haitian society for the third centennial of the Haitian nation."[29]

Casseus construes Vodou as an "old superstitious tradition" in Haitian history, and a tremendous hindrance to the collective progress. Accordingly, the Vodou religion has kept "the masses in a state of chronic dependency."[30] For Casseus, Haitians have espoused a destructive anthropology, predicated on a Vodouist wordview or cosmology that veils the nature of reality.

> After more than two centennials of the influence of Voodoo in the Haitian society, we should admit that we have developed this Voodoo mentality that encourages: superstitions, fear of the spirits world; fear of the neighbor, the spirits, and fear of the future. All this give birth to fatalism, inferiority complex, individualism, lack of confidence in the neighbor, the spirit of revenge, division and so on.[31]

---

27. Casseus, *Toward a Contextual Theology*, 91.
28. Casseus, *Toward a Contextual Theology*, 85.
29. Casseus, *Toward a Contextual Theology*, 85.
30. Casseus, *Toward a Contextual Theology*, 81.
31. Casseus, *Toward a Contextual Theology*, 61.

Jules Caseus and the well-respected Haitian Evangelical leader and theologian, and the Chancellor of Haiti's most conservative seminary: Seminaire de Theologie Evangelique de Port-au-Prince (STEP) Jean Duthene Joseph share common ideological stereotypes and intellectual misjudgments about Vodou and its role in Haitian history. Joseph promotes the idea that Vodou has fostered both mental and social alienation in the Haitian culture and has contributed enormously to collective psychosis, spiritual distress, poverty, and the suffering of the Haitian people. As a result, he maintains that Haitian Protestants should not associate or have "any link with vodouism."[32]

In his doctoral dissertation, defended in 2006 at Trinity Theological Seminary, he seeks to establish the symbiotic relationship between Roman Catholicism and Haitian Vodou and the impact of their association on the Protestant Church and community in Haiti. In this project, Joseph expresses clearly Vodouphobic tendency comparatively to that of Casseus. First, he seeks to articulate the theological distancing between Vodou and Christianity:

> The Vodou culture makes Haitians different from other nations in the Caribbean. This dissertation will demonstrate the distinction between the traditional religions of Haiti and Christianity as they are being intertwined and practiced in the Haitian society, and the religious gap between Vodou loa (mediums) and the true and living God who is both transcendent and immanent.[33]

With more clarity and precision, he articulates the overarching objective of the research:

> One of the objectives of this project is the removal of the veil existing within the Protestant Church that has for so long hidden the Vodou vestiges, vestiges that emerged from the symbiosis of the Roman Catholicism and Haitian Vodou; a coexistence that goes back to the colonial days on the island of Hispaniola.[34]

From a pastoral and theological perspective, Joseph is traumatized that the Haitian church, which professes true knowledge of God, is still "stigmatized by Vodou vestiges. The Church finds itself caught between the devotion to a Holy Trinitarian God and the traditional Vodou

---

32. Valcin, *Development and Implementation of a Training Program*, 61; Fils-Aimé, *Vodou, je me souviens*, 192.

33. Joseph, "Symbiotic Relationship," 3.

34. Joseph, "Symbiotic Relationship," 7.

beliefs."[35] On one hand, Joseph understands Vodou as a "steady religion"[36] that many Haitian Protestants "find it difficult to stay away from Vodou practitioners."[37] On the other hand, he informs us that Vodou is a religion of fear, associates the Afro-Haitian faith with magic, evil spirits, evil spells, and that the fear of Vodou is widespread among former Vodouists who converted to Protestant Christianity.

Joseph acknowledges that Vodou is gaining momentum in the Haitian society—a phenomenon which he interprets as a major religious crisis in the Caribbean nation—and that the Protestant community in Haiti should be proactive "to be free from the snare of Vodouism."[38] Consequently, the aim of his project is to:

1. Unveil the residuum of Vodou rituals and beliefs that persistently underlay the very mindset and behavior of Haitians in general and Christians in particular.
2. Help educate Haitian believers with reference to Vodou practices and the crucial reality of the interplay of Vodou and Roman Catholicism.
3. Prescribe proper biblical remedy to eradicate Vodou vestiges in the Protestant church and community.[39]

Further, Joseph questions the very notion of Vodou as a viable and legitimate religion like Christianity, Islam, or Judaism. He states that he affirms Vodou's religiosity "not by conviction but simply by convention."[40] He rejects the monotheist nature of Vodou when he writes "To claim that Vodou is essentially a monotheistic religion raises some legitimate questions. . . . By nature, Vodou is simultaneously animistic, polytheistic, and pantheistic."[41] Most religious scholars will disagree with Joseph's conclusion about the Vodou faith. Such statement also expresses his misunderstanding of the nature of African religions in general. Joseph is resuscitating or rearticulating the old missionary false ideologies and misconceptions of the nineteenth century and early twentieth century about African religions in general and the Vodou religion in particular.

35. Joseph, "Symbiotic Relationship," 16.
36. Joseph, "Symbiotic Relationship," 15.
37. Joseph, "Symbiotic Relationship," 16.
38. Joseph, "Symbiotic Relationship," 17.
39. Joseph, "Symbiotic Relationship," 17.
40. Joseph, "Symbiotic Relationship," 103.
41. Joseph, "Symbiotic Relationship," 105, 138.

Moreover, it is evident from Joseph's language that the ultimate goal of the Protestant Church is "to eradicate Vodou vestiges in the Protestant church and community." As he adds, the greatest threat to Protestant church and its ensuring growth in Haiti is "not only by the presence and practice of Vodou in the society, but also by the symbiosis of Roman Catholicism and the Vodou community."[42] As we will examine further, unlike Jean Fils-Aimé and Laennec Hurbon who call for frank ecumenical or interreligious dialogue between Vodou and Christianity, both Joseph and Caseus, and other evangelical leaders in Haiti maintain that "no real fellowship can occur between righteousness and unrighteousness, or between Christians and Vodouisants. There can be no communion between the two entities."[43]

Counter Narratives: Hurbon and Fils-Aimé Talk Back

In reaction to the anti-vodou narrative or vodouphobic discourse, Laënnec Hurbon and Jean Fils-Aimé have contended that the religion of Vodou is "the cement of the Haitian culture," and Vodou is an unavoidable reality in the Haitian experience and culture. They also maintain that "Vodou is the mode of being Haitians in the world." By this declaration, they convey the idea that Vodou for the Haitian is a philosophy, a way of life, a worldview, and a metaphysical vision of the world. Because Vodou constitutes the fundamental base and value of the Haitian culture, they suggest that the faith must be transmitted from generation to generation. These thinkers recommend the Haitianisation of Christianity—not the Christianization of the Haitian culture and Haitian people—in order to preserve the richness of Haitian culture and appropriate the Vodou tradition within the Christian religion. The true religion of the Haitian people is Vodou; the Haitian people were Christianized, and that Christianity is a foreign faith. In short, both Hurbon and Fils-Aimé are optimistic that a "thick inculturation" process would help rehabilitate the local culture in Haiti, and solve the religious conundrum in the "Black Republic."

Hurbon is regarded as one of the most respected intellectual voices in Haiti, in Caribbean contemporary thought, and in cultural and political criticism. He received a doctorate degree in theology from the Institut Catholique de Paris in 1970, and a doctorate in sociology from the University

---

42. Joseph, "Symbiotic Relationship," 18.
43. Joseph, "Symbiotic Relationship," 56.

of Paris (Paris IV-Sorbonne) in 1976. He pursued postdoctoral studies in anthropology at École des Hautes Etudes de Paris in 1973. Hurbon became a specialist on Haitian Vodou and culture, engaging the intersections of religion, culture, and politics in the Caribbean.

Hurbon is a prolific writer who has authored and edited more than a dozen books and hundreds of scholarly articles. His signature text, Dieu dans le vaudou haitien, was published in 1972, in which he explores the concept and various manifestations of God in Haitian Vodou. He interprets God as the "common ground" for ecumenical dialogue between Haitian Catholics and Haitian Vodouists. Hurbon articulates a poignant critique of Haitian Catholicism toward Vodou in which he rejects the claim of the supremacy of Christianity above other religions and its message of universal salvation.

First, he posits that Western Christianity contributed enormously to the development of the idea that the Afro-Haitian culture and Vodou were inferior—an ideology that is shared by many Haitians. Second, he argues that Christian teachings have obscured the real battlefield—the political sphere—and have hampered the transformation of economic and social conditions. Third, he maintains that Christianity, as it has been presented in Haiti, has imposed a new system of reference that devalued ancestral traditions and the original modes of existence of Haitians. Fourth, as he reasons, if the Catholic religion is presented as the religion of civilization and sociability, then the Vodou religion is cast aside as the religion of the primitive, a superstitious faith. As a result, he contends, the Vodou adept is forced to imitate the white man, his worldview, his city, his society, as well as his lifestyle in the modern world.

Hurbon defends the Vodou faith by stressing its importance in the survival of Haitian cultural life, traditions, and spiritual practices. According to the author, Vodou has been the catalyst that helped enslaved Africans survive the terror of slavery and white supremacy in colonial Saint-Domingue. He maintains the idea that Vodou is a fundamental aspect of Haitian life and culture, and remains the country's national patrimony. Through Vodou, the Haitian peasant has preserved his African identity and ancestral traditions. In addition, Hurbon argues that Vodou is a monotheistic religion, and that the supreme deity of Vodou is the God of the Abrahamaic faiths: Judaism, Christianity, and Islam. He concludes that Christians should respect the beliefs and practices of Haitian Vodou, just as they do in the so-called higher religions.

In *Dieu dans le Vodou haitien*, Hurbon brilliantly demonstrates that Vodou is a meaningful religion and has both personal and collective values in the everyday experience of the Haitian people. He maintains that Vodou is "an authentic religious experience, a valid cultural language like any other language—one which satisfies the Haitian practitioner in the quest for an understanding of things in this world in the attempt to give meaning to human existence."[44] He examines three facets of Vodou: (1) Vodou as a personal religion, (2) Vodou as a family and collective religion, and (3) the significance of Vodou as family and collective religion. As a personal faith, through the work of the tuterary spirits/lwa, the individual receives guidance and protection "in all of his understandings and in difficult moments."[45] In the second level, that is, Vodou as family and collective religion, family members come together in the *ounfo* and forge a brotherhood community. The *ounfo* facilitates a sense of community in which family members who have been disconnected "through the year come together on different occasions to celebrate their faith in the *lwa*."[46]

The relevance of Vodou to the adherents in matters of life and faith can be explained through the practice of Vodou rituals and ceremonies. Hurbon highlights three principal objectives of Vodou pilgrimage: (1) "to fulfill their duty as sons of Guinea, (2) to do penitence for their negligence in serving the lwa, (3) and to regain their favor."[47] Yet, the telos of Vodou retreats is to allow the participant to "have the opportunity to surrender themselves to a lengthy retirement in order to reaffirm their bond and their beliefs to the *lwa*.[48] This spiritual dimension of Vodou is often ignored in contemporary religious scholarship. Since Vodou is primarily interpreted as a family and collective faith, what is then its significance to families and the collective? Hurbon accentuates the vitality and practicality of Vodou in the Haitian life which entails a number of implications: the process of reestablishing links with Africa, rehabilitating fellowship with dead ancestors, rediscovering the ancestral identity of the Haitian people, and forging the spiritual union with African gods through religious ritual.

---

44. Hurbon, "Vodou," 787.
45. Hurbon, "Vodou," 787.
46. Hurbon, "Vodou," 788.
47. Hurbon, "Vodou," 790.
48. Hurbon, "Vodou," 790.

What Hurbon has done for Catholic Christianity in Haiti, Fils-Aimé has done the same for Protestant Christianity in Haiti. Both theologians make an urgent appellation to the Haitian people to change their attitude toward the Vodou religion and to acknowledge the various meaningful ways Vodou has enhanced the Haitian way of life and thinking. By contrary, as seen above, in the examined works of Haitian Protestant theologians and leaders, Vodou provides an alternative paradigm which hinders progress—spiritual, economic, political, cultural, social, etc.—in the Haitian society.

Jean Fils-Aimé received a master's degree in medieval history from McGill University and a PhD in theology from the University of Montreal. His scholarship engages the intersections of faith and culture in modernity and postmodernity, and the relationships between Christianity and Vodou in Haiti. A prolific writer and brilliant thinker, among his most influential works include *Vodou, je me souviens*, published in 2007, and the provocative titles *Et si les loas n'etaient pas des Diables* published in 2008, and *Le nécessaire dialogue entre le vaudou et la foi chrétienne: l'inculturation de la foi chrétienne au contexte du vaudou*, published in 2010.

In his original and controversial work, *Vodou, je me souviens*, Fils-Aimé declares that the religion of Vodou is "the cement of the Haitian culture"[49] and it is an unavoidable reality in the Haitian experience. For Fils-Aimé, Vodou is the mode of being absolutely Haitians in the world (*"Le vaudou est le mode d'être des Haïtiens au monde. Le vodou est carrément le 'mode d'être' de l'haïtien au monde"*).[50] In other words, it is not possible to be Haitian without being a Vodouist (*"Il n'est pas possible d'etre Haitien sans etre Vodou"*). Here, Fils-Aimé conflates religious affiliation and nationality. Second, he misconstrues existence with being religious. By this declaration, he conveys that Vodou for the Haitian is a philosophy, a way of life, a worldview, and a metaphysical vision of the world.[51] Because Vodou constitutes the fundamental base and value of the Haitian culture, Fils-Aimé suggests that it "must be transmitted from generation

---

49. Fils-Aimé, *Vodou, je me souviens*, 116. The book stemmed from his doctoral dissertation, "*L'inculturation de la foi chrétienne au contexte du vodou haïtien.*"

50. Fils-Aimé, *Vodou, je me souviens*, 114, 117; "Le vaudou à la lumière de la Bible," *Le Nouvelliste*, May 20, 2008, http://lenouvelliste.com/lenouvelliste/article/57359/Le-vaudou-a-la-lumiere-de-la-Bible.

51. Fils-Aimé, *Vodou, je me souviens*, 117.

to generation."⁵² Fils-Aimé embraces the dual perspectives about Vodou in Haitian intellectual history: that (1) Vodou as culture, and (2) Vodou as religion.

> To pronounce that "Vodou is an important place in Haitian cultural identity," and religious tradition is to maintain that "Vodou is a proper way for the Haitian to perceive life and make sense of his place in the cosmos. Hence, Vodou is and has been the most effective religion for Haitians; following the Price-Marsian rhetoric that legitimizes Vodou as a religion, Fils-Aimé provides many riveting reasons to justify the viability and relevance of Vodou today:

> 1. Vodou has aided the Haitian people to survive the trauma of slavery, and to adjust to the hell of Saint-Domingue, and to take charge and build an environment in which nothing is left to chance.
> 2. The Vodou universe or cosmology reconciles man to nature.
> 3. It bridges the gap between the living of today and that of yesterday, that is to say, the deceased.
> 4. It integrates the fate of humans and the spirits.
> 5. It reminds us that everything is energy and that energy never dies. It transforms, metamorphoses, and passes from visible to invisible registry; but, it remains. It is available for and to the service of humans.⁵³

The Christian theologian Jean Fils-Aimé advances the notion that "Vodou is more than an ordinary religion and more than a cultural trait of Haitian cultural identity."⁵⁴ His reasoning is predicated upon his insightful discernment and articulation of five compelling propositions:

> 1. Since the statistics lead us to establish a precise figure that Vodou remains the religion of the Haitian majority, some would have the tendency to argue that Vodou is a religion among others in Haiti. However, as regards to the impact of Vodou on the Haitian population, it would be too simple to say, without affirming that it remains the religion of the majority, it is

---

52. Fils-Aimé, *Vodou, je me souviens*, 116.
53. Fils-Aimé, *Et si les loas n'étaient pas des diables?*, 178.
54. Fils-Aimé, *Vodou, je me souviens*, 128.

a religion with equal influence as Christianity on the Haitian people.[55]

2. Vodou is much more than that for the Haitian. It seems that even when the Haitian is converted to another religious faith, the Vodouist beliefs or the Vodouist vision of the world continues to explain his attitude and vis-a-vis the behavior of others and life in general. This attitude is particularly noticeable in Protestant churches that stand as the alternative to Vodou. The fact remains that the Haitian reclaims the Protestant faith in what he was looking in Vodou.[56]

3. Vodou is so rooted in the Haitian soul; it seems to forge a chorus within the Haitian collectivity. Whether Protestant or Roman Catholic, the Haitian remains Vodou in his vision of the world and in his way of living in the universe. This is the reason that the statistics are not reliable as to the percentage of Vodou adepts in Haiti. In summary, the Vodou faith is the religion of the Haitian soul. Even though other faiths may superpose it, but they can never replace it.[57]

4. The religion of an individual or human group is a "*Totalite sens*" ("whole way"). There exists neither true religion nor a generation that is spontaneous born and disappears as it arises. The Vodou religion is rather a reality *sui generis* stemmed from the origin of African religions and it is maintained in what many authors have called 'the collective memory.[58]

5. The religion of most Haitian is Vodou, known to most of Americans as Voodoo. This does not mean that Haitians do not see themselves as Roman-Catholics. There are no major differences between the two systems of religion. The syncretism of African practices and certain elements of Catholicism is complete and deep.[59]

Furthermore, Like Hurbon, Fils-Aimé reasons that one must understand the colonial project in terms of the deculturalization of the African in the name of Western civilization and the Christian West.[60] The Christian mission was a civilization campaign as well as cultural

55. Fils-Aimé, *Vodou, je me souviens*, 128.
56. Fils-Aimé, *Vodou, je me souviens*, 128–29.
57. Fils-Aimé, *Vodou, je me souviens*, 130–31.
58. Fils-Aimé, *Vodou, je me souviens*, 130.
59. Fils-Aimé, *Vodou, je me souviens*, 132.
60. Fils-Aimé, *Vodou, je me souviens*, 11.

deracination. As he remarks, "We [Haitians] were not evangelized. We were Christianized. Christianity is a white and Western appropriation of the gospel that was imposed on our blackness."[61] In this same text, Fils-Aimé explains in copious details the extent to which missionary activities in Haiti have altered the local culture in Haiti. To resolve the religious tension between Vodou and Haitian Protestantism, Fils-Aimé and Hurbon propose interreligious dialogue between the two religions and urges for the inculturation of Vodou in Haitian Protestantism. What are the basses for this interfaith dialogue between Vodou and Protestant Christianity?

First of all, Fils-Aimé and Hurbon advance the idea that the Catholic-Vodouist practices of Haitians reflect a faith inherent to the Haitian culture.[62] Second, the history of Christian evangelization in contemporary Haitian society has been/is a failure, and that it is not feasible to totally divorce Vodou and Haitian Protestantism. For example, Fils-Aimé reports that sociologists of religion have observed that Haitian convert to Protestantism for the same reasons they return to Vodou.[63] Also, the history of relations between Christianity—both Protestant and Catholic—and Vodou in Haiti is marked by a high degree of combativeness, hostility, and discomfort.[64] Third, Fils-Aimé and Hurbon assert that Christianity as practiced in Haiti has caused social division and alienation between religious and non-religious people in Haiti, Vodouizan and Protestants too.

Yet, in matters of religion, it is not convenient to establish a relationship of superiority or inferiority, but to talk in terms of efficiency.[65] In other words, while Christianity might be a superior religion to many people, but it is not and has not been the most efficient and liberative religion in Haitian history.

For both thinkers, the ground for a genuine dialogue between Vodou and Christianity is rooted in the very logic of the Christian message of radical love and inclusive tolerance. From a biblical perspective, the Christian faith, a religion of love, should not seek to combat any religion or to eradicate any culture, but rather to transform all civilizations and

61. Fils-Aimé, *Vodou, je me souviens*, 22–23.
62. Fils-Aimé, *Vodou, je me souviens*, 11.
63. Fils-Aimé, *Vodou, je me souviens*, 1.
64. Fils-Aimé, *Vodou, je me souviens*, 2.
65. Fils-Aimé, *Et si les loas n'étaient pas des diables?*, 177.

to produce civilizations of love.[66] In a comparable note like Hurbon, he proceeds to underscore the reality and relevance of the Vodou religion in Haitian life: "Vodou is not only the religion of the majority of Haitians, but also the substance of the culture of the Haitian people."[67] Therefore, both Fils-Aimé and Hurbon reject the idea of Christian proselytization because it is incompatible with the Vodou faith; for it is a question of the right of the Haitian people as Christian conversion is viewed as a challenge to their cultural identity and cultural integrity.

Some Shortcomings in Fils-Aimé and Hurbon's Work

In this section of this chapter, we shall focus on three vital matters: the culture question, the social question, and the religious question—as a way to critically evaluate the arguments made by Fils-Aimé and Hurbon.

The Culture Question

Foremost, pertaining to the idea of culture, both Fils-Aimé and Hurbon have subscribed to the idea of culture as biological that is cultural essentialism. They have wrongly equated religion with culture, as some thinkers in the nineteenth century perceived race as a biological phenomenon—not a social construct. They conflate without clear distinction culture, identity, nationalism, and religion in the context of the Haitian experience and history. Finally, in their intellectual reasoning, both Hurbon and Fils-Aimé make no room for Haitian skeptics, atheists, non-theistic humanists, or simply individuals who make no commitment to any religious dogmas, creed, or theological doctrine—such as the major Haitian thinkers like Anténor Firmin, Jean Price-Mars, Jacques Roumain, Jacques Stephan Alexis, and other Haitian atheist Marxists and Communists of the twentieth century.

The question of the relationship between culture and identity is and has been an important and sensitive issue in the history of ideas. As Magesa has observed:

> What has complicated the issue has been the rise and spread of the phenomenon called globalization, a situation where,

---

66. Fils-Aimé, *Vodou, je me souviens*, 2.
67. Fils-Aimé, *Vodou, je me souviens*, 2.

through the development of science and technology, the whole world has been brought closer together than ever before. The major agent of this development has been information technology in the form of instant communication via the mass media, particularly of the electronic kind—radio, television and the computer. Through easy and fast travel, there has also been extensive contact among peoples, religions, ideas, and cultures. There has developed, as well, an intensification of commercial exchanges between nations and regions that could not have been imagine even a century ago.[68]

Magesa has also stated that "globalization and postmodernity affect cultural configurations and identifies among peoples to the extent that some academics now assert that cultures in Tylor's (1871) and Geertz's (1973) classical anthropological models of clearly defined, internally integrated, consistent, and unique meaning-generating symbol systems do not exist. Today it is argued increasingly that people factually experience themselves as belonging not to one particular identity, but to multiple identifies . . . [on the other hand]."[69] In addition, Tanner has informed us that

> change is possible because culture and society no longer form, as in the modern understanding of culture, an expressive totality, every aspect reinforcing all the others by virtue of their following the same structures or principles. Culture is never independent of social processes, and social interactions never occur apart from cultural interpretations; but culture and social interactions fall out of sync with one another, at the very least because of a time lag. . . . Innovation is a possibility even in cases where determinate cultural forms function as rules direction action.[70]

The Haitian culture is not monolithic, but heterogeneous. The Haitian people have inherited a triple heritage: African, indigenous (Native American), and European, which reflects in their taste, music, cuisine, painting, art, religion, worldview, languages, etc. Fils-Aimé and Hurbon do not consider the different cultures and traditions Haitians who live in the Diaspora or outside of Haiti share and practice. It is observed that more than 1 million Haitians live outside of Haiti, and the Haitian

68. Magesa, *Anatomy of Inculturation*, 150.
69. Magesa, *Anatomy of Inculturation*, 150.
70. Tanner, *Theories of Culture*, 52.

Diaspora in the United States, France, and Canada are a hybrid people who possess more than one culture, national or religious identity. These individuals embrace multiple identities as Haitian American, Haitian Canadian, Haitian French, etc., and practice Buddhism, Hinduism, Christianity, Vodou, etc.

In our postmodern world, cultural identity is fractured, destabilized, and decentered. The self is fragmented and shifted, and it is an on-going project. According to Ricoeur, "The self is essentially a fiction through which we understand our lives as coherent stories ('narrative identity'). We are the stories we inhabit and tell about ourselves."[71]

The Social Question

Both Fils-Aimé and Hurbon failed to address the role of Vodou and Christianity in modernizing Haiti and improving the plight and social condition of the Haitian poor, the peasant, and the underclass. They have also failed to address the social function of these two religious traditions in improving infrastructure and strengthening institutions, work toward increasing access to education health and other services, and stimulate investment. Evidently, both Vodou and Christianity are not/have not been actively involved in the everyday struggle of the Haitian masses, and have been passive in responding to their dire needs. According to a research study done by World Bank:

> Haiti remains the poorest country in the Americas and one of the poorest in the world with a GDP per capita of $ US 856 in 2014 with significant needs in basic services. According to the latest household survey, more than 6 million out of 10.4 million (59%) Haitians live under the national poverty line of $ 2.44 per day and over 2.5 million (24%) live under the national extreme poverty line of 1.24 dollars per day.[72]

The Haitian poor and oppressed need more than spiritual consolation or comfort from religion—bet it Vodou or Christianity. The Haitian people are need scholar-activists who care deeply concerned about their holistic development and understand that true religion is that which that feeds the needy, clothe the naked, and aid the widow, the outcast, and the disfranchised, and the underrepresented class.

71. See Ricoeur, *Ricoeur Reader: Reflection and Imagination*.
72. World Bank, "Haiti," http://www.worldbank.org/en/country/haiti/overview.

Both Vodou and Christianity have failed in these accounts. Fils-Aimé and Hurbon have overlooked the social question and the urgent material needs of the Haitian people because their emphasis is on spirituality and culture. The current status of Vodou and Christianity in the Haitian society is far from being transformative faiths in the Haitian culture. Unless Vodou and Christianity reform and address the holistic concerns of the Haitian individual, their impact will be minimal.

The goal of a transformative and socially engaged religion is to sympathize with the poor and the sick by actively partaking in their suffering and in the trajectories of their life experiences, life troubles, and life worlds. The task is more than paying lip service; rather, it is active collaboration, genuine partnership, and sacrificial service and giving.

The Religious Question

As already observed in the previous paragraph, both Hurbon and Fils-Aimé bring in proximity the issues of religious affiliation, Haitian national identity, and the construction of self and collective identity based on certain religious tradition or system—the Vodou religion. They have overlooked that the religious experience could be both personal and collective, and that religious piety is not spirituality. Religious affiliation is a choice—at least in most Western societies and nation-states. (I understand it may not be a personal choice in certain countries where religious freedom is limited or not prized!) It is also observed that some countries in the Middle East, for example, have adopted a state religion such as Islam. For example, while a person may be born into a particular religious tradition or system—such as Haitian Vodou, Christianity, Judaism, Taoism, Hinduism, Buddhism, Islam, etc.—genuine religious affiliation, however, should be a personal choice of the individual. As we say in Kreyòl, "*Yo pa achte Lwa*" ("One cannot buy a Lwa/Spirit"). (Nonetheless, I do understand that Vodou is also a family religion, and the religious heritage can be passed on from one generation to the next. However, that in itself does not qualify a family member to automatically become a Vodouizan, a Hougan or Mambo. Allow me to share a personal example: my grandmother from my mother's side was a mambo [Vodou priestess], and my grandfather from my mother's side served many lwa, even married to several of them [spiritual marriage in Vodou]. Nonetheless, my mother never practiced Vodou nor has she inherited the tradition or passed it on to her children. My father's parents [my grandparents] were not Vodou practitioners.) From this vantage point, religious affiliation is certainly not an entitlement.

Hence, to be born into a Haitian family does not automatically make one a Vodouizan or Vodouist. Haiti is a country. Haitian is a national identity. Vodouizan is a religious affiliation. These three things are not the same and certainly not synonymous or interchangeable. To reiterate, Haitians, both in Haiti and the Haitian Diaspora, have embraced various and competing religious affiliations. Haitians are Muslims, Buddhists, Christians, Catholic practitioners, Protestants, Agnostics, Atheists, Secular humanists, Jehovah Witnesses, Mormons, etc. As a result, Haitians are free to embrace any religious worldview or system.

Vodou is one among other religions practiced by Haitians both in Haiti and the Diaspora. Haiti's ancestral faith is not monolithic; it is rather pluralistic. (In fact, Vodou itself is not a homogeneous religion.) The African ancestors who were brought by force to the island of Saint-Domingue brought with them various traditions, practices, customs, and competing religious practices and worldviews including Christianity, African Traditional religions, Islam, etc. While living on the island, they also adopted the religions of the Native Americans, and incorporated them into the religion of Vodou; they have also integrated Christian rituals and theology, and Masonic humanist morality and rituals into Vodou. While a large number of the enslaved population practiced what is now labelled as Haitian Vodou, not all of them were Vodou practitioners.

To embrace another religion other than Vodou should not be construed as the devalorization of the Haitian culture—since religions and cultures are human inventions and part of the process and theory we call social constructionism. In a true democratic state, the individual is granted the right of religious freedom and preference.

The common ideology in contemporary Haitian scholarship is that to be Haitian is to be a Vodouizan. Many Haitianist scholars have "essentialized Vodou" as the religion of all Haitians, just like certain individuals have "essentialized" race and culture. This tendency among scholars, both in the Anglophone and Francophone worlds, does not do justice to the reality and the lived-experiences of the Haitian people—both in Haiti and the Haitian Diaspora. From a historical perspective, Vodou, Christianity, and Islam had played a pivotal role in the Haitian Revolution since Vodou itself is a syncretized faith which integrates Christian moral theology and ritual into its own brand of practice. Second, Francois Makandal,

Dutty Boukman, and other important maroon leaders, and revolutionary leaders embraced Islam; they were also Vodouizan. Third, the founding fathers Toussaint Louverture and Alexandre Petion were devout Roman Catholic by confession. In 1816, President Petion had invited Protestant Christianity in Haiti—what is now called today "Evangelical Christianity"—only twelve years after the founding of the new nation of Haiti (I do understand there is a great divide between Evangelical Christianity of the nineteenth century and that of the twenty-first century, as to their political affiliation and theological confessions). Fourth, a large number of the enslaved Africans practiced Vodou as a religion; on the other hand, the enslaved Congolese who were brought to Saint-Domingue at the end of the 18th century were equally Catholic Christians as Catholicism became the state religion of Congo in early fifteenth century—even before Christopher Columbus visited the Americas. A large number of the enslaved Senegalese who were brought to the island were Muslims—an important point Jean Price-Mars affirms in chapter 3 ("*L'Afrique, ses races et sa civilisation*") in "*Ainsi parla l'Oncle.*"

In summary, in Haiti's contemporary society, there are three major religious practices: Vodou, Protestant/Evangelical Christianity, and Roman Catholicism. (Islam is growing rapidly in Protestant Christianity is practiced by 45–50 percent of the Haitian population. It is probably more in 2016—giving the wide spread of Evangelical Christianity in post-earthquake Haitian society.) While Vodou is among the most practiced religions by Haitians in Haiti, Haiti does not have "one single religious tradition." The ancestral faith of the Haitian people is also Vodou, Christianity, and Islam.

Finally, to be a Haitian Muslim or Christian does not make one an inferior Haitian Patriot. In the same line of thought, the Vodouizan is not a superior Haitian than the Haitian atheist or agnostic. Freedom of religion means the opportunity one has to choose or reject a certain faith among others. Religious freedom means a person who is affiliated with a certain religious tradition is free to share his or faith with another individual of a different religious persuasion or to someone who has no religious affiliation. Since religion like culture is a social construction or human invention, no religion or culture has the monopoly. In our perspective, the pivotal issue that remains is this important conversation is as follows: in contemporary Haitian society, how have both dominant religions (Vodou and Christianity) collaborated to offer to the Haitian people an alternative way of living and in dealing with forces of poverty, hunger, unemployment, health issues, as well as coping with the human existence and condition in Haiti characterized—to a larger degree—by alienation, exclusion, shame, and cynicism.

CHAPTER SIX

Holistic Transformation

*Justice as Solidarity and the Poor
in Aristide's Theological Tradition*

IN THE PREVIOUS CHAPTER, we have examined the problem and hope of the Vodou religion in the writings of Laennec Hurbon, Jean Fils-Aimé, and other prominent Protestant leaders and theologians. While both Hurbon and Fils-Aimé have argued that Vodou has inaugurated a paradigm shift in the Haitian life and experience in the modern world, as the Vodou religion, according to their claim, is pervasive in all aspects of the Haitian life. They have also contended that Vodou has contributed enormously to the emancipation and independence of the Haitian people in the era of slavery and colonial rule in Saint-Domingue. What's often missing in their argument is the contemporary utilization of the Haitian Vodou in the Haitian society as a means to deal effectively with the social problems and political ills of the country; they have not demonstrated the possibility of Vodou to effectuate radical change in Haiti's current state of poverty, high unemployment, illiteracy, and economic independence on the United States and the international community such as France, Canada, Germany, Dominican Republic, World Bank, etc. In other words, these Haitian thinkers have undermined the use of religion in making social change and instilling in the Haitian people a life and existence marked by future possibilities and optimism.

In this final chapter, we bring Jean-Bertrand Aristide in the conversation, as he himself accentuates the use of the Christian religion and its resources to deal adequately with the social problems in contemporary Haitian society and to address affectively the plight of Haitian poverty and alienation. For Aristide, the Christian understanding of God as Liberator and God of the Poor may provide the remedy to respond in solidarity with the Haitian poor, the outcast, the disinherited, and the underprivileged Haitian families. Aristide has summoned us to participate in the plight of the poor and the oppressed through a life of service, self-giving, and commitment to their welfare. Aristide envisions holistic change and transformation through the use of both Christian resources and non-religious potentials and resources.

Consequently, this final chapter of the book argues that Aristide's theology of the poor should be construed as a robust theology of relationality; it calls for an ethics of participation and collaboration in the plight of the poor. In this sense, we situate Aristide's theological discourse not only in the liberation theology framework but also in the politico-theological and democratic tradition, what Douglass Sturm has termed "a politics of relationality."[1] A theology of relationality focuses on the horizontal relations between the poor and the theologian-activist. The horizontal aspect defines and shapes the ethics of democratic participation and collaboration by cultivating a dynamic alliance with the poor and fostering genuine bond between the poor and theologian-activist. Hence, a theology of relationality promotes democratic values, rights, freedom, and the welfare of the oppressed and poor. This participatory approach to theology of liberation might be the zone for active collaboration with the collective poor, oppressive communities, and Third World countries.

Jean-Bertrand Aristide's felicitous Haitian Creole explosive declaration "*Tout Se Moun*" refers to the self-evident and egalitarian principle that "Everyone is a Person." Everyone matters in Aristide's theological inquiry including the poor and those living in the margins of modernity. This essay examines the concept of "the poor" in Aristide's theological discourse and explores Aristide's theology of relationality. "The poor" not only plays a major role in modern social ethics and modern theological discourse but also an important conceptual category in liberation theology. The phrase is a dominant theme in Aristide's theological discourse and social preaching. He uses the concept both as a rhetorical code and theological trope (or strategy) in his theological imagination—as he expounds on God's relationship with the world and history, and his active engagement with the social and political order. More importantly, the

---

1. Sturm, *Solidarity and Suffering*.

phrase is deployed to elaborate on the God-poor encounter in history and in the biblical narrative. Aristide has given special attention to material poverty as a tragic condition defining the precarious existence and experience of the world's poor.

Prolegomena to a Theology of Relationality and an Ethics of Solidarity and Justice

Current scholarship on Aristide have failed to recognize and engage Aristide's articulation of a theology of relationality rooted in a robust liberating theological anthropology and the radical idea of justice as solidarity based in the biblical narrative.[2] Hallward has wrongly misconstrued Aristide's affirmative and egalitarian principle *tout moun se moun* ("Everybody is a Person")—the idea that everyone matters and that "everyone is endowed with the same essential dignity."[3] Hallward has contended that this particular aspect in Aristide's anthropological vision is not "dependent on any sort of supernatural domain."[4] Further, Hallward portrays Aristide explicitly as a political scientist rather than a theologian-politician whose political worldview and theory are deeply influenced by a particular theological school of thought. I argue that Aristide's Christian anthropology is based on the notion of imago dei, the image of God which humans are said to be created. The idea of imago dei has shaped Aristide's theology of relationality and his Christian commitment to articulate a justice theology of care and solidary with the poor and the oppressed. Accordingly, theological anthropology is dependent on our understanding that God as Trinity is a social or relational being, and as relational beings, human beings are called to fulfill the imago deity in them and that the character of our lives are evolved and developed within the communal matrix of life. As Carol C. Gould states, "Individuals act fundamentally in and through social relations. The individuals are therefore ontologically primary, but the relations among them are also essential aspects of their beings. However, these relations do not exist

---

2. The most important studies on Aristide in the English language are as follows: Dupuy, *Haiti in the New World Order*, and *Prophet and Power*; Hallward, *Damming the Flood*; Wilenz, *Rainy Season*; Greene, *Catholic Church in Haiti*; Fatton, *Haiti's Predatory Republic*; Abbott, *Haiti: A Shattered Nation*; Deibert, *Notes from the Last Testament*.

3. Hallward, *Damming the Flood*, 21.

4. Hallward, *Damming the Flood*, 21.

independently or apart from the individuals who are related. Rather they are all relational properties of these individuals."[5]

Dupuy depicts an Aristide who was hungry for power like his predecessors, and that he "had betrayed the trust and aspirations of the poor majority."[6] He provides a careful analysis of Aristide's liberation theology; yet, his analysis is limited to a Marxist reading of Aristide's political commitment. He fails to notice that Marxism was used simply as a tool of analysis by Latin American liberationist theologians including Aristide. We maintain here that Aristide is not fully committed to Marxism and to historical materialism. His circle of influence incorporates various traditions and schools of thought including the biblical prophetic tradition, liberation theology, postcolonialism, decolonization, etc. Dupuy is unable to see the intersections of Aristide's liberating theological anthropology, the idea of justice as solidary, and relational reciprocity in Aristide's thought. Finally, like Hallward, Fatton does not take Aristide's theological ideologies seriously. He has given scarce attention to the interplay between Aristide's theology of relationality and politics of relationality. By merging these ideas almost as one, Aristide's theology of relationality has substantially influenced his politics of justice as solidarity and social activism on behalf of the poor and those living in the margins of modernity. This essay is an attempt to reframe Aristide's thought and writings as a "theology of relationality" and an "ethics of mutuality and reciprocity," with an emancipative intent.

Evidently, there exists an intellectual gap in contemporary studies on Aristide that neglects an important aspect of Aristide: the intimate relationship between his theology of relationality and politics of relationality. This essay is attempt to correct these grave misunderstandings mentioned above. It also proposes that the kind of relationality Aristide distinctively theologizes is that of liberation and justice as solidarity with the poor. Aristide's theology of relationality and justice as solidarity with the poor, the hungry, and the naked is critically important, as it pertains to the role of theology within the confinement of the public sphere and social order. By considering Aristide's thought on this important subject and the existential issues mentioned above, contemporary Christians and churches will be able to develop a theology of care, sacrificial giving, and justice as solidarity—considering the plight of the poor, the

---

5. Gould, *Rethinking Democracy*, 105.
6. Dupuy, *Prophet and Power*, 165.

orphans, the immigrant, and the life condition of the outcast and the disheartened in their own communities. For example, in his excellent text, *Generous Justice: How God's Grace Makes Us Just*, Timothy Keller makes several important remarks about how contemporary Christian culture and churches in North America and Western societies generally have continued to nurture a life that disregards social justice and concern for the poor and the needy.[7] They have also failed to establish and cultivate genuine relationships with them on a human level. Hence, there are many existential reasons for the urgent practice of a theology of relationality in contemporary Christianity. As Keller observes,

> The youth culture in Western countries have imbibed not only an emotional resonance for social justice, but also a consumerism that undermines self-denial and delayed gratification. Popular youth culture in Western countries cannot bring about the broad change of life in us that is required if we are to make a difference for the poor and marginalized. . . . While many young adults have a Christian faith, and also a desire to help people in need, these two things are not actually connected to each other in their lives. They have not thought out the implications of Jesus's gospel for doing justice in all aspects of life. In the twentieth century, the American church divided between the liberal mainline that stressed social justice and the fundamentalist churches that emphasized personal salvation. In the mind of many orthodox Christians, therefore, "doing justice" is inextricably linked with the loss of sound doctrine and spiritual dynamism. When the Spirit enables us to understand what Christ had done for us, the result is life poured out in deeds of justice and compassion for the poor.[8]

Recent research has repeatedly shown that the probability of being poor follows racial, class, ethnic, and gender lines.[9] It is from this perspective Aristide has relentlessly argued that the drama of the life of the poor necessitates God to be in loving solidarity with the poor and earnestly seek their integral liberation. This essay argues that Aristide's theology of

---

7. Keller, *Generous Justice*.
8. Keller, *Generous Justice*, x–xiii.
9. Recent studies on global poverty, social inequality, and economic disparity in the United States include this impressive selected list: Piketty, *Capital in the Twenty-First Century*; Sachs, *End of Poverty*; Collier, *Bottom Billion*; Sen, *Development as Freedom*; Wilson, *Declining Significance of Race*, and *When Work Disappears*; Rank, *One Nation, Underprivileged*; Petrella, *Beyond Liberation Theology*.

the poor should be construed as a robust theology of relationality; it calls for an ethics of participation and collaboration in the plight of the poor. In this sense, we situate Aristide's theological discourse not only in the liberation theology framework but also in the politico-theological and democratic tradition, what Douglass Sturm has termed "a politics of relationality." Because we perceive a strong correlation between a theology of relationality and a politics of relationality, we reference some of Sturm's ideas in his excellent study, *Solidarity and Suffering: Toward a Politics of Relationality* to help us articulate an ethics of relational reciprocity and communal collaboration. This rapport is also valuable for us since Jean-Bertrand Aristide worked/works primarily as a theologian-politician; subsequently, the merging of his politics and theology is inevitable in his thought and life of liberation.

At the heart of the politics of relationality is a "principle of justice as solidarity."[10] By the political, we refer to fundamental idea, basic structure and content of our interaction and engagement with other individuals, as Sturm remarks, "Which may or may not assume the character of a power struggle. They key political question is not so much, who gets what, when, where, and how? As it is, how shall we live our live together? Politics is the designed structure of our togetherness."[11] Sturm defines the politics of relationality as a "form of communitarian theory . . . a communitarianism that is consistent with a robust pluralism and an inclusive public forum whose aim is the conjunctive participation of us all in a unity of adventure."[12]

The politics of relationality, when perceived rightly and practiced with gentleness, kindness, and mutual respect (or respect of other), could be a remedy even a threat to human annihilation, solitude, and isolation. In the same vein, a theology of relationality, when practiced rightly with the poor and the needy in mind, could potentially be a threat to social injustice, the life of meaningless and anxiety, which arguably defines modern societies and human interactions in the West.

Sturm defines outlines the principle of relationality in these words. First, he observes that "the principle of relationality within whose dynamics life is a continuous dialectic between participation and individuation provides us with an alternative that is more fitting given the urgent needs

---

10. Sturm, *Solidarity and Suffering*, 7.
11. Sturm, *Solidarity and Suffering*, 211.
12. Sturm, *Solidarity and Suffering*, 15.

of our time."[13] Second, "Our identity is determined in no small part by the coming together of all these relationships. We are, in this sense, members of each other, located on a grid that is in constant motion, that extends far and wide, embracing an entire ecosphere."[14] Third, "We are participants in the community of life as it is configured at this historical moment and cannot be adequately understood independently of that community."[15] Fourth, "Each of us, on the other hand, is, to some degree and within some circle of influence, a creative agent, making our own way through the concourse of these interrelationships. We do something with our inheritance. We place our own individual stamp on the flow of life."[16] Finally, he asserts, "the dialectic between participation and individuation is, within this worldview, a constant of our life. But the quality of that dialectic is not a constant, it is a matter susceptible to manipulation and transformation. The quality of relations may be refined or impaired; it may be redirected or radically altered.[17]

A theology of relationality focuses on the horizontal or rhizomic relations between the poor and the theologian-activist. The horizontal aspect of theology defines and shapes the ethics of democratic participation and collaboration by cultivating a dynamic alliance with the poor and fostering genuine bond between the poor and theologian-activist. Hence, a theology of relationality promotes democratic values, rights, freedom, and the welfare of the oppressed and poor. This participatory approach to theology of liberation might be the zone for active collaboration with the collective poor, oppressive communities, and Third World countries.

My argument is that Aristide articulates a theology of relationality rooted in the idea of (biblical) justice as solidarity (with the poor). For him, true justice is to be in companionship with the poor, which entails an ethics of rights and ethics of care. That is, to avenge their rights and defend their cause. As Yahweh proclaims himself to be "Father of the fatherless and protector of widows."[18] God is the defenders of the poor, the vulnerable, and the outcast in our midst. He is "who executes justice for

---

13. Sturm, *Solidarity and Suffering*, 231–32.
14. Sturm, *Solidarity and Suffering*, 231–32.
15. Sturm, *Solidarity and Suffering*, 231–32.
16. Sturm, *Solidarity and Suffering*, 231–32.
17. Sturm, *Solidarity and Suffering*, 231–32.
18. Ps 68:5.

the oppressed, who gives food to the hungry. The Lord sets the prisoners free; the Lord opens the eyes of the blind. The Lord lifts up those who are bowed down; the Lord loves the righteous. The Lord watches over the sojourners; he upholds the widow and the fatherless, but the way of the wicked he brings to ruin."[19] This biblical tradition that informs Aristide's theology of relationality and life, and an ethics of care for the poor and the needy is amplified in God's character and relationship with the oppressed of the world: "The LORD your God . . . defends the cause of the fatherless and the widow, and loves the immigrant, giving him food and clothing."[20]

Working within this tradition, Aristide postulates that genuine theology must engage the social order and fosters social change. A theology of relationality seeks to remedy the problem of individual and collective alienation. In other words, the kind and quality of relationality we cultivate may reduce greatly the level of individual and communal solitude and social annihilation. As Sturm puts it, "In Stressing our dependency on that nexus of relationships that constitutes our matrix and that is part and parcel of our very selves, I do not mean to detract from our creativity. What each of us feels, what each of us thinks, what of us does make a difference in the world."[21] The poor, the needy, and the immigrant live a life of intense suffering—which includes discomfort, alienation, annihilation, deprivation), and "in large part, that suffering is a consequence, directly or indirectly, of patterns of human interaction."[22] As Aristide himself observes, "A person is a human being through other people. People become persons through the community. A person is a human being when he or she treats others well."[23]

Sturm defines a politics of relationality as a "form of communitarian theory . . . a communitarianism that is consistent with a robust pluralism and an inclusive public forum whose aim is the conjunctive participation of us all in a unity of adventure." In Aristide's politico-theology of relationality, the singular attention is given to the community of the poor, the needy, and the oppressed, in which the faith community and the state work collaboratively and actively to engage scrupulously the social order,

19. Ps 146:7–9.
20. Deut 10:17–18.
21. Stum, *Solidarity and Suffering*, 10.
22. Stum, *Solidarity and Suffering*, 8.
23. Aristide, *Haïti-Haitii*, 19.

which may also involve economic relations and development in order to promote and sustain justice as solidarity. Aristide's politico-theological of relationality and ethics of life and care emphasize justice, compassion. It confronts the entire life of the human life and community and more particularly, every aspect of the life of the poor community. This basic principle engages social and structural oppression, and is against forces, ideologies, powers, movements that exploit the poor if not annihilate them from the social life. This particular philosophy is a commitment to life.

Relationship is the essence of the Christian faith and the idea that members of the Christian community—the body of Christ—belong together and share a life in common in Christ. This principle is articulated as Jesus establishes in precise terms the relational aspect of the central message of the law and the prophets: ""You shall love the Lord your God with all your heart and with all your soul and with all your mind. This is the great and first commandment. And the second is like it: You shall love your neighbor as yourself."[24] The Christian life is a life relations and relational reciprocity.

Aristide contends that the exodus event was the pivotal manifestation of "God's preferential option for the poor," in which Yahweh had made himself known clearly as "the Slave God" who had rescued the enslaved Israelites from Egyptian oppression and pharaonic imperialism. In the same line of thought, Aristide posits that the irruption of the kingdom of God on the human scene through the messianic work and charismatic leadership of Jesus was a watershed moment for the poor and the wretched of the earth. Jesus intended his revolutionary message and social preaching exclusively for the poor and the oppressed, which shows God's taking sides with the most weak and the marginalized in history. Aristide underscores that God's commitment to be in solidarity with the most vulnerable and the most excluded in the world is intentional and based on his unmerited love graciously extended to them.[25] Yet, Aristide clarifies that God's option for the poor does not "mean an option against the rich. . . . The preferential option for the poor is preferential, not exclusive."[26]

24. Matt 22:36–40.

25. The idea of God's commitment to the poor and the oppressed are explored in Aristide, *Jean-Bertrand Aristide Presents Toussaint Louverture*; *In the Parish of the Poor*; and *Autobiography*.

26. Aristide, *Jean-Bertrand Aristide Presents Toussaint Louverture*, xxiii; Aristide, *In the Parish of the Poor*, 68.

To provide a sense of intellectual orientation to the reader, below I summarize five general themes characterized Aristide's theology of the poor. Foremost, Aristide makes the theological claim that poverty is a crisis of faith. This assertion is based on Aristide's deep moral conviction that poverty is an evil to God the Liberator; as a result, God deliberately seeks the integral liberation of the poor and the oppressed whose lives have been dehumanized by poverty. Seeing poverty as a theological conundrum, Aristide has called our attention to the biblical text in Proverbs, "Whoever oppresses a poor man insults his Maker, but he who is generous to the needy honors him."[27] In other words, while those who exploit the poor commit a grave sin against God of the oppressed, those who favor the poor make a preferential option for the needy. Second, Aristide argues that poverty is an unacceptable human condition which reduces the poor to nonbeings. Therefore, being in solidarity with the poor in their suffering entails a theology of rationality and ethics of compassion. Third, Aristide traces poverty in the modern world and the intolerable state leading people in being poor and oppressed to transatlantic slavery and colonialism. He underscores that slavery and colonialism as forms of oppression and social evils exploited the production of the enslaved workers and colonial subjects. Like the master, the colonialist became exceedingly rich through the economic exploitation of the laborers; like slavery, colonization demonized people, produced social death and objectification, and ultimately reduced them to nonbeings. The exploitation is double: economic and ideological. In the context of colonization, Achille Mbembe remarks:

> Of the subject of the colony, he or she is nothing but an appearance. He/ she has a body. The colonizer can seize, harass, lock up the native, compel forced labor, make him or her pay taxes or serve as cannon fodder. . . . The colonized belongs to the *universe of immediate things*—useful things when needed, things that can be molded and are mortal, futile and superfluous things, if need be. . . . To colonize is to put the two-faceted movement of destroying the creation, creation to create, and destroying to destroy.[28]

The unholy trinity of neocolonialism, global capitalism, and modern slavery as forms of oppressive structures and systems treat the poor

27. Prov 14:31.
28. Mbembe, *On the Postcolony*, 186–89.

and international workers as objects and commodities, what Aristide has phrased rightly "a market exchange, and a human exchange."[29] Aristide interrogates the very logic of globalization and capitalism. He argues that as transnational schemes or systems, they make false promises to people and poor nations and failed to carry out those promises. Notably, he remarks, "Globalization, the integration of world markets, has promised to 'lift all boats,' rich and poor, to bring a global culture of entertainment and consumer goods to everyone—the promise of material happiness."[30]

The final characteristic of the poor as a conceptual category in Aristide's thought is articulated as a theological claim; it is originated in his interpretation of the irruption of the kingdom of God on the human scene through the mediatorial works of Jesus. Aristide puts for the idea that the messianic vision and intervention of Jesus was emancipative and designed to bring integral liberation to the poor Jews and Gentiles who had been oppressed by Imperial Roman and the Jewish religion (Judaism). He links Jesus' preaching of a "Gospel of Liberation" to the poor with the exodus narrative in which Yahweh's revolutionary move in history to deliver a colonial subject (the Hebrew slaves) from Egyptian bondage. Israel's Deity and Jesus his Messiah are clearly portrayed as anti-imperial, anti-colonial, and anti-oppression, and anti-oppression. It is from this angle that Aristide reconstructs and reappropriates both the exodus event and Jesus' liberative message in the context of the Haitian poor majority and the marginalized peasants. Yahweh the God of the Slaves then became *le Dieu pauvre* of the Haitian poor, and the Haitian people became the people of God. Hence, Haiti is "the land" of God's people, the poor. Aristide's intellectual precision and exercise can be conceived as a form of political theology. Aristide's political theology is chiefly narrated in his book *Theologie et politique*.[31] The reenactment of the exodus in the context of the Haitian reality is clear and deliberate in Aristide's political theology.[32]

> We are working among a people who believe deeply in God. So we create an approach that does not reject their faith. Our work is rooted in this faith and the faith illuminates the experience. We are building a community of faith. And because of this

---

29. Aristide, *Eyes of the Heart*, 10.
30. Aristide, *Eyes of the Heart*, 10.
31. See Aristide, *Théologie et politique*.
32. Aristide, *Eyes of the Heart*, 65.

we can go quickly.... The struggle is transcendent; it crosses borders of time and place. As the Exodus is transcendent, we are ever crossing the desert, moving from Egypt to the Promised Land.

Giving our emphasis on Aristide's politico-theological of relationality, this essay also explores the meaning of and various ways Aristide employs the concept of "the poor" as a rhetorical and theological motif or category in his theology. It also considers how the phrase is linked to an existential condition, chiefly poverty. Aristide's theological imagination and his engagement with the poor and oppressed are rooted in three complementary traditions: the Biblical Prophetic Tradition, Prophetic Tradition of Liberation Theology, and Black Atlantic Radical Tradition. Aristide's theology of relationality is always in conversation with the poor, the needy, the outcast, and the oppressed. It engages their life condition and refuses to exclude them from the political and theological life.

In the first part of the essay, we explore briefly some important historical accounts that lead us to the conclusion that Jean-Bertrand Aristide should be considered as the "Theologian of the Haitian poor." The second part of the essay explores the relationship between the poor and poverty as an existential condition in Aristide's thought. Aristide is deliberate when he posits that the poor are made poor because poverty exists as a devastating form of human oppression; it threatens human existence and our pursuit of shalom and integral liberation. Working in the tradition of liberation theology, Aristides contends that the oppressed community and the outcast of this world are victims of historical oppression and poverty as a painfully inflicting-human tragedy with a multifaceted aspect. The final section of the essay is a careful study of the relationship between Aristide's theology of the poor, politics of relationality, and theology of relationality. Aristide's politico-theology of relationality considers the oppressed community and suggests that we should come together with a sense of participation, collaboration, responsibility, and the conviction that everyone counts. For the reader who is not familiar with the name Jean-Bertrand Aristide—our subject of inquiry—and his writings, I shall provide a brief account of his entrance into Haiti's political scene.

Aristide: The Theologian of the (Haitian) Poor

After the fall of the hereditary Duvalier regime in February 1986, Jean Bertrand Aristide became the first democratically elected liberationist theologian-president of the Caribbean nation of Haiti (and perhaps in the Americas) in the free elections of December 16, 1990, with an overwhelmingly vote by the majority of the Haitian population. Aristide's prophetic political vision and revolutionary theology of liberation had contributed enormously to a promising democratic future and social transformation in Haiti. Participatory democracy, justice and social equality for the poor marked Aristide's presidential campaign rhetoric and strategy. His early presidency was also marked by active social interaction with the poor and political activism on behalf of the general masses. With the tremendous support of the ecclesiastical grassroots movement known as *Ti Legliz* ("Little Church") and Haiti's underclass majority, Aristide was able to foster and articulate an alternative vision of Haitian politics and civil society which was post-dictatorial, post-macoutism (a reference to Duvalier's military regimes and Haitian totalitarianism), anti-imperialist, and anti-oppression. Aristide was deeply influenced by the ideas and promises of liberation theology.

Aristide employed liberation theology as a mechanism to mobilize the Haitian poor and the underclass workers and peasants. The tenets of liberation theology facilitated a wide range of future possibilities for the president-theologian; the historic movement of liberation theology in Haiti resurrected a people who were seeking for life, hope, and guidance. As Aristide himself states:

> What weds the movement within the Church to the movement within Haitian society as a whole is liberation theology, which has filtered into the youth of our country, which invigorates them, which purifies their blood.... It is liberation theology that is lifting our children up against a corrupt generation, against a mentality of the Church and the society which sees corruption as the comfortable norm.[33]

Haitian liberation theology may orient us to an understanding of human history as a dialectic between alienation and solidarity and the possibility of creating collaboratively a quality of social interaction conducive to the flourishing of a vibrant community of life across Haiti and the world.[34]

Jean-Bertrand Aristide was born poor and black in July 15, 1953, in Port-Salut, a poor village in the south of Haiti. As a seminary student, he

33. Aristide, *Eyes of the Heart*, 15; Wilenz, *Rainy Season*, 113.
34. Sturm, *Solidary and Suffering*, 11.

distinguished himself academically and intellectually. He went to study aboard and completed doctoral work in biblical studies in Israel as well as in psychology in Canada. Aristide holds a PhD in literature and philosophy from the University of South Africa, an MA in biblical theology from the University of Montreal, and a BA in psychology from Haiti State University. He is a prolific writer and eloquent speaker.

Aristide was ordained a Catholic priest on July 3, 1982. A proponent of liberation theology and a prophet, he was the priest of St. Jean Bosco Catholic Church. As an eyewitness explained,

> Father's Aristide Sunday masses were attended by thousands of the Haitian black poor who lived in nearby La Saline, one of the slums in the capital. His sermons were broadcast across the country on Radio Soleil, Catholic Church radio. The slightly built priest would remind his parishioners of the Haitian proverb *Tout moun se moun* (every human being is a human being), instantly transforming the deliberating pain of his individual parishioners into a galvanizing new summons to purpose for millions of the poor.[35]

In various instances, Aristide had escaped several assassination attempts by the Haitian army and militia who tried to murder him for his radical philosophy and preferential option for the poor. Eventually, in 1987, Aristide was removed from the Salesian Order for using his pulpit to preach politics and liberation theology, which challenged the Catholic Hierarchy in Haiti. He became the first democratically elected President of Haiti on December 16, 1990. Aristide's victory was a victory for the Haitian poor, the general masses, and for the country that had been oppressed by years of dictatorship and social violence. As Aristide explains,

> The emergence of the people as an organized public force, as a collective consciousness, was already taking place in Haiti in the 1980's, and by the 1986 this force was strong enough to push the Duvalier dictatorship from power. It was a grassroots popular movement, and not at all a top down project down by a single leader of a single organization. It wasn't an exclusively political movement, either. It took shape, above all, through the constitution, all over the country, in many small church communities or *ti legliz*. It was these small communities that played the decisive historical role.[36]

---

35. Robinson, *Unbroken Agony*, 29.
36. Robinson, *Unbroken Agony*, 32.

Alex Dupuy states that "Aristide had emerged as the single most important symbol of resistance to the ignominious, larcenous, and barbaric neo-Duvalierist dictatorships" in Haiti.[37] Peter Hallward reasons, "If in 1986–87 Father Jean-Bertrand Aristide emerged as the leading figure in the popular mobilization it is because he understood the nature and depth of this antagonism as clearly as other members of the *peuple* ('the people') themselves."[38] Robert Patton argues that Aristide entered the political race to "stop reactionary forces from legitimizing their continued hold on privilege and to empower the marginalized poor majority."[39] It is good to note here, after his ordination as a priest in July 1982, Aristide had already shown concern for Haiti's marginalized poor majority uncommon among Haiti's ruling classes by establishing *Lafanmi Selavi* ("Family is Life"), a foster home for homeless orphans and street children.[40] Aristide's historic entrance into Haiti's politics was a challenge to Haiti's bourgeois class, the oppressive Church hierarchy, the international community (i.e., United States, Canada, France, England, etc.); nonetheless, the Aristide turn in Haitian politics symbolized promises of hope, democracy, equality, inclusion, as well as a better future for the poor majority in the nation and the opportunity for the nation's underclass people to integrate fully into the mainstream society. Aristide's historic candidacy and ultimately Presidency was a powerful statement on behalf of the suffering Haitian masses.

The force of Aristide's theology of resistance and theological sensibility had allowed him to inspire sustaining hope and prophetic faith to the Haitian people in their struggle against abject poverty, despair, social injustice and evils, political totalitarianism, and oppression. Jean-Bertrand Aristide presented himself as a theologian of the poor and a theologian of hope correspondingly to the community of faith in Haiti and those living in the margins of modernity.

One of the most historic moments and most compassionate sociopolitical actions in Haitian politics occurred during Jean-Bertrand Aristide's first presidency. The liberationist theologian-president held a banquet at the Presidential "Palais National" (the "National Palace") and invited the poor in the slums across the country, street children, street

---

37. Dupuy, *Haiti in the New World Order*, 72.
38. Hallward, *Damming the Flood*, 19.
39. Fatton, *Haiti's Predatory Republic*, 77.
40. Girard, *Haiti: The Tumultuous History*, 117–18.

vendors and merchants, beggars, and factory workers, as well as the peasant majority who heard him on Radio Haiti-Inter and Radio Soleil, and those living in the "popular zones" in the capital city (Port-au-Prince) to dine with him and Haiti's highest governmental officials. Aristide's gesture of solidarity with the poor was symbolic; the Haitian poor majority were treated with the highest human dignity and incredible worth as important and equal citizens in Haiti's civil society and culture. As Aristide himself remarks, "The simple fact of allowing ordinary people to enter the palace, the simple fact of welcoming people from the poorest sections of Haitian society with in the very center of traditional power—this was a profoundly transformative gesture."[41] Aristide's radical action made a substantial impact on the national conscience. Nonetheless, it was Aristide's radical philosophy and preferential option for the scandalous poor that would lead to two coups d'état during his presidency.

By opening the gates of the National Palace to the poor and holding a "banquet of the poor"—as he called it—Aristide went in public to acknowledge the significant role of Haiti's underclass in making important political decisions for their country. The poor are agents of and shapers of history. Aristide defines the meaning of democracy and a politics of inclusion in the following words:

> Women, children and the poor must be the subjects, not the objects of history. They must sit at the decision-making tables and fill the halls of power. They must occupy the radio and airwaves, talking to and calling to account their elected leaders. Their participation will democratize democracy, bringing the word back to its full meaning: *Demos* meaning people, *Cratei* meaning to govern.[42]

The misery endured by Haitian poor majority made a profound impression on the liberationist theologian-president. In his politico-theological writings, Aristide presents himself as the champion of the cause of the poor and the voice of the voiceless. Aristide's "preferential option for the poor" led to "the unfolding of the connecting thread of a theological view which surely brings one back to the one God, that of the excluded, manipulated by the more privileged to maintain an ancestral domination of the poor."[43] Amy Wilentz reports that "like other Lib-

---

41. Robinson, *Unbroken Agony*, 31.
42. Aristide, *Eyes of the Heart*, 41.
43. Dupuy, *Haiti in the New World Order*, 72.

eration theologians in Latin America, who use Jesus' teachings to raise the political consciousness of the poor, Aristide tried to make connections between the struggle of the Haitian people for freedom and what liberation theologians see as the struggle of Jesus for the liberation of Jerusalem."[44] Christopher Wargny makes a poignant observation about Aristide's intimate relationship with the Haitian poor:

> His abiding and exclusive concern for the marginal, what liberation theologians call the preferential option for the poor, has changed him into a spokesperson for the dammed of the earth—the eighty percent in Haiti who live below the threshold of absolute poverty.... He has slowly built up a power without any structure, alongside a great many structures that are utterly lacking in power.[45]

It is good to note here in September 1991, just seven months after Aristide's inauguration, supported by the United States government, Canada, France, the resentful Haitian bourgeois class overthrew Aristide in a bloody military coup. As a result, the abrupt demise of Aristide's political party (*Lavalas*) and Haitian prophetic liberation theology movement—that was made up of various ecclesial-base communities—ended. For some individuals, Aristide's overview occurred because of his closeness to the poor and those longing for change who had voted for him. Furthermore, it is also reported that the army, police, and militia terrorized the country and Aristide's supporters, and those who were supporters of liberation theology.

> About 5,000 people were murdered and 400,000 went into hiding. Civil liberties, press freedom, trade unions, and peasant organizations gave way to censorship and military dictatorship under civilian puppets. To force the putschists to relinquish power, the United Nations and the Organization of American States imposed an economic embargo on Haiti. Trade sanctions did little to dislodge the military leadership and their allies, who obtained their merchandise through contraband from the Dominican Republic. Worse, these sanctions had the unintended effect of further worsening the economic conditions and health problems of the impoverished Haitians. Exiled in Caracas,

---

44. Wilentz, *Rainy Season*, 112.
45. Aristide, *Autobiography*, 7.

Venezuela, and in Washington, D.C., Aristide tirelessly searched for a political accord that would reinstate him to power.[46]

After several years in exile, on October 15, 1994, Aristide returned to Haiti to resume his Presidency. Elected president in 2000, Aristide was again deposed four years later by former members of the disbanded army, sponsored by Haiti's business class, Canada, France, and the United States government. Aristide stated that he was abducted with his wife to a French military base in Central African Republic and then to South Africa where he found refuge. Similar to the 1991 coup, Haiti returned to illegality. Harsh political reprisals were carried out against the poor, Aristide's supporters, and government officials.

On March 17, 2011, Aristide left South Africa for Haiti. The permission was granted to him by the new elected Haitian president Michel Joseph Martelly and the international community. Aristide arrived in Port-au-Prince on Friday, March 18, 2011; he was warmly greeted by the Haitian people and the former *Lavalas* supporters who had been waiting impatiently for his return. Currently, Aristide's future engagement in Haiti's political is unknown to many. However, some have recently argued that his political party would participate in Haiti's future presidential elections. It is good to point out here, at the departure of Aristide, the Haitian liberation theology movement had lost the major influence it once enjoyed in Haitian politics and civil society; however, various grassroots and popular movements had emerged since Aristide's return to Haiti. These movements are non-church-affiliated or related.

To move our conversation forward, it is noteworthy to inform the reader that current scholarship on Jean-Bertrand Aristide has focused exclusively on his political life and Aristide as a politician. Evidently, there exists an intellectual void that neglects an important aspect of the man—his theological vision and imagination, and how his theology has influenced his politics and social activism on behalf of the Haitian poor and peasants, as well as those living in the margins of modernity. Subsequently, our chief goal in this essay is to study precisely Jean-Bertrand Aristide as a theologian and not as a politician. This approach will allow us to explore more directly and fully Aristide's theological discourse as a theology of the poor, resulting in a better understanding and appreciation of him among the theologians and social activists. Hence, this present essay intends to be a theological reflection on Aristide's deployment of "the

---

46. Florival, "Haiti's Troubles," 179.

poor" as a concept, with some implications for social transformation and social activism.

Poverty as an Existential and Theological Crisis

A clear understanding of Aristide's theological method will assist us in discovering the precise meaning of "the poor" as a rhetorical device and conceptual category. Two factors are fundamental in Aristide's theological method: the sociopolitical reality of the written Word (the Bible) and the social context of theological method and interpretation. First, Aristide establishes the dynamics between biblical exegesis and theological discourse, and the *Sitz im leben* that shape both phenomena. In other words, all theological methods, conceptualizations or formulas, and theological traditions are social constructs. Aristide presupposes that theological reflection must first begin with a critical and responsible evaluation of the life condition of the poor and the phenomenon of poverty as a harassing social reality.

Aristide reasons that if the Word of God was proclaimed in a particular social context and that God revealed himself exclusively to the poor, then it is an imperative that the social world of the poor must be the litmus test of the liberation theologian and true theology. Aristide posits that the Bible is God's good news to the poor and the marginalized; more than ever a message of liberation, it proclaims loudly liberty for those who are oppressed and those who are deprived of it.[47]

Aristide proposes two theoretical formulations. He called the first one "the presence of a theological consciousness" as the first act of theology; he phrased the second one as the event of "theological reflection" as the second act of theological thinking. The former makes sense only within human reality—that is the everyday experience of men and women. Hence, there is a sense one can speak of theological emancipative praxis as the necessary result or ingredient of a robust theological consciousness and rigorous theological reflection.

> The reality of infra-human misery described previously is the first act from which emerges the second act, which we call theological reflection. Far from being abstract, it is an articulated

---

47. Aristide, *Autobiography*, 51, 53.

response directed to social and political reality, here and now. This approach is within the biblical tradition.[48]

The cultivation of a critical theological imagination is imperative in the constructive stage of a liberative theological method. For Aristide, liberation of theology is rooted in a deliberate theological awareness of the existential condition of the poor and the oppressed, and thinking theologically from the perspective of the poor describes the very task of liberation theology. Almost in the same line of thought, Gutierrez communicates a parallel view:

> Discourse about God comes second because faith comes first and is the source of theology. . . . The first stage or phase of theological work is the lived faith that finds expression in prayer and commitment. To live the faith means to put into practice, in the light of the demands of the reign of God. . . . The second act of theology, that of reflection in the proper sense of the term, has for its purpose to read this complex praxis in the light of God's word.[49]

Leonardo Boff and Clodovis Boff find a way to bring together theological method and theological praxis in the process of liberation:

> Before we can do theology we to "do" liberation. The first step for liberation theology is pre-theological. It is a matter of trying. It is a matter of trying to live the commitment of faith: to participate in some way in the process of liberation, to be committed to the oppressed. . . . So first we need to have direct knowledge of the reality of oppression/liberation through objective engagement in solidarity with the poor.[50]

What Aristide calls "a presence of theological consciousness," the Boffs name "pre-theological," and Gutierrez, "the lived faith that finds expression in prayer and commitment" (or "reflection" in the proper sense of the term); these three ideas complement each other in the theological work of liberation and the liberation of theology. This liberating task works concurrently with the active commitment to be in living solidarity with the poor and the oppressed. It is from this particular worldview that Aristide articulates these words of admonition: "The orientation of the theological thought must involve this point of engagement and

48. Aristide, *Nevrose vetero-testamentaire*, 108.
49. Gutierrez, *Theology of Liberation*, xxxiii–xxiv.
50. Boff and Boff, *Introducing Liberation Theology*, 22–23.

thus avoid any attempt to flee its responsibility."[51] Moreover, Aristide contrasts the theological methods and approaches of two dominant theological schools or systems: traditional theology (Western theology) and liberation theology. The concentric target and subjects of interest of each theological tradition differ greatly from each other.

Traditional theology and liberation theology insinuate themselves with different ways of doing theology or/and thinking theologically. Theologians working in these traditions have articulated competing discourses dealing with theological doctrines, sociopolitical and cultural issues, and other phenomena such as God, Jesus, sin, redemption, humanity, history, human systems, identity, race, gender, sexuality, poverty, human suffering and oppression, economics, wealth, and the social and political order. For example, according to Aristide, Traditional theology gives special attention to the Christian and the Atheist. It seeks a way to explain the revealed truths, as interpreted as so. The methodology of traditional theology its methodology relies heavily on the philosophy of Aristotle and Aquinas. Traditional theology tends to evoke a God falls from the sky for the salvation of man.[52] By contrast, liberation theology gives special attention to the oppressed, the rejected, the exploited, the marginalized, the *anawims* of Yahweh, and the human person who is reduced to a mere object and trash. In this school of thought, the preferential option for the poor—without any pretension to exclude the rich—is valorized and central. Liberation theology begins with the human experience (from below), the praxis of the poor (the privileged theological site) to discover the face of God revealed in Jesus, the true prototype of man.[53]

The consensus among liberation theologians is that modern theology "has been a class-bound discipline of interest primarily to the bourgeois, middle-class audience which had been chiefly responsible for fostering the Enlightenment in the first place."[54] In other words, traditional theologians put the poor and the oppressed in the back seat in their lofty theological discourse and reasoning. By contrary, liberationist theology maintains that the true subjects of Christian theology are not the educated bourgeoisie, but the uneducated poor, the marginalized, the social outcast who have been made nonpersons by the forces of a

---

51. Aristide, *Nevrose vetero-testamentaire*, 108.
52. Aristide, *Nevrose vetero-testamentaire*, 108–9.
53. Aristide, *Nevrose vetero-testamentaire*, 108–10.
54. Rubenstein, "Political Significance of Latin American Liberation Theology," 43.

bourgeois-capitalist order and repressive structures of neocolonialism and neo-imperialism.[55]

Liberation theology rejects bourgeois Christianity and the socially class-ordered society that oppresses the poor and those living in the margins of modernity. Jose Miguez-Bonino describes liberation theology as a new theological discourse that was born in a new post-bourgeois Christianity in the struggle to find meaning and construct a postbourgeois society in the world.[56] Aristide underscores that the goal of the liberationist theologian is therefore to muster up the courage "to reject the reign of injustice established through time. . . . This process reserves a special place for the poor"[57] and to construct an ethics of liberation.

Summarizing the main tenets of liberation theology, Aristide reiterates that as an enterprise, liberation theology rejects any system of sin such as capitalism and neocolonialism and a conception of the reign of God without dichotomy: the above and the below, the profaned and the sacred, the spiritual and temporal. Similarly, liberation theology as a prophetic sociopolitical movement does not divorce practical faith from the political life while following Jesus. Intellectually, liberation theology is interdisciplinary and cross-sectional in content and form; it draws inspiration from the disciplines of social sciences and humanities and modern social theories.

Elsewhere in an article entitled, "The Church in Haiti—Land of Resistance," Aristide argues that the birth of liberation theology was a "turning point" in human history, in which members of the progressive Church (ecclesial-based communities) opposed the despotic state and the church hierarchy that oppressed the poor.[58] He also explains that, following the Second Vatican Council, with the historic conferences of Catholic Bishops at Medellin, Columbia in 1968, and Puebla, Mexico in 1979, the Catholic Church in Latin America articulated "an ecclesiology from those at the bottom, rising from the world of the poor."[59] From the perspective of this watershed moment, Aristide prioritizes the irruption of the poor in history: "The poor were no more considered the object of charity, but rather, the subject of history. In the voices of the poor,

55. Rubenstein, "Political Significance of Latin American Liberation Theology," 44.
56. Bucher, "Toward a Liberation Theology for the 'Oppressor,'" 520.
57. Aristide, *Nevrose vetero-testamentaire*, 109.
58. For further details, see Aristide, "Church in Haiti," 108–13.
59. Aristide, "Church in Haiti," 110.

theologians learned to discover the voices of God. In the struggle against misery, hunger, exploitation and slavery, they found Jesus Christ."[60] Miguel A. De La Tore is correct to affirm that "the Church of Jesus Christ is called to identity and stand in solidarity with the oppressed. The act of solidarity becomes the litmus test of biblical fidelity and the paradigm used to analyze and judge how social structures contribute to or efface the exploitation of the marginalized."[61]

Aristide explains that liberation theology is a new theology and the search for a new beginning, liberty, democracy, human rights, and a new way of life.[62] Liberation theology also means "the force of solidarity at work, a recognition that we are all striving toward the same goal and that goal is to go forward, to advance, and to bring into this world another way of being."[63] He reinforces that

> liberation theology finds in the Bible a flat rejection of the exclusion of the poor. Jesus answered John the Baptist, "Go and tell John that the good news is preached to the poor" (Matt. 11:5). Henceforth all were compelled to demonstrate a commitment to implementing God's directive: "You will love your neighbor the way you love yourself" (Lev. 19:18). From this it follows that, if you do not want to be a slave, you must not enslave your neighbor. These words from the gospel contains the seeds for the emergence of a new society, in which human relationship are rooted in respect, equality and dignity—a way forward from slavery to freedom, from social exclusion to inclusion.[64]

Aristide's prophetic liberation theology involves an active engagement with critical issues such as human rights, the right of the Haitian marginalized peasants and poor—their right to eat and feed themselves and their children—and the right to life. These rights are fundamental to human existence. Aristide's theology of the poor promotes holistic human care and inclusive democracy. Giving the precarious life of the world's poor and the material deprivation the oppressed community continues to suffer without the fault of their own, Aristide could argue that we must democratize democracy. On the democratization of democracy, Aristide writes, "Democracy asks us to

60. Aristide, "Church in Haiti," 110.
61. De La Tore, *Doing Christian Ethics from the Margins*, 15.
62. Aristide, *In the Parish of the Poor*, 5, 8, 3.
63. Aristide, *In the Parish of the Poor*, 4.
64. Aristide, *Jean-Bertrand Aristide Presents Toussaint Louverture*, xxiii.

put the needs and rights of people at the center of our endeavors. This means investing in people. Investing in people means first of all food, clean water, and education and healthcare. These are basic human rights. It is a challenge of any real democracy to guarantee them."[65] These are the demands of democracy and the idea that justice means the active engagement with the poor in their suffering and pain.

The priest-theologian champions the dignity of the poor by reminding us that "the theology of liberation started from the day-to-day life of the people, seeking to discover the real face of God in their midst, revealed through Jesus Christ present among them."[66] The intellectual and practical role of liberation theology is then to give way to the liberation of traditional theology and to incite collective consciousness on a grassroots popular level. Aristide could also argue that Jesus Christ is the liberator of the oppressed/poor consciousness.

In his short book *Eyes of the Heart*, Aristide explains that globalization as a transcultural and transnational phenomenon. Aristide rejects the idea that globalization means human progress and that it is "an automatic process inherent to natural capitalist dynamics."[67] By contrary, he argues that globalization has become "a machine devouring our planet"[68] and the world's poor and underdeveloped countries are its victims. They are forced to make a choice between life and death. While the First World countries are experiencing rapid economic growth, Third World countries are declining substantially and millions of individuals continue to undergo both social and physical death as a result of dire poverty in the collective and global sense. Aristide insists that globalization is a system that puts the market before the individual; as a system of global order and market exchange, the poor are dumped in zones of social abandonment. Petrella defines the zone of social abandonment as "the place where those who have no one and nothing wait for death—a place in the world for populations of 'ex-humans.' . . . To be dumped like trash is to be socially dead; society declares you dead before your biological death. Insofar as you are socially dead yet biologically alive, you've overextended your lease on life. Your future is dead, yet you live on."[69] In this age of global-

65. Aristide, *Eyes of the Heart*, 35–36.
66. Aristide, *Autobiography*, 110.
67. Petrella, *Beyond Liberation Theology*, 21.
68. Aristide, *Eyes of the Heart*, 6.
69. Petrella, *Beyond Liberation Theology*, 9.

ization and the so-called human progress, the poor face death every day and they lack the means of living and actual opportunities of living.[70]

Aristide recognizes that the magnitude of the global problem of poverty in the world is truly enormous. He defines poverty as a social condition and the consequential result of oppressive systems: "Whether someone is poor or poor of heart because he is the victim of an oppressive system, it remains what he is: poor."[71] He claims that the poor are the ones who are abused, weak, mistrusted. Alone, they are weak; together, they are strong, and together they are the flood.[72] Yet, the poor and the underclass are also forced to live in "a system of social apartheid . . . and face death and death every day."[73] Aristide reports that

> today, as many as two-thirds of the world's population is marginalized because of their social condition. . . . Day after day the poor are becoming poorer. In a clear rupture with the pattern over previous decades, global inequality has increased sharply since the 1980s, while global economic integration has grown. This expansion of extreme poverty coincides with an explosion of wealth. . . . Today the poor still bear the cross of marginalization, racism and misery.[74]

Poverty here is described as a socioeconomic and political dilemma, which makes the world's poor poorer. Furthermore, Aristide traces the historic causes or roots of modern and ongoing poverty and the social stigmatization of the poor to colonialism, transatlantic slavery and capitalism. Aristide also links the abject poverty in the modern world to white violence and oppression, white supremacy, institutionalized racism, and Western imperial hegemony in the world. Poverty is also rooted on the mistreatment and exploitation of a group people, the weakest in society. Having shown that poverty is a crisis of modernity, Aristide describes it in its multilayered dimension:

> Poverty is deeply rooted in colonialism, neoliberalism and globalization. The colonialism project and those who led it prioritized financial capital over human capital; centuries later, neocolonialists remain motivated by this same interest.

---

70. Sen, *Development as Freedom*, 253.
71. Aristide, *Nevrose vetero-testamentaire*, 69.
72. Aristide, *In the Parish of the Poor*, 90, 104.
73. Aristide, *Eyes of the Heart*, 44, 20.
74. Aristide, introduction to *Toussaint L'Ouverture*, xxxiii–xxiv.

For the most part, this motivation, reflects an obsessive whose roots extend back to transatlantic slave trade, a crime against humanity of immense magnitude and incomparable suffering. Institutionalized racism became embedded in Western society; it generated social pathologies and schizophrenic economics in the colonies where slavery flourished.[75]

Poverty is not only a crisis of faith, as Aristide underscores, but it is also a threatening occurrence in the modern life in Western and postcolonial societies. Liberation theologian Gustavo Gutierrez is correct to insist that the poor and the exploited are the crucified people in history; "it is a slow but real death, caused by poverty, so that the poor are those who die before their time."[76] Jon Sobrino speaks of the "Crucified Peoples" in the manner:

> "Crucified Peoples" is useful and necessary language on the factual level. "Cross" means not only poverty but death. And death is what the peoples of the Third World suffer in a thousand ways. . . . It is swift and violent death caused by repression and wars, when the poor decide simply to escape from their poverty and live. And it is indirect but effective death when poor peoples are deprived even of their own cultures, in order to subjugate them, weaken their identity and make them more vulnerable.[77]

How do then oppressed communities and the poor around the globe cope with uninterrupted social deaths and zones of social abandonment? Could they be hopeful? Aristide reasons that the poor are courageous because they maintain their human dignity in the midst of incredible suffering and social evil. In addition, they hang on to life because "We know that the Lord created us in his image."[78] So *the Imago dei* in the poor has enabled them to resist oppression and find existential meaning in God himself. The *Imago dei* is that which gives the poor hope because God is the Champion of the Oppressed; God regards them as equal members in society: "We are poor, it is true, but we are people nonetheless."[79] Aristide prompts us to consider further that the collective poor are bound together under the banner of collective solidarity and a

75. Aristide, *Jean-Bertrand Aristide Presents Toussaint Louverture*, xxviii–xxix.
76. Quoted in Sobrino, *Jesus the Liberator*, 254.
77. Sobrino, *Jesus the Liberator*, 254.
78. Aristide, *In the Parish of the Poor*, 90.
79. Aristide, *In the Parish of the Poor*, 90.

politics of relationality. As individuals, they strive to find creative ways to resist oppression and foster collective hope and create emancipative future possibilities: "Must deprivation, misery, insecurity, and despair find their refuge in resignation, emigration, hatred, or warfare?"[80]

In the sociopolitical and economic context of the Haitian poor and peasants, in a sermon, Aristide identifies the poor generally as the people, the slum-dwellers, poor peasants, poor soldiers, the poor jobless multitudes, the hungry, the masses, the workers, the market women, the street children of the Church, and the powerless.[81] Aristide also employs the Fanonian language, "the wretched of the earth" to identity the non-being, the downtrodden and the marginalized in society.[82] Lamenting on their social condition, he declares, "The experience of the poor, not only in Haiti, but around the world, is a kind of museum of humanity."[83] He moves on to stress that the poor have been affected by "the detritus of the deadly economic infection called capitalism"[84] resulting in material, ideological, structural and historical poverty.

Because material poverty is evil and dehumanizes human beings, resistance is the most natural way subjugated people and nations respond to this form of repressive domination, a relationship between the powerful and the powerless, the oppressor and the oppressed, the colonizer and the colonized. Affirming the economic and political content and nature of poverty, Gutierrez notes that "social classes, nations, and entire continents are becoming aware of their poverty, and when they see its root causes, they rebel against it."[85] As Pierre Bigo comments, poverty is "a phenomenon of migration in every country but the third world as a whole is marginal. Cut loose from its customs by new modes of existence, it still lives on the margin of industrial society. It is not just a poor relation; it is the stranger at the gate."[86] Within the Marxist framework, Enrique Dussel recapitulates in strong metaphorical language the dynamics between the poor and poverty, the rich and the poor, the oppressor and the oppressed:

---

80. Aristide, *Dignity*, 120.
81. Aristide, *Autobiography*, 22, 104–7.
82. Aristide, *Autobiography*, 107.
83. Aristide, *Eyes of the Heart*, 6.
84. Aristide, *Eyes of the Heart*, 5–7.
85. Gutierrez, *Theology of Liberation*, 163.
86. Bigo, *Church and Third World Revolution*, 19–20.

> Poverty is a dialectical concept, embracing several terms which mutually define each other. Just as there is no father without a child, and the child is defined by its father, so the poor are defined by the rich and vice versa. Poverty is in no way a pure case of someone lacking something. . . . The oppressor belongs to very substance of the concept of being poor. There are no poor people without the corresponding rich. Nor is there any absolute poverty in the face of God. There are real poor people in God's sight, since there are real oppressors confronting God, who make the poor what they are: oppressed and lacking their proper possibilities in life, deprived of the product of their work.[87]

To recapitulate our analysis, in the tradition of liberation theology, the poor constitutes a social class, a group whose destitute circumstances are the product not of chance misfortune, but of systematic exploitation and oppression.[88] They are the member of the proletariat struggling for the most basic rights; they are also the exploited and plundered social class. One can also speak of the poor countries struggling for independence and liberation from neocolonial forces. In Aristide's thought, both the collective poor and poor countries struggle for the same goal: human rights, the right to life, and freedom from repressive structures and domination. Victoria Araya posits that not only the poor live in the hard reality of material poverty—what liberation theologians have phrased "a subhuman situation" and "a scandalous condition"—the poor and the oppressed also suffer the unjust burden of real, historical poverty; the poor are truly "the crucified of history, condemned to a slow death before their time by reason of oppressive structures, and a more rapid death by reason of repressive structures."[89]

The collective poor and Third World countries continue to struggle against First World hegemony and neoimperialism in the form of exploitative first-world economic policies. To challenge this global predicament, liberation theologians employ the rhetoric of human rights and democratic freedom to respond to the demands of the oppressed and exploited people in the world. Liberationist action is the only possible action available for the poor and the liberationist theologian. Hence, one could contend that the goal of the liberationist theologian is to critique

---

87. Dussel, *Beyond Philosophy*, 90.
88. Tucker, *Marx-Engels Reader*, 354.
89. Araya, *God of the Poor*, 115.

thoroughly the oppressive social structures and social inequality, which deepen the suffering and poverty of the oppressed. In his useful remark, Araya infers that "if poverty is a destructive, structural, material reality to be fought, and if the poor are poor, not individually but as a collective subject, then the option for the poor leads unfailingly to the world of the political, and to the logic, the reasoning, peculiar to that world."[90] Liberation theologians remind us that God is the God of the Oppressed and, as their Liberator, he has willingly committed to their freedom. Aristide has prompted us to ponder upon the idea that God has a preferential love for the poor and the poor are not individuals being punished by God.[91] Aristide rejects the idea that "the poor are poor because they are stupid"[92] or lazy, as traditionally believed. He also repudiates the belief that "poverty will come from those who are poor"[93] but reminds us that poverty is everyone's struggle who concerns about justice, equality, and a better world.

Aristide insists that poverty is a crisis of faith and modernity has failed the poor and the oppressed. We already stated that he perceives poverty as the result of oppressive capitalist systems, imperial globalization, and economic exploitation and the poor are the victims. Aristide describes *the Sitz in Leben* of this human dilemma and the dynamics between the poor and the sociopolitical order provocatively:

> Behind this crisis of dollars there is human crisis: among the poor, immeasurable human suffering; among the others, the powerful, the policy makers, a poverty of spirit which has made a religion of the market and its invisible hand. A crisis of imagination so profound that the only measure of value is profit, the only measure of human progress is economic growth. We have not reached the consensus that to eat is a basic human right. This is an ethical crisis. This is a crisis of faith.[94]

Poverty is a theological predicament in the sense that it is "an evil and therefore incompatible with the Kingdom of God, which has come in its fullness into history and embraces the totality of human existence."[95]

90. Araya, *God of the Poor*, 23.
91. Gutierrez, *On Job*, 40.
92. Aristide, *Eyes of the Heart*, 20.
93. Aristide, *Eyes of the Heart*, 20–21.
94. Aristide, *Eyes of the Heart*, 6.
95. Gutierrez, *Theology of Liberation*, 168.

Elsa Tamez judges that poverty as a theological conundrum because it challenges "God the Creator; because of the insufferable conditions under which the poor live, God is obliged to fight at their side."[96] Persistent poverty and enduring suffering of the world's poor is the most serious challenge to their belief in the God of love and life. Aristide declares that there is a common consensus on poverty when it comes to addressing the issue from the moral vision of Scriptures, Jesus' gospel of liberation, and liberation theology. He argues that poverty is anti-gospel and inhuman by declaring, "We also know that for Jesus, as it were for the Bishops assembled in Puebla, poverty itself is not desirable. In solidarity with the poor, we condemn as anti-evangelical extreme poverty that affects many social sectors of the continents."[97]

Aristide reiterates that the God of the Poor brings abundant comfort to the oppressed community and is present with them along the way in the struggle. God accompanies the poor in their pilgrimage, allowing them to feel joy throughout their journey and battle for existence. In *Théologie et politique*—an important work on the relationship between faith and politics, and the intersections of theological praxis, politics, and social activism—Aristide is more blunt describing the plight of the global poor and the impoverished majority; he expounds on the puzzling relationships between the oppressed and the oppressor, the exploiter and the exploited:

> Life reveals a politics that does not look for the common good, but which is based on the relations between the exploited and exploiters. The exploiters justify and legalize the exploitation of a majority by a minority. From this human reality emerges a negative force; because it does not respond to the common good and is opposed to justice; there also emerges an opposing force. Hence, we have the strength of a politics in which the weak is exploited by the strong, and the divine power from which the weak rises to restore the balance of justice.[98]

Using Marxism as a tool of analysis and social theory, Aristide highlights the socioeconomic organization of the capitalist order, whereby some (the workers) are subjugated, while others (the peasants, the ordinary people, the suffering masses, the underemployed, and other

---

96. Tamez, *Bible of the Oppressed*, 74.
97. Aristide, *Nevrose vetero-testamentaire*, 68.
98. Aristide, *Théologie et politique*, 17.

marginalized peoples) are excluded from the production altogether. Alex Dupuy echoes that "this exploitation and exclusion result in denying the poor access to adequate food, housing, health care, an education, as well as respect for their personal dignity, self-expression, and freedom."[99]

Liberation theologians tell us that the poor suffer as the collective poor and the popular masses, and their suffering is multilayered and multidimensional. On the social level, the collective poor suffer collective expression, collective exclusion, and collective marginalization. On the cultural level, the culture and traditions of the collective poor are marginalized and ridiculed. On the socioeconomic level, the collective poor are exploited and abused. On the political level, the collective poor are alienated from political decision and right, and have no say in the political future of their country. They are deprived of basic human rights and the right to breathe as members of their own community and human race. On the religious level, the collective poor are victims of social sinfulness and religious oppression, contrary to the plan of God the Liberator and Creator and "the honor that is due to him."[100] Finally, on the psychological/mental level, the collective poor and oppressed community

> internalize the negative image projected upon them by the dominant society. They cower before the masters, but are also filled with a self-contempt which makes them self-destructive and fratricidal toward their fellows within the oppressed community. Typically, the oppressed turn their frustration inward, destroying themselves and each other, not the masters.[101]

While Aristide has given special care to the material aspect of poverty—its socioeconomic frame—he has also defined poverty multidimensionally and insisted that the sufferings and exploitations of the poor and oppressed affect their whole being and shape (and reshape) their existence. His treatment on poverty as an existential human condition has social, cultural, ideological, political, psychological, religious, theological, and gender dimensions or ramifications. To reiterate, Aristide speaks of the "integral liberation" of the oppressed; hence, the "socioeconomic poor," the sociocultural poor, and the new poor of industrial societies who are deprived of basic necessities needed to

---

99. Dupuy, *Prophet and Power*, 79.
100. Boff and Boff, *Introduction to Liberation Theology*, 3.
101. Ruether, *Liberation Theology*, 12.

live a life of dignity also need integral liberation.[102] It is from this context Aristide could invoke and advocate a robust theology of relationality and an ethics of collaboration with the poor.

Toward a Theology of Relationality for the Poor

What is then the relationship between the liberation theologian and the oppressed community in Aristide's theology? Aristide articulates what we might call a theology of relationality. Once again, we believe Sturm's politics of relationality is effective and meaningful in reframing Aristide's thought and life as a theology of relationality. Thus, I am indebted to Sturm's language here. I attempt to articulate what a politics of relationality means theologically in Aristide's theology of the poor. A theology of relationality stresses the significance of *Imago Dei* for cultivating effective and productive human relations and common understanding. Human beings including those who are made poor are created in the Image of God to pursue collaboratively the common good and the welfare of humanity. We are made for each other, and we are successfully when we are and work together. The ethics of *caritas* and reciprocal solidarity—the ability to sympathize and identity with the pain and sufferings of others—are important markers of a theology of relationality. This thought is particularly expressed in Aristide's words below:

> Too often we hear of people fighting against one another in the name of God. We say hunger has no religion, exploitation has no religion, injustice has no religion. What do we mean when we say God? We mean the source of love; we mean the source of justice. We mean woman and man, black and white, child and adult, spirit and body, past and future, that thing which animates all of us. . . . We begin with what is in front of us. I cannot see God, but I can see you. I cannot see God, but I see the child in front of me, the woman, the man. Through them, through this material world in which we live, we know God. Through them we know and experience love, we glimpse and seek justice.[103]

James Gustafson, admitting that it is an intractable problem that human sufferings will not go away, admonishes us that "one needs no sophisticated argument to sustain some sense of obligation to persons

102. De La Torre, *Doing Christian Ethics from the Margins*, 90.
103. Aristide, *Eyes of the Heart*, 63.

and communities that are in such straits."[104] Third, a theology of relationality accentuates the importance of valorizing the humanity of every individual including the poor at every circumstance of life and championing the subjectivity of each human agent to construct a better world. Fourth, a theology of relationality acknowledges that the *imago dei* also means—what Sturm has phrased—"the thick interdependency of our lives." Sturm explains the expression brilliantly:

> We cannot be what we are, we cannot do what we do, we cannot accomplish what we accomplish apart from one another. Perhaps more than we can ever fully discern, our lives are but expressions, albeit creative expressions of a communal matrix that sustains us, inspires us, and constitutes the origin of our dreams and yearnings, our obligations and our rights. We are members of each other. We belong together. That is the source of our joy in life, although that is, as well, the source of tragedies of life, the dark side of our history, which, on all too many occasions, makes us shudder and anxious about our destiny.

At the center of the theology of relationality is the principle of caring for others—especially the poor, the needy, and the oppressed—and walking in solidarity with them; practically, these are genuine acts of love and human compassion—with the needy and the oppressed. A theology of relationality that practices an ethic of hospitality, dialogue, and human solidarity can encourage meaningful encounters with otherness and the disinherited; it facilitates the access to take risk in being a servant to the needy and the immigrant. It enables to cultivate compassion and empathy, and exercise justice and loving-kindness toward others. A theology of relationality is desperately needed in the Christian community and the world at large; for it offers various possibilities and potential resources to change and make us better human beings and relational people and relational communities—in the process of character formation. Consider the following words from Aristide:

> There are many kinds of hunger. Those who have enough to eat may be crying out from spiritual hunger. During the past few years I have traveled and spoken to groups around the world: to students at dozens of U.S. universities, at conferences in Europe, Latin America and Asia. Each time I address a new group I am struck—the same questions, the same hunger for spirituality, for morality in politics, for recognition of the humanity and

---

104. Gustafson, *Ethics from a Theocentric Perspective*, 219.

dignity of each of God's beings. In Japan, speaking to a group of university students I said, "When someone is hungry, I am hungry; when someone is suffering, I am suffering." And there, through translation, across culture, I saw the unmistakable flash of recognition in their eyes.[105]

Elsewhere, Aristide establishes the dynamics between the politics of relationality and the theology of relationship. He also emphasizes an ethics of care for the poor and the needy and the needy in this politico-theological vision. Yet, he informs us that theology is pivotal in his enunciation of a politics of freedom and life, and human rights. He does not divorce the political and the theological:

> Shall I be a priest or the president? One shades easily into the other. But as head of state and of the resistance, I have to walk the tightrope, sometimes playing one role and then another. I have never experienced difficulties in living this convergence of theology and politics. The theological justices feed a life in the service of others. We have given a voice to those who had none. I am fighting for them to keep that. Politics leads me to serve, to protect, and to transform the promise of dignity into living dignity on the daily level. I am what I am in order to be what I shall be. And what I am is not different from the priest celebrating the mass in the service of his brothers and sisters. For the respect of their elementary rights. I am helping them go to school, receive medical care, meet, face the criminals who have taken over the country.[106]

Such politico-theology of relationality moves individuals to exercise compassion, empathy, and compel them to be participants and agents of social transformation. The objective here, as Aristide expresses it, is not simply for individuals to move by compassion but to plant lasting acts of kindness and become actors of change and individuals who will actively engage the public sphere and fight against structural oppressions and forces of poverty, as clearly pronounced in the words below:

> At the beginning of 1994, dozens of Haitians left their country, in spite of surveillance on the high seas, and perished by drowning. Tragedy within a tragedy; one woman, whose child had died of illness on board ship, jumped into the sea rather than be repatriated. It is as if she were perpetuating the

105. Aristide, *Eyes of the Heart*, 69–70.
106. Aristide, *Dignity*, 147–48.

three-century-old tragedy by which our people resist slavery. Always striving to live a human existence. If that is not possible, then death. How could I not be shaken by such a drama and exasperated by the slowness of political solutions that would reduce the horror? How can I endure the prolongation of the unbearable?[107]

Moreover, we stress the connection between Aristide's politico-theology of relationality and the principle of justice as solidarity. As he remarks, "I was asking myself what I could do to protect their lives. How can I show solidarity? How can I go at this pace? Thanks to a system of connected vessels! I draw energy from the wellspring of the Haitian people and redistribute it as I can"[108] The clarion call to cultivate relational reciprocity, an ethics of care and service, and self-giving or self-denial is more expressive in these words:

> Now the boat is sinking. Every effort can be made to piece it back together and to prevent it from sinking forever, body and soul. I appeal to all people of goodwill to conceive of every possible measure, all means of keeping it afloat. Give the salvage operation any name you want. I acquiesce, I applaud. Let us define as well as possible the Haiti that we want to keep afloat. Let us use the help of all men and women with expertise and ideas. That is, all Haitian men and women. The agronomists form the mountains, the doctors from the hills, the fishermen from Port-Salut, the peasants from the Central Plateau, the rise growers of the Artibonite, the *tap-tap* drivers, the *madanm Sara*, the workers from the mountains factories, the industrialists. These people and all the movements with which they identity.[109]

After all, for Aristide, that is what justice as solidarity looks like in real life. Complementarily, Aristide's theology of relationality is also informed by the African concept of *Ubuntu*. *Ubuntu* is a Zulu word that can be translated as humanity. As Aristide explains it cogently:

> The philosophy of *Ubuntu* is embodied in three key words:
> *Umuntu ngumuntu ngabantu*, which mean:
> A person is a person through other human beings.
> A person becomes a person through the community.

---

107. Aristide, *Dignity*, 144.
108. Aristide, *Dignity*, 145, 147.
109. Aristide, *Dignity*, 153.

> A person is person when she/he treats other well.
> In the philosophy of Ubuntu there is no room for selfishness or egocentricity.
> A person's existence is intertwined with the community.[110]

Aristide postulates that "in the philosophy of Ubuntu, there is no room for selfishness or egocentricity. A person's existence is intertwined with the community."[111] Aristide contends that a theology of relationality and ethics of care is "grounded in solidarity, cooperation, unity, respect, dignity, justice, liberty and love of the other."[112] Take for example, this important renouncement of injustice and violence against the human family:

> One lone injustice, one lone crime, one lone illegality, especially if it has been officially registered and confirmed; one lone insult to humanity, one lone insult to justice and the law, especially if it is universally, legally, nationally, and comfortably accepted—one lone crime destroys and suffices to destroy the social pact, the entire social contract; one lone felony, one lose disgrace suffices for losing honor, for disgracing an entire people.[113]

Therefore, he challenges us that "we must honor debts and promises. Pride? Respect? And what term dignity?"[114] Although Aristide's theology of relationality embraces a form of theological cosmopolitanism and humanism, we should not forget that the preferential option for the poor is at the heart of Aristide's theological reflection and discourse. A theology of relationality can be connected to the three levels of liberation theology: professional, pastoral, and popular. Aristide speaks about being on the side of the poor and being in a compassionate and loving solidarity with them—what Leonardo and Clodovis Boff have classified as the "pastoral level" of liberation theology. According to Aristide, the liberation theologian should struggle with the poor, love the oppressed, fight for the disinherited, and sacrifice for the marginalized. In the "professional level," the first of the three levels of liberation theology, the liberation theologian learns from the experience of the poor. Aristide testifies that "at the school of the poor, the theologian learns to discover the path

---

110. Aristide, *Haïti-Haitii?*, 16.
111. Aristide, *Haïti-Haitii?*, 16.
112. Aristide, *Haïti-Haitii?*, 17.
113. Aristide, *Dignity*, 158.
114. Aristide, *Dignity*, 158.

and the voice of the God of Jesus Christ fighting against poverty, hunger, exploitation, slavery."[115] This pedagogical lesson is crucial and instructive because the poor are actors and artisans of their own liberation and "should speak for all their brothers and sisters"[116] Aristide accentuates. He moves on to elucidate how he has applied the third level of liberation theology in the context of the Haitian poor majority:

> I spoke words of Jesus then . . . preached food for all men and women. . . . I have participated in many struggles in my life, but none has pained me so greatly as the struggle within our Church over the depth of that Church's preferential option for the poor of our parish. There are those of us, usually younger and eager for change, who believe that the commitment should be total, unrelenting, and intransigent. There are others, often with grayer heads and more comfortable with the ways of the world, who do not mind conciliating the powers that sit around the great table, who believe that collaboration and compromise are a valid means in taking up our preferential option for the poor.[117]

Jean-Bertrand Aristide, working in the tradition of liberation theology, presents himself as "the theologian of the poor people." He accompanies them in their everyday struggle in the process of creating a promising future world and a new humanism. On the professional level, Aristide thinks about the faith in solidarity from the vantage point of those living in the margins of history. While on the popular level of liberation theology, the theologian gives emphasis to the liberative function of the spoken word (orature/orality)—hence it is a spoken theology—on the pastoral level, the theologian inspires the poor and the church for liberation in their own lives and communities. As the Boffs underscore, pastoral liberation theology "is a theology in its own right: it follows the same basic line as liberation theology as it is generally known. They both share the same root: evangelical faith; they both have the same objective: the liberating practice of love."[118] In the words below, Aristide attempts to attain this singular goal by bringing in conversation both pastoral and popular levels of liberation theology.

---

115. Aristide, *Nevrose vetero-testamentaire*, 109.
116. Aristide, *Autobiography*, 53; Aristide, *Dignity*, 94.
117. Aristide, *Eyes of the Heart*, 15–18.
118. Boff, *Introducing Liberation Theology*, 17.

> We speak the words that the spirit of the poor breathes into us. That is our humble role, a simple role, one that requires no learning, no pride, no soutane, no miter. It requires faith only, and of faith we have plenty. It requires a willing to serve the people, and no machete, no fusillade of rocks, no bullets or riffles or Uzis, no tear gas or bombs, will ever dissuade us from that willingness, from the faith. We are unshakable. Like the poor, we will always be with you. Kill one among us, and we rise us again a thousand strong.[119]

Aristide's "spoken theology" is more pronounced and noticeably defined in his homilies. He emphasizes that the role of the theologian is to be with the people: "I have always lived among the dispossessed. . . . I may consider myself to be a privileged poor man living in the midst of the poor."[120] In the statement, Aristide attempts to show how theology of relationality works in practice. By living among the poor, his goal is to provide "theological enlightenment of the community on its pilgrim way"[121] and to help effectuate integral freedom. It is also a commitment to cultivate justice in the midst of injustice, and hope in the midst of despair and desolation. In an interview with political philosopher, Peter Hallward, Aristide declares, "For me the people remain at the very core of our struggle. It isn't a matter of struggling for the people, on behalf of the people, at a distance from the people; it is the people themselves who are struggling, and it's a matter of struggling with and in the midst of the people."[122] By this statement, Aristide seeks to convey that his goal is to accompany the people, the impoverished, not to replace them. Aristide's relational theological approach is grounded in the philosophy of *Ubuntu* which celebrates, as Aristide reminds us, "solidarity, cooperation, unity, respect, dignity, justice, liberty and love of the other"[123]

Aristide highlights the importance of collective self-agency and subjectivity of the poor: "The starving themselves spoke of their hunger, often uneasily and without eloquence, but they spoke."[124] He does not see the theologian as the voice of the oppressed community; rather the liberationist theologian, as Aristide insists, works in solidarity with the

---

119. Aristide, *In the Parish of the Poor*, 48.
120. Aristide, *Autobiography*, 176.
121. Boff and Boff, *Introducing Liberation Theology*, 19.
122. Aristide, "One Step at a Time."
123. Aristide, *Haïti-Haitii?*, 17.
124. Aristide, *Autobiography*, 46.

collective poor to achieve holistic freedom: "Like Jesus, we spoke of our own reality, and we poured out all the words of Christ in light of our own situation of suffering and injustice."[125] This declaration should be understood in the context of Aristide working among the Haitian poor, in which he compares the suffering poor with the historic suffering of the historical Jesus. Liberationist theologian Juan Luis Segundo is correct to declare that "when the poor start to talk, when they become the voice of their own voice, we begin to see a theology of liberation."[126] Finally, a theology of rationality accentuates the need for radical inclusion of the poor in the public discourse and theological creativity. The emphasis on God's credulous inclusion of the poor in the grand narratives of human history is a central distinctive in Aristide's theology of the poor and theology of relationality.

Concluding Thoughts

The poor as a rhetorical force and category in Aristide's theology of the poor is associated with God the Liberator who is totally committed to the radical freedom and welfare of the poor and the oppressed communities in the world. His theological outlook focuses on the idea that suffering men, women, and children who are poor are created in the image of God. This God of life and of freedom speaks through the poor; he inspires hope and faith in them, and ultimately calls them to a life of freedom, meaning, and shalom. As he remarks, "Whenever the poor are heard and respected, the face of God is illuminated. The gift of Christ is his humanity, his presence among the living, among the poor. Jesus is not only the God of glory; he is the God of suffering."[127] By the phrase, "Jesus is the God of suffering," Aristide seeks to inform us that Jesus's suffering are relative to the sufferings of the world's poor majority. It also communicates the notion that God has intentionally sided with the poor and has a plan of integral liberation for them. God has not abandoned the poor; hence, Aristide's theology of relationality encourages an ethics of inclusion and participation grounded exclusively in God's radical love and active solidarity with the oppressed of this world. God does not reject

---

125. Aristide, *Autobiography*, 66.
126. Aristide, *Autobiography*, 110.
127. Aristide, *Eyes of the Heart*, 73.

anyone; yet, he shows special favor to the poor, the oppressed, and the wretched of the earth.

Aristide maintains that liberation theology as a discourse about the God-poor encounter and his relationship with the outcast and disheartened in our communities is a liberative discourse: "We know that the innocents are still perishing in the flame of violence, but we do not fall into the sea of despair because God continually frees us with the miracle of life."[128] God's practice of a theology of relationality fosters hope and faith in the midst of poverty, human oppression, life disappointment, and tragic faith. This is where exactly Aristide brings theology and social activism together. As he notes elsewhere, "I call liberation theology the Christian impulse that does not separate belief from action, that exasperates conservatives, and annoys so many people on the left who dream of realizing the happiness of others . . . without the others."[129] And the commitment to the preferential option for the poor should be "total, unrelenting, and intransigent."[130]

Aristide's theological outlook and the rhetoric of the poor is clearly identified with the struggle of the Haitian poor and suffering masses, in particular, and the socially oppressed classes in the world, at large. His pastoral work prioritizes the poor and insists that we take into account the reality and life condition of the wretched of the earth by giving careful consideration to their socioeconomic context. Aristide's liberation theology is a theology committing to the transformation of the social order and the emancipation of the poor. God's undivided commitment to the freedom of the oppressed in the world and to the creation of a new humanity (New creation theology) is clearly affirmed in Aristide's theology of the poor. Inspired by the revolutionary actions of God Liberator and rooted in the prophetic traditions of the biblical narrative and liberation theology, Aristide maintains that the socially mistreated and disinherited of this world are agents of revolutionary change in the world. The gospel of the historical Jesus and the Jesus of Faith is a message of integral liberation from oppression. It is a prophetic message about social transformation and social newness.

For Aristide, the Bible is God's good news to the poor and the marginalized; more than ever a message of liberation, it proclaims loudly

---

128. Aristide, *Eyes of the Heart*, 68–69.
129. Aristide, *Nevrose vetero-testamentaire*, 103.
130. Aristide, *Nevrose vetero-testamentaire*, 18.

liberty for those who are oppressed and those who are deprived of it.[131] If there is one thing we need to learn and appreciate from Aristide's theology of the poor is the sense of prophetic hope and the urgency to care for and remember the poor and the wretched of the earth. This is not an individual project but a collective one; being in solidarity with the poor and the oppressed of this world is an everyday process that is worth pursuing. It has communal, societal, and ultimately cosmic value. Jean-Bertrand Aristide's theology of relationality is a prophetic vision for justice, freedom, love, peace, and healing, with special attention given to the plight of the cast-down people and marginalized majority of this world.

I want to conclude this analysis with some memorable words Aristide delivered in a speech in December 16, 1993:

> *Tan an move, li mare minn li. Se vre. Men soley delivrans la kouche. Li pa mouri*—"The horizon is somber and the sky is dark. It's true. But the sun of deliverance is only hidden. It is not dead. They can count on no other silence except a deafening and boiling silence that can be heard to the four corners of the Earth. Tomorrow, we shall be free."[132]

---

131. Aristide, *Autobiography*, 51, 53.
132. Aristide, *Dignity*, 156.

Bibliography

Abbott, Elizabeth. *Haiti: A Shattered Nation*. New York: Overlook Duckworth, 2011.
Adams, Elie Maynard. *Religion and Cultural Freedom*. Philadelphia: Temple University Press, 1993.
Adams, R. L. "African American Studies and the State of the Art." In *Africana Studies: A Survey of Africa and the African Diaspora*, edited by Mario Azevedo, 5–32. Durham, NC: Carolina Academic Press, 2005.
Allen, Troy D. "Cheikh Anta Diop's Two Craddle Theory: Revisited." *Journal of Black Studies* 38 (2008) 813–29.
Ampère, Jean-Jacques. *Voyage en Égypte et en Nubie*. Paris: Lévy, 1867.
Araya, Victorio. *God of the Poor: The Mystery of God in Latin American Liberation Theology*. Maryknoll: Orbis, 1987.
Aristide, Jean-Bertrand. *Aristide: An Autobiography*. With Christopher Wargny. Maryknoll: Orbis, 1993.
———. "The Church in Haiti—Land of Resistance." *Caribbean Quarterly* 37 (1991) 108–13.
———. *Dignity*. Charlottesville: University of Virginia Press, 1996.
———. *Eyes of the Heart: Seeking a Path for the Poor in the Age of Globalization*. Monroe, ME: Common Courage, 2002.
———. *Haïti-Haitii? Philosophical Reflections for Mental Decolonization*. Boulder, CO: Paradigm, 2011.
———. *In the Parish of the Poor: Writings from Haiti*. New York: Orbis, 1993.
———. Introduction to Nesbitt, *Toussaint L'Ouverture*, vii–xxxiii.
———. *Jean-Bertrand Aristide Presents Toussaint Louverture and the Haitian Revolution*. New York: Verso, 2008.
———. *Nevrose vetero-testamentaire*. Montreal: CIDIHCA, 1994.
———. "One Step at a Time." Interview with Peter Hallward. July 2006. http://www.aristidefoundationfordemocracy.org/about/one-step-at-a-time-an-interview-with-jean-bertrand-aristide/.
———. *Théologie et politique*. Montreal: CIDIHCA, 1992.
Asad, Talal. *Formations of the Secular: Christianity, Islam, Modernity*. Palo Alto: Stanford University Press, 2003.
Asante, Molefi. *The Afrocentric Idea*. Philadelphia: Temple University Press, 1987.
———. *Afrocentricity: The Theory of Social Change*. Trenton: Africa World, 2003 [1980].

———. "Afrocentricity: Toward a New Understanding of African Thought in the World." May 4, 2009. http://www.asante.net/articles/5/afrocentricity-toward-a-new-understanding-of-african-thought-in-the-world/.

———. *Kemet, Afrocentricity and Knowledge*. Trenton: Africa World, 1990.

Austin, J. L. *How to Do Things with Words*. Cambridge: Harvard University Press, 1975.

Baker, Lee. *Anthropology and the Racial Politics of Culture*. Durham: Duke University Press, 2010.

———. *From Savage to Negro: Anthropology and the Construction of Race, 1896–1954*. Los Angeles: University of California Press, 1998.

Banner-Haley, Charles Pete. *From Du Bois to Obama: African American Intellectuals in the Public Forum*. Carbondale: Southern Illinois University Press, 2010.

Bastien, Remy. "Vodoun and Politics in Haiti." In *Religion and Politics in Haiti*, edited by Harold Courtlander and Remy Bastien, 39–68. Washington: Institute for Cross-Cultural Research, 1966.

Bell, Madison Smartt. *Master of the Crossroads: A Novel of Haiti*. New York: Vintage, 2000.

Bell, Madison Smartt. *Toussaint Louverture: A Biography*. New York: Pantheon, 2007.

Bellegarde-Smith, Patrick, and Claudine Michel, eds. *Haitian Vodou: Spirit, Myth, and Reality*. Bloomington: Indiana University Press, 2006.

———. *Vodou in Haitian Life and Culture: Invisible Powers*. New York: Palgrave Macmillan, 2006.

Benedict, Ruth. *Patterns of Culture*. New York: Mentor, 1959 [1934].

Ben-Jochannan, Yosef A. A. *Africa: Mother of Western Civilization*. Baltimore: Black Classic, 1971.

———. *African Origins of the Major "Western Religions."* Baltimore: Black Classic, 1970.

———. *Black Man of the Nile and His Family*. Baltimore: Black Classic, 1972.

Benot, Yves. "The Insurgents of 1791, Their Leaders, and the Concept of Independence." In *The World of the Haitian Revolution*, edited by David Patrick Geggus and Norman Fiering, 99–110. Bloomington: Indiana University Press, 2009.

Berlinerblau, Jacques. *Heresy in the University: The Black Athena Controversy and the Responsibilities of American Intellectuals*. New Brunswick, NJ: Rutgers University Press, 1999.

Bernal, Martin. *Black Athena: The Afroasiatic Roots of Classical Civilization*. Vol. 1, *The Fabrication of Ancient Greece, 1785–1985*. New Brunswick, NJ: Rutgers University Press, 1987.

———. *Black Athena: The Afroasiatic Roots of Classical Civilization*. Vol. 2, *The Archeological and Documentary Evidence*. New Brunswick, NJ: Rutgers University Press, 1991.

———. *Black Athena: The Afroasiatic Roots of Classical Civilization*. Vol. 3, *The Linguistic Evidence*. New Brunswick, NJ: Rutgers University Press, 2004.

Bigo, Pierre. *The Church and Third World Revolution*. Maryknoll: Orbis, 1977.

Boff, Leonardo, and Clodovis Boff. *Introducing Liberation Theology*. Maryknoll: Orbis, 1987.

Bonino, Jose Miguez. *Doing Theology in a Revolutionary Situation*. Minneapolis: Fortress, 2007 [1975].

Boyd, Gregory A., and Paul R. Eddy. *Across the Spectrum: Understanding Issues in Evangelical Theology*. Grand Rapids: Baker Academic, 2002.

Brueggemann, Walter. *Theology of the Old Testament: Testimony, Dispute, Advocacy.* Minneapolis: Fortress, 1997.
Bucher, Glenn R. "Toward a Liberation Theology for the 'Oppressor.'" *Journal of the American Academy of Religion* 44 (1976) 517–34.
Bunson, Margaret, ed. "Ka-aper Statue." In *Encyclopedia of Ancient Egypt.* New York: Facts on File, 2002 [1991].
Burke, Kenneth. *A Rhetoric of Motives.* Berkeley: University of California Press, 1969.
Cannon, Mae Elise. *Social Justice Handbook: Small Steps for a Better World.* Downers Grove: InterVarsity, 2009.
Carter, J. Kameron. *Race: A Theological Account.* New York: Oxford University Press, 2011.
Casséus, Jules. *Eléments de Théologie Haïtienne.* Port-au-Prince: La Presse Evangélique, 2007.
———. *Toward a Contextual Haitian Theology.* Port-au-Prince: Imprimerie Media-Texte, 2013.
Castelar, Emilio. *Habitations of Modernity: Essays in the Wake of Subaltern Studies.* Chicago: University Of Chicago Press, 2002.
———. *Las guerras de América y Egypto.* Madrid, 1883.
Césaire, Aimé. *Discourse on Colonialism.* Translated by Joan Pinkham. New York: Monthly Review Press, 2000.
———. *Toussaint Louverture: La révolution française et le problème colonial.* Paris: Présence Africaine, 1962.
Chakrabart, Dipesh. *Rethinking Working Class History: Bengal, 1890–1940.* Princeton: Princeton University Press, 1989.
Champollion, Jean François. *Grammaire égyptienne.* Arles: Solin-Actes Sud, 1997.
Clavin, Matthew. *Toussaint Louverture and the American Civil War.* Philadelphia: University of Philadelphia Press, 2010.
Collier, Paul. *The Bottom Billion: Why the Poorest Countries Are Failing and What Can Be Done about It.* New York: Oxford University Press, 2008.
Cox, Harvey. *The Future of Faith.* New York: HarperOne, 2009.
Dash, J. Michael. Introduction to *Masters of the Dew*, by Jacques Roumain. Translated by Langston Hughes and Mercer Cook. London: Heinemann, 1978 [1947]. Originally published as *Gouverneurs de la rosée.* Port-au-Prince: Imprimerie de l'Etat, 1944.
———. "Nineteenth-Century Haiti and the Archipelago of the Americas: Antenor Firmin's Letters from St. Thomas." *Research in African Literatures* 35 (2004) 44–53.
———. *The Other America: Caribbean Literature in a New World.* Charlottesville: University of Virginia Press, 1998.
Davis, Gregson. *Aimé Césaire.* Cambridge: Cambridge University Press, 1997.
Dawkins, Richard. *The Selfish Gene.* 30th anniversary ed. New York: Oxford University Press, 2006 [1976].
Dayan, Joan. *Haiti, History, and the Gods.* Berkeley: University of California Press, 1995.
Debbasch, Yvan. *Le marronage: Essai sur la désertion de l'esclave antillais.* Paris: Presses universitaires de France, 1962.
Debien, Gabriel. *Les esclaves aux Antilles françaises: Dix-septième au dix-huitième siècle.* Basse-Terre, Guadeloupe: Société d'histoire de la Guadeloupe, 1974.
Deibert, Michael. *Notes from the Last Testament: The Struggle for Haiti.* New York: Seven Stories, 2005.

De La Tore, Miguel A. *Doing Christian Ethics from the Margins*. Maryknoll: Orbis, 2004.
Denis, Watson R. Review of *The Equality of the Human Races (Positivist Anthropology)*. *Caribbean Studies* 34 (2006) 325–34.
Desmangles, Leslie G. *The Faces of the Gods: Vodou and Roman Catholicism in Haiti*. Chapel Hill: University of North Carolina Press, 1992.
De Vastey, Baron. *Le système colonial dévoilé*. Cap-Henry: Roux, 1814.
De Vries, Hent. *Philosophy and the Turn to Religion*. Baltimore: Johns Hopkins University Press, 1999.
———. *Religion and Violence: Philosophical Perspectives from Kant to Derrida*. Baltimore: Johns Hopkins University Press, 2002.
Diop, Cheikh Anta. *The African Origin of Civilization: Myth or Reality*. Edited and Translated by Mercer Cook. Chicago: Hill, 1974.
———. *Civilization or Barbarism: An Authentic Anthropology*. New York: Hill, 1991 [1981].
———. *Nations nègres et culture: De l'Antiquité nègre égyptienne aux problèmes culturels de l'Afrique noire d'aujourd'hui*. Paris: Présence africaine, 1979.
Dorrien, Gary. *Soul in Society: The Making and Renewal of Social Christianity*. Minneapolis: Fortress, 1995.
Douglass, Frederick. *My Bondage and My Freedom*. New York: Barnes & Noble, 2005 [1855].
———. *Narrative of the Life of Frederick Douglass, an American Slave Written by Himself*. New Haven: Yale University Press, 2001 [1845].
Drake, St. Claire. *Black Folk Here and There: An Essay in History and Anthropology*. Vol. 1. Los Angeles: Center for Afro-American Studies, University of California, 1987.
Dubois, Laurent. *Avengers of the New World: The History of the Haitian Revolution*. Cambridge: Belknap of Harvard University Press, 2005.
———. *Haiti: The Aftershocks of History*. New York: Metropolitan, 2012.
Du Bois, W. E. B. *The Gift of Black Folk: The Negroes in the Making of America*. New York: Washington Square, 1970 [1924].
———. *The Negro*. Mineola, NY: Dover, 2001 [1915].
———. *The World and Africa: An Inquiry into the Part which Africa Has Played in World History*. New York: International, 1992 [1946].
Duchet, Michel. *Anthropologie et histoire au siècle des lumières*. Paris: Editions Albin Michel, S.A., 1995.
Dupuy, Alex. *Haiti in the New World Order: The Limits of the Democratic Revolution*. Boulder, CO: Westview, 1997.
———. *Haiti in the World Economy: Class, Race, and Underdevelopment since 1700*. Boulder, CO: Westview, 1989.
———. *The Prophet and Power: Jean-Bertrand Aristide, the International Community and Haiti*. Boulder, CO: Rowman & Littlefield, 2007.
Durkheim, Emile. *The Elementary Forms of Religious Life*. New York: Free Press, 1995.
Durkheim, Emile, and Kenneth Thompson. *Readings from Emile Durkheim*. New York: Routledge, 1998.
Dussel, Enrique. *Beyond Philosophy: Ethics, History, Marxism, and Liberation Theology*. Lanham, MD: Rowman & Littlefield, 2003.
Elie, Jean-Gille. "Patriotism, Humanism and Modernity: Three European Concepts as a Basis for the Investigation and Affirmation of the Negro Soul in Francophone

Literature of Haiti from the Nineteenth through the Late Twentieth Century." PhD diss., University of Washington, 2002.
Ellison, Ralph. *Shadow and Act*. New York: Vintage, 1995.
Fanon, Frantz. *The Wretched of the Earth*. Translated by Constance Farrington. New York, Grove Weidenfeld, 1963. Originally published as *Les Damnés de la terre*. Paris: Éditions Maspero, 1961.
Fatton, Robert. *Haiti's Predatory Republic: The Unending Transition to Democracy*. Boulder, CO: Rienner, 2002.
Fick, Carolyn E. *The Making of Haiti: The Saint-Domingue Revolution from Below*. Knoxville: University of Tennessee Press, 1997.
Fils-Aimé, Jean. *Vodou, je me souviens: Essai*. Québec: Les Editions Dabar 2007.
Firmin, Joseph Anténor. *De l'Égalité des Races Humaines (Anthropologie Positive)*. Paris: Libraire Cotillon, 1885.
———. *De l'Égalité des Races Humaines: Anthropologie Positive*. Montreal: Mémoire D'encrier, 2005.
———. *The Equality of the Human Races*. Translated by Asselin Charles. Champaign: University of Illinois Press, 2002.
Fischer, Sibylle. *Modernity Disavowed: Haiti and the Cultures of Slavery in the Age of Revolution*. Durham: Duke University Press, 2004.
Florival, Lys Stéphane. "Haiti's Troubles: Perspectives from the Theology of Work and from Liberation Theology." PhD diss., Loyola University, Chicago, 2013.
Fluehr-Lobban, Carolyn. "Anténor Firmin: Haitian Pioneer of Anthropology." *American Anthropologist* 102 (2000) 449–66.
———. Introduction to *The Equality of the Human Races*, by Antenor Firmin. Translated by Charles Asselin. Champaign: University of Illinois Press, 2002.
Fluehr-Lobban, Carolyn, and Kharyssa Rhodes, eds. *Race and Identity in the Nile Valley: Ancient and Modern Perspectives*. New York: Red Sea, 2004.
Flyod-Thomas, J. M. "Seeing Red in the Black Church: Marxist Thought and African American Christianity." *Journal of Race, Ethnicity, and Religion* 1 (2010) 1–46.
Fontus, Fritz. *Les églises protestantes en Haiti: Communication et inculturation*. Paris: L'Harmattan, 2001.
Fowler, Carolyn. *A Knot in the Thread: The Life and Work of Jacques Roumain*. Washington, DC: Howard University Press, 1980.
———. "The Shared Vision of Langston Hughes and Jacques Roumain." *Black American Literature Forum* 15 (1981) 84–88.
France, R. T. "The Servant of the Lord in the Teaching of Jesus." *Tyndale Bulletin* 19 (1968) 26–52.
François, Kawas. "Vaudou et catholicisme." Coalition et Assistance Versus Amertume. https://cavainc.blogspot.com/2011/02/vaudou-et-catholicisme.html.
Freud, Sigmund. *Future of an Illusion*. Edited and translated by J. Strackey. New York: Norton, 1961.
Garrigus, John. "'New Christians' / 'New Whites': Sephardic Jews, Free People of Color, and Citizenship in French Saint-Domingue, 1760–1789." In *The Jews and Expansion of Europe to the West*, edited by Paolo Bernadini and Norman Fiering, 314–32. New York: Berghan, 2001.
Geggus, David Patrick. *Haitian Revolutionary Studies*. Bloomington: Indiana University Press, 2002.

———. *The Impact of the Haitian Revolution in the Atlantic World*. Columbia: University of South Carolina Press, 2011.
———. *Slavery, War, and Revolution*. Oxford: Clarendon, 1982.
———. "The 'Volte-Face' of Toussaint Louverture." In *Haitian Revolutionary Studies*, 119–36. Bloomington: Indiana University Press, 2002.
Geggus, David Patrick, and Norman Fiering, eds. *The World of the Haitian Revolution*. Bloomington: Indiana University Press, 2009.
Geiss, Immanuel. *The Pan-Africa Movement*. Translated by Anne Keep. New York: African Publishing, 1974.
George G. M. *Stolen Legacy: The Egyptian Origins of Western Philosophy*. New York: Philosophical Library, 1954.
Gilles, Jean-Elie. "Patriotism, Humanism and Modernity: Three European Concepts as a Basis for the Investigation and Affirmation of the Negro Soul in Francophone Literature of Haiti from the Nineteenth through the Late Twentieth Century." PhD diss., University of Washington, 2002.
Gillespie, Michael Allen. *The Theological Origins of Modernity*. Chicago: University of Chicago Press, 2009.
Gilroy, Paul. *The Black Atlantic: Modernity and Double-Consciousness* Cambridge: Harvard University Press, 1993.
Girard, Phillippe. *Haiti: The Tumultuous History—from Pearl of the Caribbean to Broken Nation*. New York: Palgrave Macmillan, 2010.
———. *The Slaves Who Defeated Napoleon: Toussaint Louverture and the Haitian War of Independence, 1801–1804*. Tuscaloosa: University of Alabama Press, 2011.
Girod, François. *La vie quotidienne de la société créole: Saint-Domingue au XVIII siècle*. Paris: Hachette, 1972.
Gobineau, Joseph-Arthur de. *The Inequality of Human Races*. Translated by George L. Mosse. New York: Fertig, 1999.
Gordon, Dexter B. *Black Identity: Rhetoric, Ideology, and Nineteenth-Century Black Nationalism*. Carbondale: Southern Illinois University Press, 2006.
Gordon, Lewis R. *An Introduction to Africana Philosophy*. New York: Cambridge University Press, 2008.
———. "Not Exactly Positivism: Firmin's Critique of Transcendental Idealism in His Philosophy of Race and Culture." Unpublished paper provided in communication with the author.
Gould, Carol C. *Rethinking Democracy: Freedom and Social Co-operation in Politics, Economy, and Society*. Cambridge: Cambridge University Press, 1990.
Gould, Jay. *The Structure of Evolutionary Theory*. Cambridge: Belknap of Harvard University Press 2002.
Greene, Anne. *The Catholic Church in Haiti: Political and Social Change*. East Lansing: Michigan State University Press, 1993.
Groome, Thomas. "Take and Read: Pedagogy of the Oppressed." *National Catholic Reporter*, February 22, 2016. https://www.ncronline.org/blogs/ncr-today/take-and-read-pedagogy-oppressed.
Guha, Ranajit. *Elementary Aspects of Peasant Insurgency in Colonial India*. Durham: Duke University Press, 1999 [1983].
———. *Subaltern Studies Reader, 1986–1995*. Minneapolis: University of Minnesota Press, 1997.

Guha, Ranajit, et al., eds. *Selected Subaltern Studies*. New York: Oxford University Press, 1988.
Gustafson, James M. *Ethics from a Theocentric Perspective*. Vol. 2, *Ethics and Theology*. Chicago: University of Chicago Press, 1984.
Gutierrez, Gustavo. *On Job: God-Talk and the Suffering of the Innocent*. Maryknoll: Orbis, 1993.
———. *The Power of the Poor in History*. Translated by Robert R. Barr. Maryknoll: Orbis, 1984. Originally published as *La fuerza historica de los probres*. Lima, 1979.
———. *A Theology of Liberation: History, Politics, and Salvation*. Translated and edited by Caridad Inda and John Eagleson. Maryknoll: Orbis, 1988. Originally published as *Teologia de la liberacion*. Lima, 1971.
Hallward, Peter. *Damming the Flood: Haiti and the Politics of Containment*. New York: Verso, 2010.
———. "The Will of the People: Notes towards a Dialectical Voluntarism." *Radical Philosophy* 155 (2009) 17–29.
Hamilton, Edith, and Huntington Cairns, eds. *The Collected Dialogues of Plato: Including the Letters*. Princeton: Princeton University Press, 2005.
Harris, Leonard. *The Philosophy of Alain Locke: Harlem Renaissance and Beyond*. Philadelphia: Temple University Press, 1989.
Harris, Marvin. *The Rise of Anthropological Theory: A History of Culture*. New York: Columbia University Press, 1968.
Harrison, Faye V., ed. *Decolonizing Anthropology: Moving Further toward an Anthropology for Liberation*. Arlington: American Anthropological Association, 1997 [1997].
———. "Dismantling Anthropology's Domestic and International Peripheries." *WAN E-JOURNAL* 6 (2012) 87–110.
Hauerwas, Stanely, and Jean Vanier. *Living Gently in a Violent World: The Prophetic Witness of Weakness*. Downers Grove: InterVarsity, 2008.
Heinl, Robert Debs, and Nancy Gordon Heinl. *Written in Blood: The Story of the Haitian People, 1492–1971*. Boston: Houghton Mifflin, 1978.
Hick, John. *Evil and the God of Love*. Rev. ed. New York: Harper & Row, 1952.
———. *An Interpretation of Religion: Human Responses to the Transcendent*. New Haven: Yale University Press, 1989.
Howe, Stephen. *Afrocentrism: Mystical Pasts and Imagined Homes*. New York: Verso, 1998.
Hughes, Langston. *Langston Hughes: The Collected Poems of Langston Hughes*. Edited by Arnold Rampersad and David Roessel. New York: Vintage Classics, 1994.
Hunt, Alfred N. *Haiti's Influence on Antebellum America: Slumbering Volcano in the Caribbean*. Baton Rouge: Louisiana State University Press, 1988.
Hurbon, Laënne. *Le barbare imaginaire*. Port-au-Prince: Deschamps, 1987
———. *Comprendre Haïti: Essai sur l'état, la nation, la culture*. Port-au-Prince: Deschamps, 1987.
———. *Dieu dans le vaudou haïtien*. Port-au-Prince: Deschamps, 1987.
———. "Vodou: A Faith for Individual, Family, and Community." *Callaloo* 15 (1992) 786–96.
———. *Voodoo: Truth and Fantasy*. London: Thames and Hudson, 1995.
James, C. L. R. *The Black Jacobins: Toussaint L'Ouverture and the San Domingo Revolution*. New York: Vintage, 1989 [1938].

James, William. *The Will to Believe and Human Immortality*. New York: Dove, 1959.
James, Winston. *Holding Aloft the Banner of Ethiopia: Caribbean Radicalism in Early Twentieth-Century America*. New York: Verso, 1998.
Joseph, Celucien L. "Prophetic Religion, Violence and Black Freedom: Reading Makandal's Project of Black Liberation through a Fanonian Postcolonial Lens of Decolonization and Theory of Revolutionary Humanism." *Journal of Race, Ethnicity, and Religion* 3 (2012) 1–30.
———. *Race, Religion, and the Haitian Revolution: Essays on Faith, Freedom, and Decolonization*. North Charleston, SC: CreateSpace, 2012
———. "The Rhetoric of Prayer: Dutty Boukman, the Discourse of 'Freedom from Below,' and the Politics of God." *Journal of Race, Ethnicity, and Religion* 2 (2011) 1–33.
Joseph, Jean Duthene. "The Symbiotic Relationship between Roman Catholicism and Haitian Vodou and the Impact of Their Association on the Protestant." PhD diss., Trinity Theological Seminary, 2006.
Kahn, Jonathon S. *Divine Discontent: The Religious Imagination of W. E. B. Du Bois*. New York: Oxford University Press, 2009.
Kaplan, Hilary. "Nature's Equal, or Her Conquerer: Two Island Vision Of Drought,Land, and Community." May 5, 2011. http://www.yale.edu/sangha/PDF_FILES/KaplanHilary2000.pdf.
Karenga, Maulana. "Black Studies and the Problematic of a Paradigm: The Philosophical Dimension." *Journal of Black Studies* 18 (1988) 359–414.
———. *Introduction to Black Studies*. Los Angeles: University of Sankore Press, 1993.
———. "Nommo, Kawaida, and Communicative Practice: Bringing Good into the World." In *Understanding African American Rhetoric: Classical Origins to Contemporary Innovations*, edited by Ronald L. Jackson II and Elaine B. Richardson, 3–22. New York: Routledge, 2003.
Katongole, Emmanuel, and Chris Rice. *Reconciling All Things: A Christian Vision for Justice, Peace and Healing*. Downers Grove: InterVarsity, 2008.
Keller, Timothy. *Generous Justice: How God's Grace Makes Us Just*. New York: Penguin, 2010.
Kirkland, Frank M. "Modernity and Intellectual Life in Black." In *African American Perspectives and Philosophical Traditions*, edited by John P. Pittman, 136–65. New York: Routledge, 1997.
Klaussen, Valerie. *Migrant Revolutions: Haitian Literature, Globalization, and U.S. Imperialism*. Lanham, MD: Lexington, 2008.
KMT-Sisouvong, Baruti. "Equality of the Human Races: A Review." *Radical Scholar*, http://www.radicalscholar.com/articles/publish/bkreviews/Equality_of_the_Human_Races_A_Review_printer.shtml.
Knight, George A. F. *Servant Theology: A Commentary on the Book of Isaiah 40–55*. Grand Rapids: Eerdmans, 1984.
Kuhn, Thomas S. *The Structure of Scientific Revolutions*. 50th anniversary ed. Chicago: University of Chicago Press, 2012 [1962].
Kunin, Seth D., and Jonathan Miles-Watson, eds. *Theories of Religion: A Reader*. New Brunswick, NJ: Rutgers University Press, 2006.
Miller, Carolyn R. "The Polis as Rhetorical Community." *Rhetorica* 11 (1993) 211–40.
Laguerre, Michelle S. *Voodoo and Politics in Haiti*. New York: Palgrave Macmillan, 1989.

Largey, Michael. *Vodou Nation: Haitian Art Music and Cultural Nationalism*. Chicago: University of Chicago Press, 2006.
Laurent, Gerard Mentor. *Toussaint Louverture à travers sa correspondance, 1794–1798*. Madrid: Gráficas, 1953.
Lefkowitz, Mary. *Not Out of Africa: How Afrocentrism Became an Excuse to Teach Myth as History*. New York: Basic, 1996.
Lefkowitz, Mary, and Guy M. Rogers, eds. *Black Athena Revisited*. Durham: University of North Carolina Press, 1996.
Lescot, Elie. *Avant l'oubli: Christianisme et paganisme en Haïti et autres lieux*. Port-au-Prince: Deschamps, 1974.
Lewis, C. S. *The Problem of Pain* .New York: HarperCollins, 1996 [1940].
Lewis, Gordon K. *Main Currents in Caribbean Thought: The Historical Evolution of Caribbean Society in Its Ideological Aspects, 1492–1900*. Baltimore: Johns Hopkins University Press, 2004 [1983].
Lewis, Shireen K. *Race, Culture, and Identity: Francophone West African and Caribbean Literature and Theory from Negritude to Creolite*. Lanham, MD: Lexington, 2006.
Lilla, Mark. *The Stillborn God: Religion, Politics, and the Modern West*. New York: Vintage, 2008.
Lloyd, Vincent W. *The Problem with Grace: Reconfiguring Political Theology*. Stanford: Stanford University Press, 2011.
L'Ouverture, Toussaint. "Address to Soldiers for the Universal Destruction of Slavery." In Nesbitt, *Toussaint L'Ouverture*.
———. "Letter to General Laveaux, 18 May 1794." In Nesbitt, *Toussaint L'Ouverture*.
———. "Letter to Laveaux, 20 February 1796." In Nesbitt, *Toussaint L'Ouverture*.
———. "Proclamation, 29 August 1793." In Nick, *Toussaint L'Ouverture*.
———. "Toussaint L'Ouverture to His Brothers and Sisters in Varettes, 22 March 1794." In Nesbitt, *Toussaint L'Ouverture*.
Lowry, Michael. "Ernest Mandel's Revolutionary Humanism." In *The Legacy of Ernest Mandel*, edited by Gilbert Achcar, 24–37. New York: Verson, 1999.
Magloire-Danton, Gerarde. "Antenor and Jean Price-Mars: Revolution, Memory, Humanism." *Small Axe* 18 (2005) 150–70.
Manning, Patrick. *The African Diaspora: A History through Culture*. New York: Columbia University Press, 2009.
Mazama, Ama. "The Afrocentric Paradigm: Contours and Definitions." *Journal of Black Studies* 31 (2001) 387–405.
Mbembe, Achille. *On the Postcolony*. Berkeley: University of California Press, 2001.
Mboukou, Jean-Pierre Makouta. *Jacques Roumain: Essai sur la signification spirituelle et religieuse de son œuvre*. Paris: Atelier, 1978.
Metraux, Alfred. *Le vaudou haïtien*. Paris: Gallimard, 1958.
Mokhtar, G., ed. *General History of Africa*. Vol. 2, *Ancient Civilizations of Africa*. Berkeley: University of California Press, 1990.
Moore, David Chioni, ed. *Black Athena Writes Back: Martin Bernal Responds to His Critics*. Durham: Duke University Press, 2001.
Moreland, J. P. *Christianity and the Nature of Science: A Philosophical Investigation*. Grand Rapids: Baker, 1989.
Morris, Leon. *The Atonement: Its Meaning and Significance*. Downers Grove: InterVarsity, 1986 [1983].
Mudimbe, V. Y. *The Idea of Africa*. Bloomington: Indiana University Press, 1994.

———. *The Invention of Africa: Gnosis, Philosophy, and the Order of Knowledge.* Bloomington: Indiana University Press, 1988.

Murray, John. *Redemption Accomplished and Applied.* Grand Rapids: Eerdmans, 1987 [1955].

Neibhur, Reinhold, ed. *Karl Marx and Friedrich Engels on Religion.* Mineola, NY: Dover, 2008 [1964].

Neiman, Susan. *Evil in Modern Thought: An Alternative History of Philosophy.* Princeton: Princeton University Press, 2004 [2002].

Nesbitt, Nick. *Caribbean Critique: Antillean Critical Theory from Toussaint to Glissant.* Liverpool: Liverpool University Press, 2013.

———, ed. *Toussaint L'Ouverture: The Haitian Revolution.* New York: Verso, 2008.

———. "Troping Toussaint, Reading Revolution." *Research in African Literatures* 35 (2004) 18–33.

———. *Universal Emancipation: The Haitian Revolution and Radical Enlightenment.* Charlottesville: University of Virginia Press, 2008.

Netland, Harold A. *Dissonant Voices: Religious Pluralism and the Question of Truth.* Grand Rapids: Eerdmans, 1991.

Nietzsche, Friedrich. *Thus Spake Zarathustra.* Translated by Thomas Common. Mineola, NY: Dover, 1999. Originally published as *Also sprach Zarathustra: Ein Buch für Alle und Keinen.* Germany: Schmeitzer, 1883–1885.

Nietzsche, Friedrich. *Thus Spoke Zarathustra.* Mineola, NY: Dover, 1999 [1883–1885].

Nicholls, David. *From Dessalines to Duvalier: Race, Colour and National Independence in Haiti.* New Brunswick, NJ: Rutgers University Press, 1996 [1979].

North, C. R. *The Suffering Servant in Deutero-Isaiah.* New York: Oxford University Press, 1948.

Obenga, Theophile. "Hommage a Antenor Firmin (1850–1911), egyptologue haitien." *ANKH* 17 (2008) 132–47.

Okafor, Victor Oguejiofor. "Diop and the African Origin of Civilization: An Afrocentric Analysis." *Journal of Black Studies* 22 (1991) 256–68.

Okpewho, Carole, et al., eds. *African Diaspora: African Origins and New World Identities.* Bloomington: Indiana University Press, 2001.

Ollivier-Beauregard, M. *Les divinités égyptiennes: Leur origine, leur culte et son expansion dans le monde; À propos de la collection archéologique de feu le docteur Ernest Godard.* Paris: Librairie internationale, 1866.

Otto, Rudolf. *The Idea of the Holy.* Oxford: Oxford University Press, 1958.

Ott, Thomas. *The Haitian Revolution, 1789–1804.* Knoxville: University of Tennessee Press, 1973.

Pamphile, Léon. *La croix et le glaive: L'Eglise Catholique et l'Occupation américaine d'Haïti.* Port-au-Prince: Editions des Antilles S.A., 1991.

Parham, Althéa de Peuch. *My Odyssey: Experiences of a Young Refugee from Two Revolutions.* Baton Rouge: Louisiana State University Press, 1959.

Péan, Leslie. *Comprendre Anténor Firmin: Une inspiration pour le XXIe siècle.* Port-au-Prince: Editions de l'Université d'Etat d'Haiti, 2012.

Peters, Carl Edward. *La Croix contre l'asson.* Port-au-Prince: La Phalange, 1960.

Petrella, Ivan. *Beyond Liberation Theology: A Polemic.* London: SCM, 2008.

Piketty, Thomas. *Capital in the Twenty-First Century.* Cambridge: Belknap of Harvard University Press, 2014.

Pinn, Anthony B. *The End of God-Talk: An African American Humanist Theology.* New York: Oxford University Press, 2012.
———. *Varieties of African American Religious Experience.* Minneapolis: Augsburg Fortress, 1998.
Piquionne, Nathalie. "Lettre de Jean-François, Biassou et Belair, Juillet 1792." *Annalles historiques de la révolution françaises* 311 (1998) 132–39.
Pluchon, Pierre. *Toussaint-Louverture, de l'esclavage au pouvoir.* Paris: Edition de l'école, 1979.
Plummer, Brenda Gayle. *Haiti and the United States: The Psychological Moment.* Athens: University of Georgia Press, 1992.
Pompilus, Pradel. *Anténor Firmin par lui-même.* Port-au-Prince: Pegasus, 1990.
Pratt, Cornelius B. "Managing Sustainable Development in Sub-Saharan Africa: A Communication Ethic for the Global Corporation." In *The Global Public Relations Handbook: Theory, Research, and Practice,* edited by Krishnamurthy Sriramesh and Dejan Vercic, 206–24. Rev. ed. New York: Routledge, 2009.
Price-Mars, Jean. *Ainsi parla l'Oncle: Essais d'ethnographie haïtienne.* Port-au-Prince: Imprimerie de Compiègne, 1928.
———. *Ainsi parla l'Oncle suivi Revisiter l'Oncle.* Québec: Mémoire d'Encrier, 2009.
———. *Joseph Anténor Firmin.* Port-au-Prince: Imprimerie du Séminaire Adventiste, 1978.
———. *La Vocation de l'élite.* Port-au-Prince: Chenet, 1919.
———, ed. *Témoignages sur la vie et l'œuvre du Dr. Jean Price-Mars, 1876–1956.* Port-au-Prince: Imprimerie de l'Etat, 1956.
———. *Thus Spoke the Uncle.* Translated by Magdaline W. Shannon. New York: Three Continents, 1983.
———. *Une Etape de l'évolution haitienne.* Port-au-Prince: Imprimerie "La Presse," 1929.
Quatrefages, Jean Armand de Bréau. *L'espèce humaine.* Paris, 1877.
Ramsey, Kate. *The Spirits and the Law: Vodou and Power in Haiti.* Chicago: University of Chicago Press, 2011.
Rank, Mark Robert. *One Nation, Underprivileged: Why American Poverty Affects Us All.* Oxford: Oxford University Press, 2004.
Ratner, Sidney, et al. *The Evolution of the American Economy: Growth, Welfare, and Decision Making.* New York: Basic, 1980.
Rawls, John. *A Theory of Justice.* Cambridge: Harvard University Press, 1971.
Richardson, Michael and Krzysztof Fijalkowski. *Refusal of the Shadow: Surrealism and the Caribbean.* New York: Verso, 1996.
Robinson, Cedric J. *Black Marxism: The Making of the Black Radical Tradition.* Foreword by Robin D.G. Kelley. Chapel Hill: University of North Carolina Press, 1983.
Robinson, Randall. *An Unbroken Agony: Haiti, from Revolution to the Kidnapping of a President.* New York: Basic Civitas, 2007.
Rodriguez, Junius P. Rodriguez, ed. *Slavery in the United States: A Social, Political, and Historical Encyclopedia.* Vol. 1. Santa Barbara: ABC-CLIO, 2007.
Rorty, Richard. *Contingency, Irony, and Solidarity.* New York: Cambridge University Press, 2006 [1989].
Rosenberg, Roy A. "Jesus, Isaac, and the 'Suffering Servant.'" *Journal of Biblical Literature* 84 (1965) 381–88.

Roumain, Jacques. *A Propos de la campagne "anti-superstitieuse."* Port-au-Prince: Imprimerie de L'Etat, 1944.
———. *Analyse schématique.* Publication of the Comité Central du Parti Communiste Haitien. Port-au-Prince: Valcin, 1934.
———. *Bois d'ébène, suivi de Madrid.* Montreal: Mémoire d'encrier, 2003 [1937].
———. *Gouverneurs de la rosée: Roman.* Montreal: Mémoire D'encrier, 2007.
———. "Griefs de l'homme noir." In *L'Homme de couleur*, edited by S. E. le Cardinal Verdier, 8–15. Paris: Librarie Plon, 1939.
———. *Jacques Roumain: Œuvres complètes.* Edited by Léon-François Hoffmann. Collection Archivos. Madrid: ALLCA, 2003.
———. *La Montagne ensorcelée.* Prefaced by Jean Price-Mars. Port-au-Prince: Chassaing, 1931.
———. "Le Sacrifice du tambour-assoto (r)." Port-au-Prince: Imprimerie de l'Etat, 1943.
———. "L'Ecroulement du mythe nationaliste." In *Jacques Roumain: Œuvre complètes*, 653–55.
———. "Lettre à Tristan Remy." *Haïti-Journal*, January 4, 1933.
———. *Masters of the Dew.* Translated by Langston Hughes and Mercer Cook. Introduced by J. Michael Dash. London: Heinemann, 1978 [1947]. Originally published as *Gouverneurs de la rosée.* Port-au-Prince: Imprimerie de l'Etat, 1944.
———. "Réplique Finale au Révérend Père Foisset." *Le Nouvelliste*, March 30–31, April 10–11, 21 and 24, 1942.
Rousseau, Jean-Jacques. *The Social Contract and Other Later Political Writings.* Cambridge: Cambridge University Press, 1997.
Rowe, William L. *Philosophy of Religion: An Introduction.* Belmont, CA: Wadsworth, 1993.
Rubenstein, Richard L. "The Political Significance of Latin American Liberation Theology." *International Journal on World Peace* 3 (1986) 41–55.
Ruether, Rosemary. *Liberation Theology: Human Hope Confronts Christian History and American Power.* New York: Paulist, 1972.
Sachs, Jeffrey. *The End of Poverty: Economic Possibilities for Our Time.* New York: Penguin, 2006.
Said, Edward. *Representations of the Intellectual: The 1993 Reith Lectures.* New York: Vintage, 1996.
Schlesinger, Arthur. *The Disuniting of America: Reflections on a Multicultural Society.* Knoxville: Whittle Direct, 1991.
Scott, David. *Conscripts of Modernity: The Tragedy of Colonial Enlightenment.* Durham: Duke University Press, 2004.
Sen, Amartya. *Development as Freedom.* New York: Anchor, 2000.
———. *The Idea of Justice.* Cambridge: Belknap of Harvard University Press, 2011.
Sertima, Ivan Van. *Nile Valley Civilizations.* New York: Transaction, 1989.
Skinner, Elliott P. "The Restoration of African Identity for a New Millennium." In *The African Diaspora: African Origins and New World Identities*, edited by Isidore Okpewho et al., 28–45. Bloomington: Indiana University Press, 2001.
Snowden, Frank M. "Attitudes towards Blacks in the Greek and Roman World: Misinterpretations of the Evidence." In *Africa & Africans in Antiquity*, edited by Edwin M. Yamauchi, 246–75. East Lansing: Michigan State University Press, 2001.
———. *Before Color Prejudice: The Ancient View of Blacks.* Cambridge: Harvard University Press, 1983.

———. *Blacks in Antiquity: Ethiopians in the Greco-Roman Experience.* Cambridge: Belknap of Harvard University Press, 1970.
Sobrino, Jon. *Jesus the Liberator: A Historical-Theological Reading of Jesus of Nazareth.* Maryknoll: Orbis, 1999.
Spivak, Gayatri Chakravorty. *A Critique of Postcolonial Reason: Toward a History of the Vanishing Present.* Cambridge: Harvard University Press, 1999.
Stephens, Michelle Ann. *Black Empire: The Masculine Global Imaginary of Caribbean Intellectuals in the United States, 1914–1962.* Durham: Duke University Press, 2005.
Stocking, George W. *Race, Culture, and Evolution: Essays in the History of Anthropology* Chicago: University of Chicago Press, 1982 [1968].
Sturm, Douglass. *Solidarity and Suffering: Toward a Politics of Relationality.* Albany: State University of New York Press, 1998.
Sundiata, Ibrahim. "Afrocentrism: The Argument We're Really Having." *Dissonance*, September 30, 1996. https://way.net/dissonance/sundiata.html.
Tamez, Elsa. *Bible of the Oppressed.* Eugene, OR: Wipf and Stock, 2006.
———. "Good News for the Poor." In *Third World Liberation Theologies: A Reader*, edited by Deane William Fern, 189–96. Maryknoll: Orbis, 1986.
Taylor, Charles. *A Secular Age.* Cambridge: Belknap of Harvard University Press, 2007.
Theissen, Gerd, and Annette Mertz. *The Historical Jesus: A Comprehensive Guide.* Minneapolis: Fortress, 1998.
Toussaint, Hérold. "Ethnologue et Théologie en Haiti: Signification d'une problématique entre le Père Joseph Foisset et le Dr. Jean Price-Mars." In *Ainsi Parla l'Oncle suivi de Revisiter l'Oncle*, 383–94. Québec: Mémoire d'Encrier, 2009.
Trouillot, Hénock. *La pensée du Dr. Jean Price-Mars.* Port-au-Prince: Théodore, 1956.
Trouillot, Michel-Rolph. *Haiti, State Against Nation: The Origins and Legacy of Duvalierism.* New York: Monthly Review Press, 1990.
Tucker, Robert C., ed. *The Marx-Engels Reader.* New York: Norton, 1972.
Tyson, George F. *Toussaint L'Ouverture.* Englewood Cliffs, NJ: Prentice-Hall, 1973.
Vaillant, Janet G. *Black, French, and African: A Life of Leopold Sedar Senghor.* Cambridge: Harvard University Press, 1990.
Viaud, Léonce. *La personnalité de Joseph-Antenor Firmin.* Port-au-Prince: Valcin, 1948.
Volf, Miroslav. *Exclusion & Embrace: A Theological Exploration of Identity, Otherness, and Reconciliation.* Nashville: Abingdon, 1996.
Walker, J. D. "The Misrepresentation of Diop's Views." *Journal of Black Studies* 26 (1995) 77–85.
West, Cornel. *The Cornel West Reader.* New York: Basic Civitas, 1999.
———. *Keeping Faith: Philosophy and Race in America.* New York: Routledge, 1994.
———. *Prophesy Deliverance! An Afro-American Revolutionary Christianity.* Philadelphia: Westminster, 1982.
Wilentz, Amy. *The Rainy Season: Haiti since Duvalier.* New York: Simon and Schuster, 1989.
Wilson, William Julius. *The Declining Significance of Race: Blacks and Changing American Institutions.* Chicago: University of Chicago Press, 1979.
———. *When Work Disappears: The World of the New Urban Poor.* New York: Vintage, 1997.
Wright, N. T. *Evil and the Justice of God*. Downers Grove: InterVarsity, 2006.

Yelvington, Kevin A. "The Anthropology of Afro-Latin America and the Caribbean: Diasporic Dimensions." *Annual Review of Anthropology* 30 (2201) 227–60.

Zuckermanm, Phil. *Du Bois on Religion*. Walnut Creek, CA: AltaMira, 2009.

Index

Abbé Raynal, 16–17
Abbott, 174, 213
abolition, 22, 125, 137, 150
   universal, 41
abolitionist, 2, 18, 25
abolitionist movement, 16, 27
Abrahamic faiths, 159
abuses, 51, 107, 109
Abyssinia, 91
accusations, 33–34, 40
Achcar, Gilbert, 221
Achille, 221
act, 2, 13, 18, 23–24, 28, 31, 38, 47, 115–16, 124–25, 194
   creative-performative, 6
   creative speech, 45
   first, 190
   performative speech, 38
   second, 190–91
activism, 20, 23, 28, 32, 45, 141–2, 115
   intellectual, 1
   political, 21, 184
   social, 138, 175, 189–90, 201, 211
Adam, Russell, 68
Adams, 69, 213
   definition of Afrocentrism, 69
Address to Soldiers, 31
adherents, 118, 135, 141, 146, 160
Adriatic Sea, 76
Aeschylus's drama, 80
AEthiopes, 81
Aethiops, 88, 91

affirmation, 20, 34, 216, 218
   inspired, 119
   uncompromising, 39, 53
Africa, 61, 63, 65, 68, 71, 73–76, 78, 82, 84–85, 88, 91–92, 113–14, 213–14, 216, 221–22
   ancient, 65, 73, 78, 80, 221
   continental, 68, 92, 94
   distinctive role, 60
   precolonial, 1
Africa & Africans, 79, 224
Africa and ancient Egypt, 67, 95
Africana, 64
African achievement in history, 67, 69, 71
African American Christianity, 217
African American Episcopal Church, 153
African American Humanist Theology, 223
African American Intellectuals, 214
African American past, 70–1
African American Religious Experience, 141, 144–45, 148, 223
African Americans, 58, 60, 70, 141, 220
African American Studies, 69, 213
African ancestry, 5, 60, 57, 65, 70–71, 75, 100, 105, 169
Africana Philosophy, 62–63, 218
Africana Studies, 62, 213
African Christianity, 149
   classical, 84
African concept of Ubuntu, 206

INDEX

African cultural image, 71
African cultural traditions, 68, 150
African deity, 135
African Diaspora, 4, 68, 70–71, 213, 221–22, 224
African epistemological inquiry, 72
African epistemological relevance, 72
African experience, 22, 69
African flora, 89
African genius, 84
African gods, 136, 142, 144, 160
African historians, 100
African historiography, 72
African history, 23, 58–59, 69, 79, 99–100
  constructing, 67
  modern, 67
African identity, 159, 224
  restoration of, 73
African kingdoms and civilizations, 80, 84
African languages, 15, 99
African literatures, 215, 222
African-Negro culture, 114
Africanness, 59, 65–6, 81
African origin, 6, 23, 37, 59, 74, 93, 105, 214
African Origin of Civilization, 61, 73, 99–100, 216, 222
  Origins and New World, 222, 224
African peoples, 90–1, 149
African perspective, 71, 81, 163
African religions, 151, 157, 163
Africans, 1, 4, 37, 40, 53–54, 69, 71–74, 80, 82, 84, 121, 150–51, 163, 166
Africans to Western worldview and lifestyle, 151
African studies, 107
African Traditional religions, 149, 169
African World, 213–14
Africologists, 63, 69, 170
Afrique noire, 19, 216
Afro-American Revolutionary Christianity, 225
Afro-American Studies, 216
Afroasiatic Roots, 214
Afrocentric and Egyptocentric themes and ideologies, 72
Afrocentric approach, 71
Afrocentric discourse, 59, 66, 80
  idea, 59, 69, 71, 81, 213
  paradigm, 68–69, 72, 221–22
  ideology, 72
  imagination, 6, 57
  methodology, 69, 71
  movement, 74
  myth of ancient history, 75
  scholars, 7, 67
  school, 66
Afrocentricity, 59, 66, 69–71, 213–14
  label, 69
Afrocentrism, 59, 66–72, 75–6, 88, 97, 219, 221, 225
  critics of, 69–70
  performative, 64
agnostic humanist, 145
alienation, 121, 156, 179
American military occupation in Haiti, 107, 123, 137, 149
American pragmatic religious tradition, 131
American power, 224
Araya, Victorio, 199–200, 213
Aristide, Jean-Bertrand, 5, 28, 172–75, 184–89, 193–4, 203, 207
Asante, Molefi, 19, 59, 66, 68, 71–72, 76, 80–81, 84, 90–91, 97, 100–101
Antillean Critical theory, 4, 222
Asia, 77–78, 82, 90, 113–14, 204
avengers, 16–7, 30, 54–55, 216

Banner-Haley, Charles Pete, 29, 114, 224
Banner of Ethiopia, 114, 220
barbarism, 18, 61, 79, 99, 150, 216
Bastien, Remy, 150, 214
Biassou, Jean-Francois, 17, 36, 42, 47, 50, 52, 54, 223
Bell, Madison Smartt, xxx, 52
Bernal, Martin, 74–75, 88, 214

Bible, 127, 161, 190, 194, 201, 211, 225
biblical perspective, 164
biblical theology, 185
black achievement, 59, 101
black agency 79
Black Athena controversy, 74, 75, 88, 214, 221
Black Atlantic thought, 4, 5, 17, 57, 59, 61, 66, 70, 92, 114, 218
Black agency, 75
Black Bourgeoisie-Capitalist, 99
Black civilization, 59, 73
Black Christ, 144
Black church, 217
Black citizen, 26
Black diaspora, 1, 5, 68, 70, 72, 105
Black humanity, 34, 39
Black empire, 114, 225
Black genesis, 72, 74-5, 95
Black identity, 38
Black internationalism, 113
Black origins thesis, 92
Black people, 74, 78-9, 82, 116
Black pride, 60, 66, 69
Black Radical tradition, 4, 57, 113-4, 183, 223
Black Republic, the first, 62, 158
Black socialism, 113-14
Black Surrealism, 113
Black Marxism, 113-14, 117-18, 137-38
Black Jacobins, 14, 18, 33, 35-36, 50, 219
Black, Janet G. 225
blackness, 68, 76, 81, 85, 164
blacks, poor, 94, 117
blacks, the land of the, 84
Black writers, 99
blood, 3, 50, 136, 140, 143, 184, 219
Boas, Frantz, 64, 72
Bois, d'ebene, 114
Breda, Toussaint of, 15
Boff, Leonardo, 191, 202, 208-9, 214
bourgeoisie, 111, 117-18
bourgeois, Christianity, 193
bourgeois, culture, 111, 118
Brueggemann, Walter, 30, 215

capitalism, 116-17, 182, 193, 196, 198
Casseus, Jules, 154-56
Catholicism, 8, 108, 119, 121-22, 147-48, 150, 152, 163, 170, 186
Catholic church, 8, 121-25, 147, 150-51, 153-54, 161, 164, 185, 217
Christians, 2-3, 127, 151, 157-59, 169-70, 192
Christ, 88, 100, 127-28, 143-44, 154, 176, 180, 194-95, 210
Christ-Noir, 144
Christian-Vodouist compromissory tradition, 9, 147
Cedric, Robinson, 223
Césaire, Aime, 27, 54, 215
colonial, anti-, 21, 23, 30, 60, 97, 113, 122, 182
Cuba, 137-8, 140
culture, 71, 85, 87,121, 133, 158, 164
  black, 113
  racist, 94, 100
Concordat, 149, 152
color, 22, 35, 101, 109, 112-13, 207
colonialism, 26, 32, 54, 63-4, 77, 113, 181, 196, 215
colonization, 23, 122, 181
colony, 15, 22, 26, 28, 30, 33-37, 39, 42, 51-53, 85, 90, 92
community, 19, 25-26, 36, 38, 139-42, 156-58, 160, 176, 178-80, 202, 204, 206-9, 211, 219-20
consciousness, revolutionary, 139-40
culture, 39-40, 59, 63, 67-68, 79-80, 95-96, 98-101, 107, 114, 123, 131-32, 144158-59, 161-62, 164-70, 214, 216-19

Damnes, 217
Dash, Michael, 62, 65, 117-18, 215
Darwin, Charles, 60
Dayan, Joan, 4, 215

death, 28, 45, 52, 55, 61, 77, 143–44, 148, 195–97, 206
death of God theology, 143
Debbash, Yves, 48
Debien, Gabriel, 48, 215
Debs, Robert, 219
Declaration of Independence, 53
decolonization, 45–46, 49, 57, 105, 138, 175, 220
Delaney, Martin, 72
De la Torre, Miguel A., 176, 216
Delira, 212
democracy, 2, 20, 25, 125, 169, 173, 178, 187, 194
Dominican Republic, 22, 172, 188
Desmangles, Leslie, 216
Destiny, 7, 16, 38, 49, 115, 204
Dessalines, Jean-Jacques, 32, 49, 53, 62, 109, 116, 119, 222
Diaquoi, Louis, 119
dialectic, 55, 126, 178, 184
Dieu, 123–159–60, 219
    Dieu pauvre, 182
Diop, Cheikh Anta, 59, 61, 72–73, 79, 84–85, 87, 90, 93, 99–100, 213, 216, 222, 225
doctrine, 216, 22
domination, 73–74, 78, 80, 216
drought, 63, 142, 216
Dubois, Laurent, 16–7, 30, 54–55, 64, 120–22, 153, 216
Dupuy, Alex, 110–11, 174–75, 186–87, 202, 216
Duvalier regime, 62, 109–10, 116, 119, 149, 184–85, 222, 224–25
Dussel, Enrique, 198
Durkheim, Emile, 216
duty, 3, 18, 33, 37, 112, 144160
Dutty Boukman, 7, 30, 50, 170, 220
Drake, St Clair, 73–4, 78, 80, 216

economy, 14, 11, 116, 218
Eddy, Paul R., 214
Edward, Wilmot Blyden, 72073
Edward, Carl, 222
Egypt, 61, 81–2, 73, 78, 82–3, 89
    ancient, 67, 85, 91–92, 224

black, 62, 72–74, 91, 96
classical, 79, 89
history, 77, 215
Egyptology, 59, 60, 65, 72–73, 77–78, 80, 83, 88, 91, 93, 100, 108, 113
Ellison, Ralph, 7
emancipation, 21, 28, 36–37, 44–45, 55–56, 139, 172, 211
empire, 73, 87
enlightenment, 18, 63, 97, 119, 192
Engels, Friedrich, 122, 127, 144, 222
equality, human ontological, 55
Europe, 14, 54, 63, 76, 81–82, 99, 204, 217
ethics, 2, 9, 175, 177–8, 180–81, 193, 203–4, 207, 210, 216, 219
Ethiopia, inhabitants of, 70, 74, 78, 85–92, 101, 114, 217, 220
exploitation, 106–7, 116–17, 124, 128, 194, 196, 201–3, 208, 201

Fanon, Frantz, 65, 114
faith, anti-, 127
faith, crisis of, 181, 197, 200
faith, community of, 179, 182, 186
Fatton, Robert, 174–75, 186, 217
Fern, Deane William, 225
Fick, Carolyn, 36, 48, 54–55, 217, 220
Fils-Aime, Jean, 3. 5–9, 8, 146–7, 154, 158, 161–65, 168, 172, 217
Firmin, Joseph Antenor, 57–59, 61–66, 80–88, 93, 101, 105, 195, 199, 217–19, 22
Fischer, Sibylle, 31, 217
Fluehr-Lobban, Carolyn, 62–64, 82, 217
Fonds Rouge, 148, 217
Fontus, Fritz, 139
Foisset, Joseph, 118, 125–27, 130
Foucault, Michel, 29
Fowler, Carolyn, 107
Freedom, 5–8, 11, 13, 15–16, 19–23, 26–27, 31–34, 36–39, 41–50,

55–57, 105–6, 115, 117,
  199–200, 210–12
 religious, 121, 146–47, 168–70
 revolutionary, 18, 21–22, 35,
  56, 220
freedom fighter, 40, 53
freedom principle, 40, 53
French revolution, 14, 18, 22, 27, 27,
  31, 47

Garrigus, John, 149, 217
Geffrard, Fabre Nicolas, 152
Geggus, David, 15, 20, 24–25, 36,
  47–48, 54, 217–18
general emancipation, 19, 23–24, 33,
  44, 46–48
general liberty, 7, 33–34, 36–38, 44,
  46, 48–49, 52–54
Gilroy, Paul, 70
Girard, Philippe, 218
Glissant, Edouard, 4, 222
globalization, 4, 9, 124, 137, 165–66,
  182, 195–6, 213, 220
Gobineau, Joseph Arthur, 58–59,
  60, 62–63, 65, 78, 93–95,
  143, 218
God, 3–4, 9, 31, 141–43, 159, 173–
  74, 176, 178–82, 194–95,
  197, 199–203, 210–11,
  215–15
Gordon, Lewis, 38, 62–63, 65, 218
Gouverneurs de la rosée, 106, 140,
  215, 224
Greece, 73–75, 81, 96–97
Greek, classical, 75, 93, 95
Gutierrez, Gustavo, 115–16, 191,
  198, 200, 219

Haiti, 60, 112, 146, 161–63, 182–86
 post-colonial, 1
 self-determining, 111, 154
Haitian bourgeoisie class, 167, 186,
  189
Haitian Catholicism, 9, 147, 159
Haitian Creole, 15, 173
Haitian Communism, 112, 165
Haitian Christianity, 118, 151, 157
Haitian church, 130, 156

Haitian culture, 124, 156, 158, 161,
  164, 166, 168–69
Haitian indigenism, 5, 61, 105
Haitian liberation theology
  movement, 184, 189
Haitian peasants, 108, 120–21, 135,
  138, 140–41, 159
Haitian Protestantism, 9, 147, 154,
  164
Haitian renaissance, literary, 107
Haitian revolution, 1, 4–5, 14, 15,
  16–18, 20, 24, 26, 30–31, 36,
  44–48, 2124, 228, 220, 222
Haitian revolutionary studies, 14–
  15, 24–25, 46, 54, 217–18
Haitian state, 127, 152, 154,
Haitian thinkers, 5, 128, 165–69,
  224
Haitian War of independence, 43,
  218, 222
Haiti's influence on Antebellum
  America, 20, 219
Haiti's underclass population, 155,
  163, 184–87
Haiti's underdevelopment, 109, 111,
  154
Hallward, Peter, 26, 29, 55, 174–75,
  186, 219
Heidegger, Martin, 50, 219
historical Jesus, the, 210–11, 225
historiography, 1, 7, 60, 66–67, 75,
  94–5
human equality, 7, 37, 39, 49, 53, 64
human existence, 5, 21, 101, 116,
  125, 132, 146, 148, 194, 200,
  206
human flourishing, 19, 60, 131, 217
human rights, 4, 6, 13, 16, 21, 23, 33,
  37, 41, 44–45, 194, 199, 205
humanism, 3, 26, 29, 37, 39, 51, 53,
  65, 71, 73, 93, 134, 192–93,
  197–98, 203–4, 206–7, 218,
  221
Hurbon, Laennec, 5, 9, 118, 123,
  146–49, 151, 158–61, 163–
  68, 172, 219

justice, generous, 176, 220

Kemet, 85
Labat, Jean-Baptiste, 151
Laurent, Gerard Mentor, 14
Liberation theology, 175, 211,
Louverture, Toussaint, 13, 15

Magloire-Danton, Gerarde, 62, 150
Mandel, Ernest, 117, 221

Nietzsche, Friedrich, 143
Obenga, Theophile, 65

peace, world, xx, xxx
people, crucified, 197
peasant, 137, 143
Pluchon, Pierre, 48
priests, Egyptian, 90, 96, 98

race, 176, 225
    Aryan, 58, 60
    Black, 8, 27, 58–60, 57, 73, 77–80, 93–95, 100
racial hierarchy, 58
religion, 23, 67, 69, 74, 105, 120, 126, 130, 221
revolutions, world, xx
Roumain, Jacques, x–xx

Saint-Domingue, 1, 6–7, 32, 46–47, 50, 159
slavery, 21, 35, 40, 56, 115
    American, 216
    anti-, 122
    enslaved Africans, 2, 13, 16, 18–19, 26, 32, 50, 149
    transatlantic slave trade, 21
    slaves in Saint-Domingue, 49, 54
Sobrino, Jon, xxx

theory, anthropological, 63, 219
totalitarianism, 184

Vodou, x, xxx, 123, 131, 147, 150–51, 156–59, 168–69, 172, 214, 220
vodouphobia, x, xx, 31, 60, 73, 94–95, 113

worldview, x, xxx
Wright, Richard, xxx

www.ingramcontent.com/pod-product-compliance
Lightning Source LLC
Chambersburg PA
CBHW051637230426
43669CB00013B/2341